Black and Green

Black and Green

The Fight for Civil Rights in Northern Ireland & Black America

Brian Dooley

PLUTO  PRESS

First published 1998 by Pluto Press
345 Archway Road, London N6 5AA

www.plutobooks.com

British Library Cataloguing in Publication Data
A catalogue record for this book is available from the British Library

ISBN 978 0 7453 1211 8 Hardback
ISBN 978 0 7453 1295 8 Paperback
ISBN 978 1 7837 1118 5 PDF eBook

Typeset by Stanford DTP Services, Northampton, England

Contents

For Alison Dooley. Thank You.

Abbreviations

ACIF	American Congress for Irish Freedom
BPP	Black Panther Party
BTC	Belfast Trades Council
CDU	Campaign for Democracy in Ulster
CSJ	Campaign for Social Justice
DHAC	Derry Housing Action Committee
IRA	Irish Republican Army
IRB	Irish Republican Brotherhood
NAACP	National Association for the Advancement of Colored People
NAIF	National Association of Irish Freedom
NAIJ	National Association for Irish Justice
NCCL	National Council for Civil Liberties
NICRA	Northern Ireland Civil Rights Association
Noraid	Irish Northern Aid Committee
PD	People's Democracy
RUC	Royal Ulster Constabulary
SCLC	Southern Christian Leadership Conference
SDLP	Social and Democratic Labour Party
SNCC	Student Non-Violent Coordinating Committee
UNIA	United Negro Improvement and Conservation Association and African Communities League
UDA	Ulster Defence Association
UVF	Ulster Volunteer Force
WPC	Women's Political Council
YSA	Young Socialist Alliance

Acknowledgements

This book began as a footnote. In its Fall 1995 edition, the *Georgia Historical Quarterly* Vol. 76, No. 3, carried a piece by Brian Ward about Martin Luther King's visit to Newcastle University in England in 1967 ('A King in Newcastle: Martin Luther King, Jr and British Race Relations 1967–1968'). Brian suggested that King's impact on the civil rights movement in Northern Ireland was 'a subject ripe for more thorough scholarly investigation'. He was right, and I am grateful for the suggestion.

What helped make the subject ripe for investigation was the willingness of so many of the key figures of the civil rights movements in the US and in Northern Ireland to spare me the time to be interviewed. Without their cooperation, it is unlikely that the book would have appeared at all. They include St Clair Bourne, Kathleen Cleaver, Austin Currie, Angela Davis, Michael Farrell, Ann Hope, Tomas MacGiolla, Bernadette McAliskey, Eamonn McCann, Conn and Patricia McCluskey, Kevin McNamara, Martin Meehan, Fionnbarra O Dochartaigh, Edwina Stewart and Juanita Williams. There were also others who were interviewed on condition of anonymity. They know who they are, and they know I am grateful.

The staffs at the Library of Congress, the British Library, and at Queen's University Belfast were also very helpful, as were Polly Armstrong and Margaret Kimball at Stanford University. I now join that long list of authors who are greatly indebted to those at the Linen Hall Library's Political Collection in Belfast, whose expertise is phenomenal. Yvonne Murphy helped me enormously in my search through the NICRA files, and put me in contact with several former civil rights activists.

Others like Black Panther Party founder Dave Hilliard and Peter Urban of the Irish Republican Socialist Committee in San Francisco helped by sending me clippings, party newsletters, and leaflets, and gave me valuable leads to follow in finding people. St Clair Bourne also sent me a copy of his film, *The Black and the Green*, for which I am extremely grateful. A special word of thanks to Alison Dooley, who encouraged me throughout the project, transcribed some interviews, read drafts as they were produced and helped organise the index. This book is for her.

Several people read portions of the manuscript and offered helpful criticism. My thanks to Michael Crowley, Emma Ireland, Barry Sheehan and Anna Turvey for their suggestions. Their advice and improvements are appreciated; any errors remaining are my own.

Introduction

The Irish Times is a famous Irish bar in Washington DC, opposite Union Station and just a few hundred yards from the US Congress. It displays all the usual Irish-American memorabilia found in Irish-American bars all over the country – pictures of John F. Kennedy, of Michael Collins, of James Joyce. Next to a mirror promoting Jameson's Irish whiskey, there is a portrait of black American Frederick Douglass, and at first glance the picture seems incongruous – a nineteenth-century black face looking down from a row of Irish heroes. But for many years former slave Douglass agitated in Washington for Irish independence, visited Ireland twice and spoke at a political meeting with Daniel O'Connell in Dublin. Douglass is one of the largely forgotten links between black American and Irish politics, part of a tradition which goes back several centuries and which inspired the civil rights movement in Northern Ireland in the 1960s.

Civil rights activists in Northern Ireland borrowed slogans from black American protestors, called themselves 'white negroes' and identified in a positive way with the struggle across the Atlantic led by Martin Luther King. Yet the comparison had been made for generations before, usually negatively. During the 1650s, in the wake of Oliver Cromwell's invasion of Ireland, thousands of Irish peasants were shipped off to the Caribbean to work as slaves with African slaves. In Victorian Britain, it was common to regard Africans and Irish people as subhuman. Nineteenth-century British historian Charles Kingsley visited Ireland and recorded:

> I am haunted by the human chimpanzees I saw along that hundred miles of horrible country ... to see white chimpanzees is dreadful; if they were black, one would not feel it too much, but their skins, except where tarred by exposure, are as white as ours.[1]

In 1862, *Punch* magazine suggested that scientists looking for the missing link in evolution, the being between 'the Gorilla and the Negro' would find it in the Irish race.[2] A decade earlier, the

1

same magazine had pictured Irish nationalist leader John Mitchel as a monkey.[3] In the 1890s, when London Zoo acquired a new chimpanzee to replace its much-loved monkey 'Sally', it was named 'Paddy', to general amusement.[4]

The idea that the Irish and Africans were somehow a different species from the rest of humankind went far beyond jokes. English academic John Beddoe, a founding member of the Ethnological Society and later President of the Anthropological Institute, compiled an 'Index of Nigresence' in the mid-nineteenth century, and claimed that locals in the west of Ireland were so 'black' they should be categorised as 'Africanoid'.[5] The Irish as apes re-emerged as a theme in the 1970s when the *Daily Express*, the *Houston Chronicle* and several other newspapers in Britain and the US characterised Irish bombers as gorillas in cartoons.[6]

In fact, the image of the Irish as a different race was as common in the US as it was in Britain during the nineteenth century, and newly-arrived Irish immigrants, although not slaves, were often regarded as belonging to the same social, if not genetic, category as black Americans. The sense of persecution shared by black Americans and Irish immigrants did not always lead to solidarity between the two groups. Violence broke out in several northern American cities as freed blacks competed with Irish labourers in the job market and black Americans were famous for telling 'Irish jokes' during the 1800s, as laughing at Irish immigrants was one of the few ways that black Americans could openly take revenge on whites. To make fun of white Americans was not acceptable, but to join in the laughter at the Irish was. In 1876 one writer noted that black stevedores working in Cincinnati 'can mimic the Irish accent to a degree of perfection which an American, Englishman or German could not hope to acquire'.[7]

The Irish featured in the jokes told by blacks are characterised by their stupidity and laziness. One told of an Irishman who bought a gun and immediately killed his friend by trying to shoot the grasshopper on his chest, another of the Irishman who bought a watermelon and only ate the rind.[8] This tradition persisted well into the twentieth century. In the 1920s black folklorist Arthur Huff Fauset collected jokes about the Irish from blacks in Pennsylvania, Mississippi and Alabama. 'It is curious to hear a native-born southern Negro, nearly full-blooded, tell a story about Pat and Mike with all the spirit and even the inflection of voice that one might expect of an Irishman,' he wrote.[9]

No doubt these jokes fuelled the tension between blacks and Irish in America, but the history of the two groups was not consistently hostile, as the example of Douglass suggests. Throughout the nineteenth and twentieth centuries, black Americans looked to Ireland for political inspiration, and during the Irish Famine of the 1840s freed black slaves sent contributions to Ireland for famine relief, as did American Indians.[10] Much of the black nationalist ideology popularised in the 1920s by Marcus Garvey was rooted in his study of Irish Republicanism, and Garvey joined the campaign to support IRA prisoner Terence MacSwiney, who died on hunger strike in 1920. When the civil rights activists of Northern Ireland first began to protest about discrimination they followed the model of the American movement, copied its tactics, and met with some of its leaders. But the black American influence on the civil rights movement in Northern Ireland during the 1960s has been largely underplayed, even in the best accounts of the period.

Bob Purdie's excellent study of the civil rights movement in Northern Ireland, *Politics in the Streets*, concluded that

> ... although the black civil rights movement in the US had been an inspiration, strictly speaking it was not a model. There is no evidence that any of the founders or leaders of the Northern Ireland civil rights movement ever visited the Southern United States, consulted with any of the Black civil rights organisations, or even undertook a thorough study of that movement. Their information came from the media.[11]

Other studies largely agree with Purdie, that the influence was minor, that there was little or no connection between the two struggles.[12]

None the less, most – if not all – the major civil rights activists in Northern Ireland claimed they were influenced by the American experience. Some thought the influence minor, others that it was crucial. Different actors in the Northern Ireland civil rights movement appear to have empathised with particular individuals in the American movement, with younger activists like Michael Farrell having 'a bit of fellow-feeling for [US student leader] John Lewis' and more moderate leaders like Austin Currie emphasising that 'for everyone who drew a parallel with Che Guevara there were hundreds who identified with Martin Luther King.'[13] Derry radical Fionnbarra O Dochartaigh recalled 'We were the underclass ... the Catholic middle class might not have identified themselves with the blacks but we did.'[14] Bernadette Devlin McAliskey not only read about the Black Panther Party, she went to the US and met with its leading members, and visited militant black leader Angela Davis in prison in 1971. SDLP leader John Hume regularly refers to Martin Luther King as an important influence in the late 1960s, and representatives from King's Southern Christian Leadership Conference (SCLC) visited Belfast in 1972 to address a meeting of Northern Ireland Civil Rights Association (NICRA) activists. Members of Sinn Fein and the IRA also enthusiastically cite the example of the American civil rights movement as an important inspiration, and Belfast Republican Martin Meehan even claims that in prison during the 1970s 'there wouldn't have been a wing or a cell where you wouldn't have seen a book about Martin Luther King.'[15]

Whatever the level of knowledge of the American civil rights movement, there is no doubt that it proved an important guide for the Northern Ireland activists. Organisers of the historic Belfast–Derry march in January 1969 consciously modelled it on the Selma–Montgomery protest four years earlier. Civil rights leaders in Ireland had been receiving literature from the civil rights movement in the US from the early 1960s, and by the early 1970s several visits had been exchanged across the Atlantic. Moreover, the links between the black American and Irish movements in the 1960s and 1970s drew on a long tradition of mutual support.

Not only did the struggles for civil rights in Northern Ireland and in the US copy each other's tactics and identify with each other's leaders, they even shared a common political vocabulary. The Montgomery Bus Boycott of 1955, which launched Martin Luther King's career as a civil rights activist, for example, was named after an Irish example of political protest through economic sanction. In 1880 Irish labourers refused to harvest the crops of Captain Charles Cunningham Boycott, whose reputation for evicting tenants who could not meet their rents was legendary. Between 1920 and 1922, Irish Republicans urged a boycott of Belfast businesses in anger at the mass expulsion of Belfast Catholics from their employment, and King's use of the tactic in Alabama 35 years later was another example of the fingerprints of one struggle being found on the other. Irish civil rights activists used marches, sit-ins and civil disobedience campaigns in conscious imitation of the US civil rights movement. In fact, Daniel O'Connell had used the mass non-violent march and meeting as a political tactic 150 years before, and it had been exported to America, used by black Americans in the 1950s and early 1960s, then reimported to Ireland in the late 1960s and early 1970s. When Martin Luther King used the metaphor of a trail of blood to describe black civil rights experience, he was borrowing the phrase from Frederick Douglass, who in turn got it from Daniel O'Connell, who had said that following the history of Ireland was like tracing the blood of a wounded man at a party.

The language of the civil rights movements in the US and Ireland is full of such overlaps – both were familiar with gerrymandering (the drawing of unfair constituency boundaries), both demanded 'One Man One Vote' (itself now a dated slogan) and the Irish adopted the black American anthem of 'We Shall Overcome'. Both the Northern Irish and the American civil rights movements had their own 'Bloody Sunday' – in a US context it refers to the beatings sustained by civil rights marchers in Selma in March 1965, in Ireland the massacre of 13 unarmed civil rights protestors by British soldiers in Derry in January 1972. Phrases like 'mixed marriages', 'integrated schools' and 'employment quotas' are common in both contexts; the meaning either is black/white in America or Catholic/Protestant in Northern Ireland. However, there are many other terms which have a particular meaning in one context but something completely different in another, which makes for some confusion. Words like 'South', 'Republicanism', 'minority', and even 'black' mean different things depending on whether the context is Northern Ireland or black America.

For example, at the second civil rights march in Northern Ireland, in October 1968, Nationalist MP Gerry Fitt stood before a line of policemen and said 'If one of those black bastards of the Northern Ireland Gestapo puts a hand on any man here, I'll lead you through!' Fitt was referring not to the colour of the policemen's skin (there being no black police officers in Northern Ireland), but to their religion. Black, in an Irish context, is sometimes used as a derogatory term for Protestant.[16] Other odd coincidences of the struggles in Northern Ireland and the US include the surface similarities between Martin Luther King and Ian Paisley. While the American civil rights movement produced a Protestant minister, the son of a Baptist preacher and a powerful and charismatic speaker to lead it, the Northern Ireland civil rights effort witnessed the political rise of a Protestant minister, also the son of a Baptist minister and a powerful and charismatic speaker, as one of its most formidable enemies.

Similar histories of subjugation produced a similar heritage of artistic imagery in Ireland and the US. The theme of slavery runs through black American poetry, folklore and music. In Ireland, too, it is a regular theme in songs (including the national anthem).[17] There has also been a strong identification between several Irish and black American artists. 'Sean O'Casey had a huge influence on me,' said Harry Belafonte:

O'Casey led me to looking at the theater as my main center of expression ... the play that we did ... *Juno and the Paycock* [originally set in early twentieth-century Dublin], we did it as a West Indian cast living in America ... we never changed a word in the play. Everything fit perfectly.[18]

Others have noted the heavy influence of James Joyce on black American novelist James Baldwin, who regarded the Dubliner as one of his 'models'.[19] Critics of Baldwin's work point to the similarity between his *Go tell it on the mountain* and Joyce's *Portrait of the artist as a young man*, and the more than passing resemblance between the two novels' central characters – John Grimes and Stephen Dedalus.[20] Huey P. Newton, founder of the Black Panther Party, also cited Joyce as an important teenage influence: 'I identified very strongly with Stephen Dedalus in James Joyce's *Portrait of the artist as a young man*, because he went through a similar experience [of religious doubt].'[21]

More recent identification has been made by Roddy Doyle in the book (and film) *The Commitments*, whose young characters form a band to play soul music in Dublin. Why soul music? Their leader explains:

'Your music should be abou' where you're from an' the sort o' people yeh come from. – Say it once, say it loud, I'm black an' I'm proud ... – The Irish are the niggers of Europe, lads.'
They nearly gasped: it was so true ... ' – Say it loud, I'm black an' I'm proud...'.[22]

In a more serious context, those in Northern Ireland who believe they are the victims of discrimination still identify with American blacks. In 1996, almost 30 years after the first civil rights march in Northern Ireland, a controversial Orange Order parade made its way through a Catholic neighbourhood, much to the dismay of local Catholics. One told a reporter 'We're just second class citizens – white niggers.'[23] It is an identification which goes back centuries, one which is deeply rooted in Irish history and political tradition, and one which proved crucially important to the civil rights activists in Northern Ireland in the 1960s and 1970s.

1

Black and White Slaves

Irish and black American history of the last few centuries has been primarily defined by powerlessness, and a variety of responses to that powerlessness. Sometimes the resistance of the Irish to the British and of black Americans to the white power structure was violent, sometimes not. Both groups had their situations measurably improved after a civil war, yet the Irish and American civil wars also created new problems of second-class citizenship in the Irish North and the American South. Although the two minorities shared several important similarities, there were also major differences. The Irish struggle was (generally) defined in terms of nationalism: that British rule ought to be expelled and some form of Irish government installed. While black America had its own elements of nationalism, including those who advocated relocating black Americans to Africa, a more consistent theme was the struggle for American blacks to enjoy the same rights as American whites.

Nevertheless, the Irish and black American struggles for power, or rights, intersected and overlapped at crucial junctures from the mid-nineteenth century onwards. The links even predate the mid-1800s, but it is during this time that political leaders in Ireland and black America began to realise there was something common about their purpose, and took tentative steps to learn from each other's approaches, and to help each other's efforts.

Slavery was the defining historical experience for black Americans, but it also played a fundamental part in the development of early Ireland. The Irish trade in British slaves had gone on since Roman times, when Irish raiding parties took slaves from the British coast. Saint Patrick himself endured six years as a slave after being seized from the coast of the island of Great Britain in the fifth century. Written Irish history begins with his recollection of his abduction into slavery: 'I, Patrick, a sinner, the simplest of country men ... was taken away into Ireland in captivity with ever so many thousands of people.' For six years, he recalled, he tended sheep 'near the western sea' [probably in the northern part of Ireland] before escaping by walking the two hundred miles back across Ireland to the east coast where, in the company of pirates, he escaped.[1] He eventually made his way to Gaul, probably somewhere near Cannes, where he received a formal education, became a priest and, later, a bishop. In later life, he denounced slavery with a venom only a former slave could muster. St Patrick described the slave trade as this 'crime so horrible and unspeakable,' and some historians credit St Patrick with being the first writer in the history of the world to condemn slavery so unequivocally.[2] By the time of the Norman invasion of Ireland in the late 1160s, the Irish clergy opposed the practice of seizing slaves from the British coast, claiming the invasion was divine retribution for the nation's widespread slaveholding, and Ireland became the first country in the world to abolish slavery officially when it banned the trade at the Armagh Synod of 1177.

In the mid-1600s, Oliver Cromwell's English army invaded Ireland and banished many Irish to become slaves in the West Indies. Some made their way to north America and one, Goody Glover, was hanged as a 'witch' in Massachusetts in 1688.[3] Some of those who stayed in the West Indies worked side by side with black slaves in the sugar cane fields of the Caribbean, and, in Bermuda in 1661 and in Barbados in 1668, the Irish on the islands were suspected of collaborating with black slaves in planning insurrection against the British authorities.[4] The small Caribbean island of Montserrat became particularly closely identified with Ireland. From the first settlements in 1628, the white population of Montserrat was predominantly Irish. According to *Jeffreys' West Indian Atlas*, published in 1780, the vast majority of the inhabitants were either descendants of the original Irish settlers or natives of Ireland, 'so that the use of the Irish language is preserved on the island, even among the Negroes.'[5] Today, the island still uses a shamrock design for its immigration stamp, and many island families identify themselves as Irish.[6]

Although Ireland played no significant part in the slave trade, there were isolated incidents of individual Irish merchants selling slaves. In his study of Irish–American trade, Thomas Truxes notes that during the 1720s, 'Irish merchants on Montserrat imported slaves directly from Africa in their own vessels, distributing them throughout the Leeward Islands.'[7] In 1767 the *Cork Evening Post* carried an advertisement for 'a likely Negro Boy of about four years old, American born, and past all disorders' offered for sale by a ship captain.[8] Three years later, Dubliner Randall Mitchell, a merchant operating from Philadelphia, returned to Ireland from America after selling his slave called 'Dublin'.[9] Truxes reveals wider Irish involvement in the business:

A few Irish firms had more than a peripheral interest in the slave trade. Anthony Lynch and Sons, merchants and 'town agents' at Bridgetown, Barbados, conducted large slave auctions, 'At their Yarde in High-Street'. In February 1766, they advertised the sale of 'Two hundred and Seventy choice Whidah and Popo Slaves, imported in the Ship Squirrel ... from Whidah'.[10]

Although the Irish record on buying and selling slaves was not completely faultless, Irish participation in the slave trade was relatively minor, and Irishmen never figured among the great West Indian slave traders. In fact, there is some evidence to suggest that the presence of Irish servants helped stem the spread of slavery to parts of America. Typically, Irish servants in the eighteenth century were bound to an employer for four years in America in return for a free passage across the Atlantic. Such indentured servants competed with slaves and for a while helped slow the development of slavery to the middle colonies like Maryland and Pennsylvania. Not all of the Irish settlers in the new American colonies were servants. Richard Rose and others have highlighted the important influence of Ulster migration on the New World during the 1700s: 'In the eighteenth century, economic and religious pressures encouraged thousands of Ulster migrants, especially Scots, to try their fortune a second time by moving on to America. The Scotch-Irish became almost the prototypical White Anglo-Saxon Protestant.'[11] Rose's work illuminates the similarities between the development of the American South and Northern Ireland over several centuries, beginning with their official births as settlements of the English Crown in the seventeenth century. James I of England chartered a settlement in Virginia just a few months before he chartered the plantation in Ulster.[12]

Comparisons between the situation of the black slave and the Irish peasant were made with increasing frequency throughout the early nineteenth century, as those campaigning for the abolition of slavery in America sought to make common cause with powerful Irish-Americans. An early and vital Irish convert to the cause of abolitionism was Daniel O'Connell, the acknowledged leader of Catholic Ireland. O'Connell was a Kerry-born lawyer who had been educated in Europe. During the first half of the nineteenth century he led the fight for Catholic emancipation in Ireland and for the repeal of many of the penal laws which prevented Catholics from participating in public life. He became the first Catholic in the

British House of Commons since the Reformation. In the 1840s he led a campaign of massive non-violent resistance to British rule in Ireland and for the repeal of the Act of Union which legalised the sovereignty of the British parliament in Ireland.

A formidable parliamentarian and orator, he masterminded the widespread civil disobedience campaign in Ireland which would prove inspirational to American abolitionists. Douglas C. Riach's work on O'Connell and slavery dates O'Connell's opposition to slavery from 1824, when he supported the English abolitionist James Cropper in a scheme attacking the sugar-and slave-based economy of the West Indies.[13] By 1833, O'Connell had carved such a reputation as a fervent abolitionist through his comparisons between the conditions of Irish peasants and black slaves that William Lloyd Garrison, future president of the American Anti-Slavery Society, sought him out during a visit to London to enlist his help. His anti-slavery credentials growing, O'Connell was cited by the Glasgow Emancipation Society in 1835 as 'one Parliamentarian who could be relied upon not to compromise or vacillate in his efforts to abolish the system of Negro Apprenticeships', which O'Connell had attacked as a system of slavery in disguise.[14]

Three years later, he proved even more popular with the American abolitionists when he promised to 'begin the work with the vile and sanguinary slaveholders of Republican America. I want to be *directly* at them. No more side-winded attacks: firing directly at the hull, as the seaman says, is my plan'.[15] These were not empty threats. After he publicly condemned George Washington for having been a slaveholder, he famously attacked the American ambassador to London, Andrew Stevenson, for being a slave-breeder. Stung by the assault, Stevenson challenged O'Connell to a duel, which immediately boosted O'Connell's popularity among abolitionists in America. O'Connell was proud of the Irish record on slavery, and liked to remind audiences of 'Ireland, that was never stained with negro slave-trading – Ireland, that never committed an offence against the men of color – Ireland, that never fitted out a single vessel for traffic in blood on the African coast'.[16]

While O'Connell was not the only Irish public figure to condemn slavery, his attacks carried the most weight and were regarded as vital by American abolitionists hoping to win support from the Irish in America. Unfortunately for both the anti-slavery movement and O'Connell, many Irish in America were unsympathetic to the cause of blacks, whom they often regarded as economic rivals and competitors in the job market. In 1842, O'Connell's signature headed an address urging Irish people in America to support the abolitionists. About 60,000 other Irish signatures also appeared on the petition, including those of figures like Fr Theobold Mathew, the temperance campaigner and perhaps the best-known Irishman of the time after O'Connell. The signatures were collected at a series of anti-slavery meetings throughout Ireland held by Charles Lenox Remond, a prominent black American abolitionist. The American anti-slavery movement was delighted with the address. The leader of the American Anti-Slavery Society, William Lloyd Garrison, hoped

> every true Irishman will cordially respond to its sentiments. Let none of their number pretend to honour Daniel O'Connell, or revere Father Mathew, who refused to co-operate with the American abolitionist, or who is found shaking hands with southern slave drivers ... Remember, there is no neutral ground.[17]

The address urged Irish-Americans 'to love liberty – hate slavery – CLING BY THE ABOLITIONISTS – and in America you will do honour to the name of Ireland.'[18] At a meeting in Boston's Faneuil Hall, a grateful Garrison compared slaveholder claims that the slave was incapable of looking after himself with England's claim that Ireland was unfit for self-government:

> This meeting most cordially wishes old Ireland success, in all her righteous efforts to redeem the Emerald Isle from every species of English oppression, and especially in the grand movement of Daniel O'Connell, for the repeal of the fraudulent act of Union between his country and England.[19]

Despite American abolitionist attempts to make common cause with the Irish, Irish-Americans generally withheld their support for the anti-slavery effort. Some attacked O'Connell for meddling in American affairs. The Tyrone-born Archbishop of New York, John Hughes, condemned the anti-slavery address as a fake and urged that even if it be proved genuine that it should be rejected by every Irish-American as unwarrantable interference in domestic affairs.[20] Hughes maintained that slavery was 'infinitely better than the condition in which these people would have been, had they not been seized to gratify the avarice and cupidity of the white man', and recommended that the slave 'should bear with his lot and be faithful to his master'.[21]

Irish-American newspapers like the *Boston Pilot* accused O'Connell of undermining Irish-American efforts at integration into mainstream American society by his insistence on regarding them as a distinct class. Many supporters of O'Connell's Repeal Association in America condemned his position on slavery, and several withdrew their financial support. The Repeal Associations in Charleston and Natchez broke up in protest at the address, and it sparked a transatlantic debate between O'Connell and Irish-Americans, with a series of robust exhortations being exchanged across the ocean.

The most famous of these was O'Connell's Cincinnati Address of October 1843, his response to the Cincinnati Irish Repeal Association's criticism of his abolitionist position, and his most important statement of anti-slavery beliefs. O'Connell accused Irish-Americans of betraying Ireland's tradition of liberty, suggesting their support for slavery

> reflects dishonor not only upon you, but on the land of your birth. How can the generous, the charitable, the humane, the noble emotions of the Irish heart, have become extinct among you? ... it was not in Ireland you learned this cruelty.[22]

Addressing them as 'pseudo-Irishmen', he continued:

> We cannot bring ourselves to believe that you breathed your natal air in Ireland – Ireland, the first of all the nations on the earth that abolished the dealing in slaves ... It is, to be sure, afflicting and heart-rending to me to think that so many of the Irish in America should be so degenerated as to be among the worst enemies of the people of color.[23]

The Cincinnati Address hammered home a favourite O'Connell theme, that by opposing slavery in America Irish-Americans could bring honour to Ireland's cause. He concluded by imploring 'Irishmen in America, in the name of your father-land ... to abandon for ever all defense of the hideous Negro Slavery system.'[24]

O'Connell's efforts made little headway in Irish America, however, and the backlash against him forced him to emphasise the difference between himself and Garrison on religious issues. There was already widespread suspicion among Irish-Americans that the Protestant abolitionists were anti-Catholic. For instance, according to Riach, 'English Quakers reputedly refused to use the term "emancipation" in reference to the slave because it smacked too much of Roman Catholic Emancipation', and prominent abolitionists like Lyman Beecher, the president of Lane Seminary in Cincinnati and the father of Harriet Beecher Stowe, the author of *Uncle Tom's Cabin*, were regarded by many Irish-Americans as being anti-Catholic.[25]

Abolition was seen by many Irish-Americans as a Protestant cause, and prominent Catholics in America were reluctant to denounce slavery. Irish-born Bishop John England of Charleston maintained that the Catholic tradition condemned not slavery but only the slave trade, and Irish-born Bishop Francis Patrick Kenrick of Philadelphia advised that with regard to anti-slavery, 'nothing should be attempted against the law.'[26] In 1849, Garrison wrote that 'not a Catholic priest, not a Catholic journal, can be found in this great country, pleading for the liberation of the enslaved; on the contrary, they most heartily stigmatize the abolitionists and all their movements.'[27] In fact, although Pope Gregory XVI had condemned the slave trade in an apostolic letter in 1839, not a single Catholic bishop spoke out publicly in favour of abolition before the American Civil War began in 1861.[28]

When Fr Mathew visited America seven years after he had signed O'Connell's Address, he found there was no neutral position to take on slavery. A few weeks after arrival, he was met in Boston by Garrison who invited him to an Anti-Slavery Society meeting. Mathew declined, insisting that he was in America to combat intemperance, and added that although he was not in favour of slavery, he was not sure there was anything against it in Scripture.[29] Mathew's remarks, widely reported throughout America, were predictably denounced by the abolitionists and welcomed in the South. Senator Jefferson Davis of Mississippi, later to lead the Confederacy in the Civil War, said he was willing to pay homage to Mathew's work in Ireland, but not to O'Connell. Mathew further enraged the abolitionists by dining with the US President and slaveholder John Tyler, and embarking on a controversial visit to the southern slave states. Writing from Alabama in 1850, Mathew insisted that his refusal to speak against slavery had been necessary because, had he condemned the institution, he would have been refused access to the South, and so not been able to convert many Irish people in the southern states to temperance, and they would have remained 'slaves' to drink.[30]

The divisions between the abolitionists and the Catholic Church were widened by the fuss surrounding Mathew's visit and remained obvious for decades. Bostonian Wendell Phillips, who succeeded Garrison as President of the American Anti-Slavery Society, conceded that it was O'Connell who gave the abolitionists their first lessons in the techniques of non-violent mass agitation; however, Phillips's wife Ann, herself a prominent abolitionist, remained virulently anti-Catholic. In a letter to her husband in

1869, she criticised him for giving a speech supporting the labour rights of Irish immigrants:

> You ought never, even in the most [indecipherable] way, to help the Catholics. In the course of a hundred or less years, there has got to be a new Reformation and a new Luther. *Protestants* are doing the work which they [the Catholics] have got to give their lives to undo.[31]

Although O'Connell's attempts to rally Irish-Americans to fight slavery failed, he proved an inspirational figure for several American abolitionists, most notably the former slave Frederick Douglass. Douglass was the most important black figure of the era. Born in Maryland in 1817, the son of a black slave mother and a white father, he was originally called Frederick Bailey, and took the name Douglass after escaping to freedom from Baltimore in 1833, where he learned to read and write while working as a house servant. At an Anti-Slavery Society meeting in Massachusetts in 1841, he gave his first speech, recounting his experiences as a slave. He was immediately signed up by the society for a series of lectures, and became one of the nation's most powerful speakers for abolition. He toured Ireland and Britain in 1845 and 1846, delivering a series of lectures in Limerick, Dublin and – most famously – Belfast, before returning to the US to edit an abolitionist newspaper, the *North Star*. Almost a decade later, he would remember his first day in Ireland, and how he had been struck by the similarities between the Irish peasant and the black slave:

> I addressed ... a large meeting ... of the common people of Ireland. ... Never did human faces tell a sadder tale. More than five thousand were assembled ... these people lacked only a black skin and wooly hair, to complete their likeness to the plantation negro. The open, uneducated mouth – the long gaunt arm – the badly formed foot and ankle – the shuffling gait – the retreating forehead and vacant expression – and, their petty quarrels and fights – all reminded me of the plantation, and my own cruelly abused people. ... the Irishman educated, is a model gentleman; the Irishman ignorant and degraded, compares in form and feature with the negro.[32]

When Douglass spoke at a meeting of the Repeal Association in Dublin's Conciliation Hall a few weeks later, O'Connell was also on the platform. According to a newspaper report, Douglass remembered that he'd first heard the Irishman's name through the curses of his master, 'which made me love him [O'Connell],' and admire him because he had 'heard him condemned and denounced by those who oppressed the slave'.[33] The former slave also told the meeting that the idea of escape from slavery had first been suggested to him by two Irishmen he met on the docks in Baltimore. The Irishmen, he remembered

> advised me to run away to the north; that I should find friends there and be free. I pretended not to be interested in what they said, and treated them as if I did not understand them; for I feared they might be treacherous.[34]

Douglass's tour of Ireland coincided with the Famine years of 1845 and 1846, and left an indelible impression on the former slave and his audiences, as he recounted first-hand the reality of slavery and the fight for abolition to packed halls across the country. Though fascinated by his presence in Ireland, local press reaction to Douglass was mixed. At the start of his tour, the *Waterford Freeman* suggested that American abolition should be a secondary consideration to Ireland's own troubles, as 'people in serfdom cannot afford to make new enemies', a view echoed by the *Tipperary Free Press*, which suggested that 'when we ourselves are free, let us then engage in any struggle to erase the sin of slavery from every land. But, until then, our own liberation is that for which we should take counsel, and work steadily.'[35] Nevertheless, Douglass's oratorical skills were widely admired, and he drew large crowds everywhere he spoke. When he spoke in Cork in October 1845, the *Cork Examiner* declared itself impressed with Douglass's speech to 260 people and what it called his rendition of a 'Nigger song'.[36] A month later in Limerick he made a forceful impression on his audiences by showing some torture equipment used against slaves, including an iron collar which still had some flesh of a slave woman on it, and a pair of handcuffs.[37]

It was in Belfast, however, that Douglass encountered serious controversy. A fierce debate over the proper position for religious ministers to adopt over the question of slavery had been raging for months. Abolitionists had been urging Irish Presbyterian ministers to exclude pro-slavery foreign churchmen from their pulpits. Douglass stepped into the furore even before he arrived in Belfast, when he complained about the record of American churches in opposing slavery during a speech in Cork. 'The Presbyterian body also had done as much to uphold slavery as the Episcopalian,' he is reported to have said by the *Cork Examiner*. 'Indeed they went farther, for they justified it by reference to Abraham ... and particularly instanced the act of St Paul, who caused a runaway slave to be sent back to his master.'[38] Douglass himself was a Methodist, and, notwithstanding the American Catholic Church's poor record on abolition, added that 'if the majority of the persons at the meeting ... were Roman Catholics, it showed they felt more sympathy with the slave than other sects.'[39]

Local religious disagreements in Belfast had resulted in some Presbyterian ministers announcing that they would stay away from his meetings in protest at local abolitionists' uncompromising language, and rumours were circulating that Douglass was an imposter. The visitor was initially hesitant about venturing north, regarding Belfast as 'a hotbed of Presbyterianism and Free Churchism', though he insisted on making the trip because he thought 'a blow can be struck here more effectively than in any other part of Ireland.'[40]

The Mayor of Belfast, Andrew Mulholland, chaired the first of Douglass's six lectures in the city in December 1845. Douglass gave a straightforward and witty narrative of his life in slavery, his escape and his voyage to Ireland, and was received enthusiastically by the audience.[41] A few weeks later, however, at a meeting of the Belfast Anti-Slavery Society, he confronted the rumours about his credibility. 'Although the admission was not gratuitous,' reported the *Belfast Newsletter*, 'the Meeting-House was crowded to excess, not a spare seat attainable.'[42] After a lengthy introduction, Douglass rose to deny that he was an impostor, and insisted that the rumour that he had no credentials was false:

I have been in Ireland four months, and have delivered upwards of fifty lectures in different parts of the country, and it was not until I reached Belfast, that I had even been asked for credentials. No enquiries were made of me in Dublin, for I had been known to the Abolitionists of that city for the last four years, through the American papers.[43]

He then launched into an attack on the Free Church of Scotland for its poor record on abolition, and on the American Baptists, whose president was a slaveholder.

Despite the difficulties surrounding Douglass's visit to Belfast, his trip was largely successful, and within a month of his departure for Britain a female anti-slavery society had been formed in Belfast. Although Douglass did not return to Ireland until 1883 (on honeymoon), he took an intense interest in Irish affairs, and often referred to O'Connell in his speeches. He repeatedly quoted O'Connell's assertion that 'the history of the Irish people might be traced, like a wounded man through the crowd, by the blood' to illustrate the brutality of the slave system on blacks.[44]

Inevitably, Douglass joined in the furore over Fr Mathew's visit to America in 1849. Douglass had taken the pledge of alcohol abstinence from Fr Mathew when Douglass was in Ireland in 1845, and was dismayed at Mathew's refusal to condemn slavery when he arrived in the US four years later.[45] Douglass said he was 'grieved, humbled and mortified' at Mathew's silence, and compared him with others from outside the US who had spoken out against slavery while abroad but who, once in America, 'deserted their principles, abandoned the cause and linked themselves with the oppressors and haters of liberty, finding it much easier to sail with the popular breeze, than to maintain their integrity'.[46]

Douglass remained faithful to the Irish struggle until his death in 1895, appearing on platforms with Irish leader Charles Stewart Parnell and declaring his support for Irish Home Rule. Douglass addressed a reception for two Irish MPs in Washington DC in 1887, where he dutifully declared himself 'an out-and-out Home Ruler for Ireland'.[47] He also remembered how, 40 years earlier, he had stood on the banks of the Liffey 'side by side with the great Daniel O'Connell. ... He called me then the Black O'Connell of America,' recalled Douglass with some pride. 'At that time I declared, before a vast audience in Conciliation Hall, my conviction of the justice, the wisdom, the necessity, and the final triumph of the repeal of the Union.'[48]

Not all supporters of Irish Home Rule reciprocated Douglass's support, however, and in the second half of the nineteenth century some prominent Irish leaders were happy to associate themselves with the idea of black slavery, most notably John Mitchel of the Young Ireland movement. Impatient with O'Connell's slow parliamentary approach to repeal, the Young Irelanders were formed in 1842 to promote a more radical nationalism. Mitchel, the son of an Ulster Presbyterian minister, called for an uprising in 1848. The failed insurrection resulted in Mitchel being sentenced to fourteen years' transportation. Escaping from Australia in 1853, he made his way to America, where he supported the Southern cause. Mitchel proposed that the slave trade should be reopened, and even foresaw the possibility of an Irish Republic with 'an accompaniment of slave plantations'.[49]

Mitchel published a newspaper in America called *Citizen*, in which he denied that it was wrong 'to keep slaves to their work by flogging or other needful coercion'.[50] During the American Civil War he edited two newspapers based in Richmond, Virginia, the capital of the Southern Confederacy, and his son was killed in the opening skirmish of the US Civil War at Fort Sumter, fighting to defend slavery. Douglass called Mitchel 'a traitor to liberty'.[51]

Irish-American immigrants fought on both sides during the war over slavery. An estimated 150,000 Irish-born immigrants joined the Unionist forces, while about 40,000 fought for the Confederacy.[52] Union commander (and later US President) Ulysses S. Grant and Confederate General 'Stonewall' Jackson could both trace Ulster Presbyterian origins. In some northern cities, despite widespread support for the Union cause, there was notable Irish-American hostility towards blacks. Many Irish immigrants feared the prospect of increased economic competition in the event of a southern defeat, predicting that thousands of newly-freed slaves would flood the North and compete for scarce jobs. While poor relations between Irish immigrants and American blacks were common, they were not universal. Seneca Village in New York, for example, appears to have integrated the two traditions quite happily by the middle of the nineteenth century. An Irish woman, Margaret Geery, served as midwife for the whole village and there was at least one interracial marriage.[53] The village was levelled in the 1850s to make way for Central Park.

However, the first military conscription bill signed in 1863 resulted in riots in New York. The bill drafted white men aged between 20 and 45, but those who could afford $300 were able to buy their way out. The draft thus fell disproportionately onto the poor, a situation exacerbated by the Union Army's refusal to accept blacks who wanted to enlist.[54] The law meant that large numbers of Irish-Americans were drafted, leaving blacks to fill their vacant jobs. Between 13 and 16 July the Irish-American community staged a series of riots in New York City. Blacks were the main target of the attacks, and for four days Irish-Americans attacked black neighbourhoods, lynching, burning and killing men, women and children.

The Union's eventual victory and the consequent abolition of slavery was due, in part, to many Irish-American infantrymen. After helping to liberate the slaves in the Southern states, many Irish-American veterans from the Union Army returned to Ireland to help train the Irish Republican Brotherhood (IRB), forerunner of the Irish Republican Army (IRA), and to prepare the IRB for war against the British. In fact, about 800 soldiers led by Colonel John O'Neill crossed the US border in 1866, attacked British-controlled

Canada and proclaimed themselves the Irish Republican Army in an attempt to strike a blow for Irish freedom. The invaders had anticipated support from the US government, but President Andrew Johnson (a first generation Scotch-Irish) had them arrested and the episode ended in failure, as did an uprising in Ireland itself a year later.[55]

The fight for Irish independence became largely a parliamentary one again in the late nineteenth century, with Parnell as the new O'Connell, hoping to win Irish freedom through the British parliament. Parnell's efforts failed, despite a widespread campaign of withholding rents, which became known as 'boycotting' after Captain Boycott, one of the landlords targeted by the campaign. A more radical alternative emerged, and by the early years of the twentieth century, the IRB was planning another attempt to remove the British by force.

When the Irish Rising eventually happened in 1916, it was not supported by the majority of the Irish public, and was put down with some ease by the British military. However, the executions of 16 of the Rising's leaders turned much Irish public opinion against the British, and contributed to a surge of sympathy for the rebels. The Rising was greeted with some enthusiasm in black American quarters. The leading black paper the *Chicago Defender* noted sympathetically:

> And now comes Ireland with a little revolution all of its own. So long has England oppressed her that a large portion of the population are even willing to take a chance and aid Germany rather than be tied longer to England's apron strings.[56]

In August, *Crisis*, the official magazine of the National Association for the Advancement of Colored People (NAACP), carried an editorial piece about the poor state of Dublin's slums, and suggested that 'where human oppression exists there the sympathy of all black hearts must go. The recent Irish revolt may have been foolish, but would to God some of us had sense enough to be fools!'[57] The piece triggered a complaint in a subsequent issue for its apparent advocacy of a 'blood sacrifice' to advance black rights.[58]

The idea of progress through violence had been supported by some blacks since the arrival of the first slaves. Violent uprisings were part of a wider repertoire of resistance to slavery, and from time to time black Americans tried to free themselves by force. Between 1663 and 1864, over a hundred slave revolts had been recorded.[59]

Some were well organised, others not. In the nineteenth century there were three major uprisings. In 1800, Gabriel Prosser led 1100 slaves in an attack on Richmond, Virginia. The attempt failed, and Prosser and 34 others were executed.[60] In 1822, former slave Denmark Vesey organised thousands of slaves around Charleston, South Carolina but, like Prosser, he was betrayed by an informer. Vesey and 46 others were executed for their part in the planning the revolt. Nine years later Nat Turner led a small band of about 60 slaves in Virginia. Turner's group forced their way into his master's house, and killed the slaveowner and his family. Turner led the slaves to other slaveholders' houses, and killed them and their families. In all, ten men, 14 women and 35 children were killed by Turner's men before they were captured. Turner was one of almost a hundred black men killed for their part in the insurrection.

In the 1920s, a militant black nationalism in the US was championed by Jamaican-born Marcus Garvey, who had founded the Universal Negro Improvement and Conservation Association and African Communities League (UNIA) in Jamaica in 1914. It aimed to instil racial pride, and acquire economic power for blacks to help build a black-governed nation in Africa. Garvey arrived in New York in March 1916, a month before Ireland's Rising, and became the most important black leader of his generation. He drew thousands of supporters into the UNIA, and soon made the UNIA the first important black nationalist movement of the twentieth century.

Garvey was one of several black nationalists who studied and admired the Irish Republican approach. Garvey's Irish influences had begun as early as 1910, when he was assistant secretary of the National Club of Jamaica, whose founder, S.A.G. Cox, had admired the Sinn Fein movement while studying in London in the early years of the century. Cox called the National Club of Jamaica's newspaper *Our Own*, roughly translated from the Irish Sinn Fein.[61] Garvey himself arrived in England in 1912 and lived there for the next two years, just as the new Irish nationalism, which eventually culminated in the 1916 Rising, became a major political issue. Garvey based many of his black nationalist ideas on the Irish model. In an essay introducing Garvey's public papers Robert A. Hill suggests: 'Far more than any other nationalist struggle, the Irish revolutionary struggle assisted in focusing Garvey's political perspective.'[62]

Garvey was not alone in taking inspiration from Irish Republicanism. Cyril V. Briggs owned *Crusader*, a black nationalist paper which exchanged subscription advertisements with its Irish counterpart, *Sinn Feiner*, and, as Hall points out, Briggs's creation of the secret African Blood Brotherhood for African Liberation and Redemption 'drew upon the example of the Irish Republican Brotherhood'.[63] It was Garvey, however, who most often cited the Irish struggle as instructive for black nationalism. Garvey organised the Black Star Line in 1919, a steamship company owned, managed and operated by blacks. It became emblematic of the UNIA's idea for an independent black economy working within white capitalism. The following year, he presided over an international UNIA conference, which adopted a Declaration of Rights of the Negro People of the World, and declared himself provisional president of an African empire the following year. Like Douglass before him, Garvey compared the condition of blacks with that of the Irish and, like Douglass, was inspired by the most important Irish leader of the time. Where Douglass had O'Connell to influence his political development, Garvey looked to Eamon de Valera, the highest-ranking Republican leader of the 1916 Rising to survive, and president of Sinn Fein.

De Valera, a former maths teacher, had been a commandant in the 1916 Rising in Dublin before being captured and sentenced to death. However, after public opinion turned so strongly against the British following the first wave of executions, de Valera and others had their sentences commuted.[64] With the top tier of Irish revolutionaries executed, the mantle of leadership fell to figures like de Valera to carry on the fight for an Irish Republic. Released from prison in 1917, the new Republican leadership began to reorganise. When Tomas Ashe, the only surviving veteran of the 1916 Rising with a Republican pedigree to match de Valera's, died on hunger strike in September that year, de Valera became undisputed leader of the Republican movement, and was elected President of Sinn Fein. The political party contested the general election called by Britain in December 1918, and although it won the overwhelming majority of seats, its representatives refused to attend the British parliament, and instead set up an alternative illegal Irish parliament, or Dail, in Dublin. De Valera proclaimed himself president of the Irish Republic, and Sinn Fein became the *de facto* government in some parts of Ireland, setting up an alternative administration, organising local government, taxes and courts.

Within a year, large-scale guerrilla war had broken out in Ireland, with the police and British soldiers targets of IRA attacks. Hundreds of soldiers died in ambushes, and hundreds more civilians were killed in reprisals. Garvey supported the Irish Republican struggle during these traumatic years. At a speech in Madison Square Garden in New York in August 1920, just before the UNIA Conference opened, Garvey announced he was sending a telegram to de Valera, whom he recognised as president of the Irish Republic (although the governments of Britain and America did not). '25,000 Negro delegates ... send you greetings as president of the Irish Republic. Please accept sympathy of Negroes of the world for your cause. ... Keep up the fight for a free Ireland,' it read.[65]

A few weeks later, Garvey was interviewed by journalist Charles Mowbray White on his hopes for the UNIA. Garvey told Mowbray he had already proposed that the organisation's colours should be red, black and green. 'Garvey said red because of sympathy with the "Reds of the world", and the Green their sympathy for the Irish in their fight for freedom, and the Black – [for] the Negro', explained White.[66] At the end of August 1920, the convention elected Garvey 'Provisional President of Africa', an idea borrowed from de Valera in declaring himself 'President of Ireland'. In December of that year, Garvey and de Valera were scheduled to speak together at a meeting organised by the UNIA. A leaflet advertising the meeting, (which never took place due to de Valera's return to Ireland) billed Garvey as 'Provisional President of Africa' and de Valera as 'Provisional President of Ireland'.[67]

Some sections of the American press began to report on the links between Irish and black nationalist groups in the US. Reporting on the UNIA Convention in 1921, the *Washington Bee* noted that a speaker from the National Committee of the Friends of Irish Freedom addressed the conference and compared Garvey with St Patrick.[68] The reporter concluded that 'by the frequent applause from the audience, it was quite evident that the aims and objectives of the two great peoples are identical and that their efforts are mutual.'[69]

Some in the US intelligence community were concerned about the Garvey–Irish link. An informer specialising in 'Negro subversion' in the Military Intelligence Division alleged that Garvey and Friends of Irish Freedom, an Irish-American organisation sympathetic to Irish Republicanism, were linked. The informer alleged that the Black Star Line had been set up with Irish help and its ships would eventually carry arms to Africa.[70] Suspicions increased a few months later when, in October 1920, Special Agent P-138 of US Intelligence observed a black nationalist meeting in New York where 'some Irish leaders spoke in high terms of Garvey and his movement and pledged their support.'[71] The meeting took place while Irish dockworkers were boycotting British ships in an attempt to get an Irish Republican prisoner, Terence MacSwiney, released from jail.

Agent P-138 reported that 'SELFRIDGE, a Negro local preacher and Garvey's hired field agent and right hand stool pigeon was sent down to the docks to urge all the Negro longshoremen not to load British ships, which act pleased the Irish strikers.'[72]

In 1920, Garvey sent a telegram to British Prime Minister David Lloyd George asking that MacSwiney, who was on hunger strike, not be allowed to die, and sent another to MacSwiney's priest which said 'Convey to McSwiney [sic] sympathy of 400,000,000 Negroes.'[73] MacSwiney's death after 74 days on hunger strike touched a deep chord in Garvey, who repeatedly expressed admiration for the prisoner's sacrifice. 'I believe the death of McSweeney [sic] did more for the freedom of Ireland today than probably anything they did for 600 years prior to his death', he said two months after MacSwiney's death. The following year Garvey compared the Irish Republican with Indian leader Mahatma Gandhi.[74]

Lloyd George became subjected to increasing national and international pressure to stop the war in Ireland. Sinn Fein stood again in the elections of April 1921, and, under de Valera's leadership, again won most constituencies. In July a truce was called, and Republican representatives – though crucially not de Valera, who decided to stay in Dublin – went to London to negotiate a settlement with Britain. A settlement was eventually reached and signed by the Sinn Fein representatives six months later. But what Britain had offered, and what the Sinn Fein representatives led by Arthur Griffith and Michael Collins had signed, was something less than an independent Irish Republic.

The Treaty, as it was known, stipulated that representatives in an Irish parliament would still have to take an oath of allegiance to the British Crown, and that the northeast of Ireland would remain under British rule. Collins and others argued it was a magnificent achievement, and presented it as a marvellous stepping-stone to a full Republic. Although it was accepted by a narrow majority when voted on in the Dail, de Valera and many others refused to accept it. Civil war broke out between those who accepted the Treaty, and those who did not. For the next 18 months, Ireland was torn apart by a bloody internecine conflict that left families divided, with fathers pitted against sons and brothers fighting against brothers. By mid-1923 the forces of the new Irish government, which had accepted the Treaty, overcame the IRA, led by de Valera. Despite Garvey's professed admiration for de Valera, however, he welcomed the Treaty which propelled de Valera into civil war. A week after the settlement was announced, Garvey said:

I am glad Ireland has won some modicum of self-government ... so I am not with my friend de Valera at this minute; I am with my friend [Arthur] Griffith. I believe he is a wise statesman in signing the pact and accepting a sort of Irish Free State. [75]

Garvey also sent telegrams of congratulation to Griffith and Lloyd George. A month later he was predicting complete Irish freedom within two or three years. Michael Collins had been killed in the war, but de Valera survived it, and in the 1930s returned to mainstream politics with a new party, Fianna Fail. De Valera dominated Irish politics in the following decades, and was either head of the government or president for 35 of the 41 years between 1932 and 1973.

Reflecting on his inspiration from Ireland a decade later, Garvey paid tribute to de Valera: 'We have watched his career for several years both in Ireland and the U.S.A., where he carried on a relentless propaganda in the interests of Irish Republicanism ... we understand him and spirit of people he represents.'[76] By the time Garvey wrote those words in July 1932, de Valera had just completed a remarkable political comeback. From being the most feared enemy of the Irish Free State government, de Valera had become its president. De Valera steered Ireland through the Second World War, successfully preserving its neutrality in the face of fierce pressure from Britain to join the allied effort. America's entry into the war resulted in large numbers of black soldiers being stationed in Northern Ireland. Arriving 100 years after Frederick Douglass had been feted in Belfast, the black GIs often encountered prejudice and discrimination.

The first US troops arrived in Northern Ireland in January 1942, and by 1944, when preparations for the D-Day landings in France were under way, there were 120,000 American soldiers based there, including several thousand black troops. Tension between black and white American soldiers was never far from the surface, and in an effort to avoid trouble the US Army issued guidelines urging

... segregation where possible (dances, accommodation, private parties, etc) but otherwise mutual respect in mixed facilities such as washrooms and Red Cross clubs. Neither race must interfere with a 'cut-in' on soldiers of the other race in company with girls.[77]

The guidelines failed to prevent a series of violent incidents from breaking out. Charlie Gallagher recalled the friction in Derry's dancehalls:

I remember in the Corinthian one night ... they had the hottest band, Paddy Lynch's String Quartet ... a lot of black soldiers came in and also a bunch of white Americans .... All the black Americans got on one side of the hall and all the [white] Americans got on the other and they began advancing towards each other and then some of them grabbed chairs and it looked like an ugly scene. The manager phoned for the Shore Patrols and then in came a swarm of Military Police with their batons and began beating every-one ... that sort of thing did go on quite regularly in certain dance halls.[78]

More serious trouble broke out between white and black troops in late September 1942, as reported by the *Belfast Telegraph*:

Wm. C. Jenkins, a negro private in the American Army ... was stabbed to death during a disturbance in the streets of Antrim about nine o'clock on Wednesday night. A white soldier was wounded. Several shots were fired ... no civilians were involved.[79]

The Belfast paper followed the incident with an insensitive feature on black troops a few days later. The piece noted some of the many things the 'dusky Doughboys' didn't understand about Northern Ireland: 'They want to know why the daylight lingers so long. ... When darkness comes they wonder what spooks are at large in these great trees – they are very superstitious.'[80] It also quoted a senior American officer who advised readers that if they wanted to make the black soldiers feel at home they could 'drive into the camp with a load of piccaninnies – and *would* the boys be happy?'.[81]

Many of the black soldiers were decidedly unhappy about the treatment they received from locals in Northern Ireland. One wrote anonymously to members of Northern Ireland's government to complain that he had been refused service in a bar in Antrim because of his colour, and that 'We hate to walk the streets of Belfast merely because we are insulted. They used the words "nigger" and "darky". ... We want to be friends of the Irish, not enemies.'[82] Not all locals were hostile, of course, and the anonymous soldier said he and his colleagues had been treated very well while stationed in Carrickfergus. There were complaints from white GIs that black soldiers were being made too welcome by local women. A white quartermaster wrote from Northern Ireland that several outfits of colored troops preceded us over here and have succeeded pretty well in salting away the local feminine pulchritude ... the girls really go for them in preference to white boys, a fact that irks the boys no end.[83]

One Unionist MP complained that local girls going out with black GIs were 'mostly of the lowest type and belong to our [Catholic] minority'.[84]

When the black troops finally went home, they returned to an America beginning to deal with civil rights. In 1948, the US Army was desegregated. Six years later, the US Supreme Court ruled that racially segregated schools were illegal, and a year after that a young Protestant minister, Martin Luther King, rose to national prominence for his part in organising a boycott of segregated buses in Montgomery, Alabama. During the 1940s and 1950s, comparisons were repeatedly drawn between blacks in America and Catholics in Northern Ireland.

Discrimination by local government was experienced by both groups, most notably in the *de facto* denial of the vote to large numbers of Catholics in Northern Ireland and blacks in America, and the denial of local government jobs to both minorities. In 1942, a Protestant offered a job as town clerk in Belfast had the offer withdrawn when it was discovered he was married to a Catholic.[85] The *Irish News* reported that at a special meeting of Armagh City Council called to appoint a clerk typist in 1949 it was suggested 'that a notice reading "No Catholic Need Apply" be posted on the City Hall door'.[86] Housing patterns in Northern Ireland during this time were unofficially segregated along religious lines, much as many American cities were divided into black and white neighbourhoods. One study of Northern Ireland during the 1950s noted how Protestants there were often alarmed if housing patterns began to break down: '"They are getting in" is the phrase one hears, and it is evident that in general a "mixed" area in the towns is regarded by Protestants as one which is going downhill.'[87]

Political integration was even more unlikely. Northern Irish Catholics traditionally repudiated the right of the British government to rule them. In the 1950s most still hoped for an eventual reunification of Ireland, and to enjoy the independence from Britain which the rest of the island had won in 1922. The ruling Unionist Party, backed by the majority of Protestants, made little effort to integrate them into Northern Irish political life. In 1959, when it was rumoured that the ban on Catholics joining the Unionist Party might be lifted, Sir George Clark, grand master of the powerful Protestant organisation the Orange Lodge of Ulster, was adamant: 'It is difficult to see how a Catholic, with the vast differences in our religious outlook, could be ... acceptable within the Unionist Party.' This view was echoed by Northern Irish Prime Minister Lord Brookeborough, who confirmed the Catholic ban would stay and added: 'If that is called intolerance, I say at once it is not the fault of the Unionist party. If it is called inflexible then it shows that our principles are not elastic.'[88]

Within this political climate, ideas of Catholic civil disobedience began to stir. In late 1948, Nationalist MP Eddie McAteer of Derry wrote a pamphlet calling for a programme of non-violent non-cooperation. *Irish Action* urged Catholics to express their resistance to British rule in small acts of defiance. When dealing with government agencies, for instance, he advised people to 'act stupid, demand explanations, object, anything at all that will clog the Departmental machinery'.[89] Citing Mahatma Gandhi's third road between violence and constitutional agitation, McAteer suggested strategies designed to make British rule untenable, including commercial and cultural boycotts. 'Irish people must not be spectators at military tattoos, parades or any function under Occupation auspices. Our attitude must be the attitude of the French to the Germans whilst France was under German occupation,' he said.

Perhaps most significant, however, was his suggestion to beat the ban on political marches. 'Surely we can walk (not march) on our own streets, and if we all walk in one direction and in perfect silence, what law do we break?' Some Nationalist marches were attempted in Derry during the early 1950s, but stimulated forceful police reaction and little media interest, and political marching was not attempted again until the civil rights era over a decade later.

Before the early 1960s, most Catholics generally accepted the situation as inevitable, and tried to make the best of it. Complaining about discrimination appeared unlikely to change things. It was a fact of life that the Protestant majority governed Northern Ireland and few outsiders were interested or took complaints seriously. As one academic from Oxford University suggested in 1955:

> From any objective point of view it cannot be said that the grievances of the Catholics are always very real. They have less to complain about than the U.S. negroes, and their lot is a very pleasant one as compared with that of the nationalists in, say, Ukraine.[90]

2

Second-class Citizens

The early years of the 1960s saw an Irish Catholic elected American President, an intensification of the civil rights struggle in the US, and a sharp increase in the number of television sets in Northern Ireland. The first television broadcasts were received in Northern Ireland in 1954, when 10,000 television licences were issued. By 1962, the number of channels had doubled to two, and 194,000 licences were issued.[1] Within a few years, most people in Northern Ireland would regard the broadcast media as the best source of news.[2]

British media coverage of the campaign for civil rights in the US in the first few years of the 1960s meant that Northern Irish viewers saw television reports of sit-ins at segregated eating facilities, the Freedom Rides of 1961 aimed at integrating public transport in the American South, thousands of people on protest marches and – most dramatically – the brutal treatment of non-violent protestors by some police forces. Republican leader Gerry Adams credits media coverage of the black civil rights movement as contributing to an increased politicisation in Northern Ireland. 'Courtesy of television, we were able to see an example of the fact that you didn't just have to take it, you could fight back,' he wrote.[3]

Michael Farrell, a student at Queen's University in Belfast in the early 1960s, and later a leader of the organisation People's Democracy, recalled that

> all young Catholics ... were very influenced by seeing on television the American civil rights movement ... by the beginning of the '60s, you were beginning to have the American civil rights struggle on television and I think there was a very general identification with it.[4]

Farrell, with about a dozen other students, set up the Working Committee on Civil Rights at Queen's in 1964. Eamonn McCann, another of the students involved in the project, remembered:

The idea was to investigate was there discrimination against Protestants in Newry which would have been complementary to the discrimination against Catholics in Derry. ... Northern Ireland being the sort of place it was, discrimination against Catholics dominated all politics but hardly anybody had quantified this or attempted to investigate it.[5]

Elsewhere in Northern Ireland, similar attempts to collect evidence on discrimination were being made. In early 1963, Dungannon was a typical town in the middle of Northern Ireland. Its population of about 7,000 was roughly half Catholic, half Protestant. Protestants tended to dominate the upper end of what social scale there was, either owning or being employed in the town's larger shops, its banks and factories. Most of the labouring jobs were done by Catholics, and there were a few Catholic nurses and teachers.

One of the few middle-class Catholics in the town was local doctor Conn McCluskey. The health of several of his patients was being damaged by Dungannon's chronic housing shortage. Due to the gerrymandering of electoral districts, the town consisted of three wards, two controlled by Unionists, the other by Nationalists. There was no points system for housing allocation, so tenancies were awarded in the Unionist wards by local Unionists, and in the Nationalist ward by Nationalists. However, as no new houses had been built in the Nationalist ward for decades, the problem was particularly acute for Catholics hoping to get a house. No Catholic family had been allocated a permanent house for 34 years. There were over 300 families on the housing waiting list, most hoping for temporary or semi-permanent homes.[6]

'In some cases families had been waiting as long as twelve years for a home', said Conn McCluskey, who found ten people living in one room of a converted house. The strain on young couples was extreme. 'Newly-weds were compelled to move in with in-laws and keep their wedding presents under the bed', recalled the doctor.[7] If children began to arrive, the tension increased. When one young mother took an overdose in desperation, a group of young married women called a meeting to discuss the housing situation in May 1963, and decided to picket the local offices of the Urban Council in protest at the housing crisis.

Television news in the weeks before the picket had shown pictures of large-scale civil rights protests in Birmingham, Alabama, as Martin Luther King led demonstrations against segregated schools, hotels, cinemas, public eating facilities, and against the city's discriminatory employment practices, its all-white police force and unfair voting systems.[8] King had been jailed during the protest, and the Birmingham police force, on the orders of Eugene 'Bull' Connor, had used hoses and Alsatian dogs against the civil rights marchers, many of whom were children.

Those on this first anti-discrimination protest of the 1960s in Northern Ireland immediately identified with the American civil rights movement. One woman on the picket, interviewed by a local paper, said: 'They talk about Alabama, why don't they talk about Dungannon?'[9] The women marched up and down the pavement, American-style, carrying placards with slogans such as 'Racial Discrimination In Alabama Hits Dungannon' and (in reference to an earlier US civil rights campaign) 'If Our Religion Is Against Us Ship Us To Little Rock'.[10] The women's petition – called the 'Declaration of Independence' – demanded a fairer housing allocation, and an end to Unionist 'ghetto' policy.[11]

Protestors in Derry the following year also made the link with Little Rock, Arkansas, where in September 1957 US President Dwight Eisenhower had despatched 1,000 paratroopers to ensure the racial integration of Central High School. The Derry protestors of January 1964 were residents of Springtown, one of the military camps built to house American soldiers during the early 1940s. Many Derry families were living in the 'temporary' accommodation 20 years after the troops had left, and it had fallen into squalor. The residents staged a protest with banners declaring 'Derry's Little Rock Calls For Fair Play.'[12]

In Dungannon, the 67 women, or 'the young housewives [who had] declared war on the local council' as the local press described them, were mostly in their twenties.[13] Patricia McCluskey, the doctor's wife, had helped them draft the petition, and obtained permission to call a meeting in a local hall to air their grievances. She recalled:

> We got permission to call a meeting in the local hall, and I didn't want any part or parcel other than to get people to express their opinion, but when nobody turned up – none of the other Catholic councillors or even the clergyman who was supposed to sponsor the meeting turned up and the hall was packed with people because the girls had brought all their friends ... and they sat for an hour and the table at the top [was] empty, and then people began to scuffle and I absolutely saw red ... and I got up and banged the table and called the meeting to order and it was just pure rage at so much hard work and so many people's hopes

being thrown out that made me take over and I found myself with the gift of the gab – I found myself organising.[14]

She chaired the meeting when the group of young women officially became the Homeless Citizens League on 18 May 1963. The League's representatives met with the council, but when they were refused any of the 142 new council houses just built in a Unionist ward, they decided to stage a series of protest marches around the town. One local paper carried a photograph of two young boys on one of the marches. One has his face blacked up, and is carrying a sign which reads: 'We are pals from Alabama/where they say we can't agree/Is there really that much difference/When you look at him and me?'[15]

With no immediate prospect of council help, some families decided to take direct action. The 142 new houses had mainly gone to Protestant newly-weds, many of whom had vacated an estate of pre-fabricated bungalows in another part of town. The women had told Patricia McCluskey that if they didn't get the vacated pre-fabs they were going to hand the responsibility for looking after their babies over to the state:

> [They] promised me that if they didn't get these houses they were all going to put their babies into homes ... welfare homes, so I rang up all the welfare homes to tell them that if these houses were knocked down that they were going to get all these children.[16]

Unperturbed, the council moved bulldozers to the site and began dismantling the pre-fabs. Some were to be sold as henhouses. That night, 28 August 1963, 200,000 people across the Atlantic stood at the Lincoln Memorial in Washington, DC to hear Martin Luther King deliver a legendary speech. 'I Have a Dream,' King declared, '[that] ... we will be able to speed up that day when all of God's children – black men and white men, Jews and gentiles, Protestants and Catholics – will be able to join hands ...'.[17] At exactly the same time King spoke his historic words in America's capital, 17 Dungannon families – led by the young women – moved into the vacant pre-fabs. 'It was the girls you see, it was the women's effort. The men were terrible sheep ... the women do the talking ... it was the thing that started the whole thing and Northern Ireland has never been the same since' said Conn McCluskey.[18]

As had happened in the US, it was women who took decisive action and offered crucial impetus to the civil rights movement.

Years before Martin Luther King became recognised as the leader of the Montgomery Bus Boycott, local black women had been agitating against their unfair treatment on the city's buses. In 1946, middle-class black women in Montgomery had formed the Women's Political Council (WPC). 'We were "women power", organized to cope with any injustice ...' recalled an early member.[19] By 1953, the women's group had lodged 30 complaints against the bus company, and when Rosa Parks refused to give up her seat on a bus in 1955, it was the WPC's several hundred members who mobilised to initiate the famous boycott.

The women's group had planned the launch of a bus boycott some time before, and within 24 hours of Parks' arrest tens of thousands of leaflets had been distributed by the WPC to Montgomery's black community asking people to stay off the buses. Although King would eventually emerge as the most prominent black leader of the boycott, it was the WPC who started the protest. While King was assuring Montgomery authorities that he was not seeking anything so radical as integration of the buses, the women's group was demanding integration. 'The women of the WPC had started the boycott, and we did it for the specific purpose of finally integrating those buses,' said Jo Ann Gibson Robinson, a leader of the women's organisation.[20]

Elsewhere in the US civil rights movement, the contribution made by women has also gone largely unrecognised. One study of the civil rights movement in Mississippi suggests that 'women canvassed more than men, showed up more often at mass meetings and demonstrations, and more frequently attempted to register to vote.'[21] Like the young mothers of Dungannon who protested about unhealthy housing conditions, many black women were drawn to civil rights activism for similar reasons. 'Various stories recounting how black women first became involved in the movement attest to their intolerance of conditions that threatened their lives and the lives of their children,' noted another study of women's civil rights activism in Mississippi.[22]

The Dungannon women's takeover of the pre-fabs was the first act of civil disobedience by the new civil rights campaigners, and it resulted in a victory. As Dungannon Council reluctantly allowed the squatters to stay (within a fortnight there were 35 families in the pre-fabs), and promised to hurry the completion of a new housing estate in the Nationalist ward, the local paper described Northern Ireland's Catholic minority as 'white negroes', similar to blacks in the Southern states.

The success encouraged the campaigners to put up candidates in the local council elections. Patricia McCluskey and three others were elected in a voter turnout of over 96 per cent. The new councillors were unable to make much of a difference to the council, however, and their attempts at housing and employment reforms were all rejected. The new councillors were deeply resented by many of the old guard, and when appointments to various committees were being made, the new intake was frozen out. Patricia McCluskey, having considerable experience of foreign travel, was proposed by her colleagues to be the council's representative on the Tourist Development Body for Northern Ireland. She was rejected by the Unionist majority on the council in favour of one of their own 'whose claim to suitability', recalled Conn McCluskey, 'was that he was an employee of Ulsterbus, and was involved in running their half-day Mystery Tours from Dungannon'.[23]

Support from local well-off Catholics for the anti-discrimination campaign was also, initially, unforthcoming. According to Conn McCluskey, the local Catholic middle class did not support the protest marches as they could not bring themselves to be associated with their poorer neighbours from the housing estates, and the local Catholic Church was similarly timid. Whereas the churches in the black community in the US had often been central to organising initiatives like the Montgomery Bus Boycott, in Dungannon 'When these squatters squatted, the church [representatives] didn't even go to see them', recalled Conn McCluskey.

> I went to one of the clergymen and said 'Look, if Christ was on earth now he would at least have gone down to see the squatters' ... well, then he got into his car and he drove down to the centre where the squatters were and he opened the window and he shouted 'We're all going to be in Crumlin Road [Prison] together' ... and he never got out and he drove home.'[24]

However, it was not long before the emergent Catholic middle class took over the leadership roles of the burgeoning civil rights movement. Just as the end of segregated education facilities in the US led to an upsurge in the number of educated blacks in the 1960s, so too the post-war education reforms in Britain resulted in a young, educated generation of Catholics.

The Butler Act of 1944, which became law in Northern Ireland in 1947, provided free grammar-school education for children lucky and bright enough to pass an exam at the age of eleven. It also provided financial assistance to voluntary Catholic schools, giving many working-class Catholic families their first chance of post-primary education. Between 1946 and 1952 the total number of secondary school pupils in Northern Ireland doubled.[25] Many working-class Catholics took educational opportunities never known to their families before. Gerry Adams, born in Belfast in 1948, made it into a local grammar school. 'We were all part of a new generation of working-class *Taigs*, winning scholarships to grammar schools and "getting chances" which, as our parents and grandparents frequently reminded us, they never had', he recalled.[26]

Several civil rights leaders shared similar experiences. John Hume passed the eleven-plus exam the first year it was introduced in Northern Ireland, in 1947, and was duly awarded a grammar-school scholarship. Under the scheme, the local authority in Derry paid Hume's tuition fees – seven pounds – which his family would never have been able to afford.[27] The Derry local authority also paid the grammar-school fees of civil rights leader Eamonn McCann, born in 1943: 'We were the first generation ever given the opportunity to climb out of our condition, and much was expected of us.'[28] Some, like McCann, even went on to university. The number of full-time students at Queen's University Belfast rose from 2,691 in 1958/59 to 4,315 in 1963/64.[29] Not all, or even most, of these students were Catholics, of course, but more Catholics than ever before were graduating from local universities in the early 1960s.

A newly-educated middle-class leadership was also a characteristic of the US civil rights movement in the early 1960s. In a study of the developing class of black leadership in New Orleans in 1963, Daniel C. Thompson found that while the average black in that city had achieved 5.7 years of schooling in 1940, by 1960 the average had risen to 7.5 years.[30] The historic Selma protests of 1965 were instigated by recently-qualified, young black teachers demonstrating outside the local court house for their right to vote.[31]

Many of the educated young Catholics had their first taste of political involvement during the protest over the location of the University of Ulster in 1965. Many believed the logical site for Northern Ireland's second university was in Derry, but the Unionist government appeared reluctant to make such a large economic and educational investment in the Catholic city. The Lockwood Report on Further Education, released in January 1965, recommended that the new university be built in the largely Protestant area of Coleraine. The report briefly unified Catholic and Protestant business and educational leaders from the Derry area against the recommendation, and a campaign to have the university located in Derry was led by John Hume. Letters were written to newspapers, petitions gathered and a protest rally held at Stormont itself. The campaign was not successful but it gave middle-class Catholics some experience of political lobbying. This newly-emerging group of educated Catholics would provide an influential impetus to the civil rights movement.

For example, while the first anti-discrimination protests in Dungannon had been largely organised by working-class Catholic women, when it came to drawing up a petition, they called on Patricia McCluskey, the doctor's wife who, she said, was 'reasonably well educated'.[32] Within a few weeks of the Dungannon protests, Patricia and Conn McCluskey set about establishing a more permanent organisation to agitate for local government reforms. By January 1964 they had appointed a committee, and the Campaign for Social Justice (CSJ) was formally launched at a press conference in Belfast. By now, the movement was male-dominated, with nine men on a committee of twelve. All of the men were middle-class Catholics (three doctors, an architect, a dentist, a teacher, a councillor, a wealthy businessman and a professor). The CSJ dedicated itself to collecting material on injustices in Northern Ireland and warned that if discrimination in housing and employment were not reformed, it would present its case to the Commission for Human Rights in Strasbourg, and to the United Nations.

Although discrimination in housing legislation had triggered the protests, a wider problem – as for blacks in the US – was voter representation. Northern Ireland's peculiar voting system dated from the years immediately following its birth in the early 1920s. The treaty which Michael Collins had signed with the British government allowed for the partition of Ireland into two parts – the northeastern six counties of the island were to become Northern Ireland, and remain under British rule; the remaining 26 counties were to have their own Irish government. The provision for partition proved the most divisive part of the new agreement, and fuelled the war between the new Irish Free State government, supported by Collins, and the anti-Treatyites, led by de Valera.

Several analysts have noted the similarities between the development of Northern Ireland in the years following the Anglo-Irish War and the development of the American South after the US Civil War 60 years before. Following the defeat of the Confederacy in the US, the central government in Washington, DC allowed the

Southern states a remarkable degree of autonomy, turning a blind eye to racist laws and practices and displaying little enthusiasm for interfering in Southern ways. So too, after the Anglo-Irish War and the establishment of the six-county Northern Ireland, the government in London preferred to keep out of the new statelet's affairs. It allowed the Northern Ireland parliament at Stormont to govern more or less as it pleased. It too pretended not to see, or claimed to be powerless to prevent, discrimination. As Richard Rose has suggested, 'The [American] South, with more than one-third of its population black, remained a white man's land politically, just as Northern Ireland, with one-third of its population Catholic, became an exclusively Protestant regime.'[33]

When King George V of England opened the Northern Ireland parliament in June 1921, many Nationalists in Northern Ireland refused to recognise the parliament, and insisted that their allegiance lay with the Dail, the Irish parliament based in Dublin. Local councils which recognised Dublin as the seat of government, instead of London, were dissolved. In April 1922, 21 local authorities controlled by councillors elected on a Nationalist ticket were dissolved and replaced by commissioners appointed by the new Northern Ireland government. The Unionists soon moved to cement their grip on government, and in 1923 abolished voting by proportional representation and redrew local voting constituencies for their own benefit. Nationalists had been invited to assist in redrawing the constituency boundaries, but were still refusing to recognise the legitimacy of the Unionist government, and so would not participate, leaving the Unionists a free hand to draw electoral boundaries wherever they wished. The effects of the new-look constituencies were obvious almost immediately. In the local elections of 1927, Unionists controlled 15 out of 27 local authorities, whereas in 1920 they had controlled only three.[34] In the elections for Omagh Rural District Council in 1927, Nationalists cast 5,381 votes more than Unionists, but lost the majority of seats.

In the following decades, most election results in Northern Ireland became wholly predictable, and most seats were uncontested as the results, thanks to the large majorities for either Catholics or Protestants, were seemingly inevitable. Between 1925 and 1955, 90 per cent of rural council seats and 60 per cent of urban and borough positions were uncontested.[35] Derry City was the most famous example of the bizarre system. In 1966, the number of Catholic voters totalled 14,429, and Protestant voters 8,781. However, because the local council electoral wards had been divided into three, with most of the Catholics herded into one ward, the Unionists kept control of the city by winning the other two wards, and thus winning a 'majority' of wards, two to one.[36]

Moreover, the strange situation was exacerbated by some people being entitled to more than one vote. Limited companies were allowed to cast up to six extra votes, and as most limited companies were owned by Protestants, the rule gave Unionists an extra electoral advantage. There was also a property qualification, and as Catholics were more likely to rent than own their house, they were more likely to be disenfranchised than Protestants.[37] Catholics were in a similar situation to many American blacks who, in the 1960s, were effectively disenfranchised through gerrymandering in the northern cities and by complicated voting qualifications in the South.[38]

In Chicago, for instance, wards on the south side of the city were gerrymandered along racial lines to keep the white administration (headed by Irish-American Richard Daley) in power. In the South, black disenfranchisement was less sophisticated. A number of Southern states passed laws complicating voter registration so that in Mississippi, for instance, someone wanting to register to vote had to fill out a 21-question form, and be prepared to interpret any of the 285 sections of the Mississippi Constitution to the satisfaction of the (invariably white) registrar.[39] In Alabama, registrars were permitted to ask someone applying to vote to summarise the American Constitution. If the registrar found the applicant's answer unsatisfactory, the applicant would not be allowed to register.[40]

While Catholics who owned property were allowed to vote in local council elections in Northern Ireland, the gerrymandered boundaries often made their vote worth far less than one cast by their Protestant neighbours. As Fionnbarra O Dochartaigh of Derry suggests, 'By confining many thousands of nationalists within the South Ward, and by refusing to allocate houses to them in the other two [Protestant-controlled] wards, greater miseries were inflicted on the mainly Catholic electorate.'[41] According to O Dochartaigh, Catholic identification with blacks was obvious: 'Many of us looked to the civil rights struggles in America for our inspiration. We compared ourselves to the poor blacks of the US ghettoes. ... Indeed we viewed ourselves as Ulster's White Negroes.'[42]

Derry was not the only place to suffer from gerrymandered boundaries and quirky voting regulations. In Magherafelt, Omagh, Armagh and several other council districts, Catholics made up a majority of the adult population, but the control of councils remained Unionist.[43] Whatever the true extent of discrimination against Catholics, it was the perception of Catholics as victims of discrimination which was crucial. In Rose's survey of early 1968, 74 per cent of Catholics questioned said they believed that Catholics were badly treated in some parts of Northern Ireland, whereas only 18 per cent of Protestants thought such a statement was valid. Of this 18 per cent, 26 per cent thought that Catholic complaints about discrimination should simply be ignored.[44]

The CSJ began to collect solid data on discrimination which avoided exaggeration and presented the first statistics on Catholic disadvantage. Within a few months of the campaign's January 1964 press conference, a pamphlet, *The Plain Truth*, was published detailing the discrimination in Dungannon and elsewhere. Called 'scurrilous propaganda' by Northern Ireland Minister for Home Affairs William Craig, the pamphlet stimulated unprecedented press interest in the issue, which in turn exposed more incidents of discrimination.[45]

It included various examples of sectarian housing policies, which made gerrymandering possible. The policy reinforced the sectarian housing patterns, so that new estates were often made up of people from one religion or the other. In 1967, the Turf Lodge estate, owned by the Belfast Corporation, had 1,175 Catholic families, and 22 Protestant families.[46] Between 1945 and 1967, of 1,048 council houses built in Fermanagh, 82 per cent went to Protestants.[47] Such segregated arrangements helped gerrymandering. Omagh, for example, was split into three electoral wards. Two – the North and South – were kept with a permanent Protestant majority, leaving the West Ward with a very heavy Catholic majority. The two Protestant wards each elected six councillors, the West Ward a total of nine. This meant that in 1967 the Protestant minority (29 per cent of the town) elected twelve Unionists to the council, while the non-Unionist voters elected nine.

To reinforce the unrepresentative system, it was important that new houses in the Protestant wards be allocated to Protestants, and newly-housed Catholics be kept in the West Ward, where they wouldn't upset the electoral balance. So between 1945 and 1968, of 116 houses built in the South Ward, 95 per cent of them went to Protestants. All 197 houses built in the North Ward went to Protestants, and none to Catholics. Similarly, 98 per cent of the 251 houses built in the Catholic West Ward went to Catholics.[48]

The CSJ, following the example of the US civil rights movement, turned to the courts for redress. Just as the National Association for the Advancement of Colored People (NAACP) had initiated and won a series of legal cases throughout the century, overturning practices of segregation and racial discrimination, so too the CSJ sought judicial rulings to prevent discrimination.[49] The British prime minister, Alec Douglas-Home, had visited Northern Ireland in March 1964 and advised that complaints about religious discrimination could be dealt with by the courts. In November 1965, the CSJ instructed a lawyer to start proceedings – on behalf of a Catholic – against the Dungannon Council for religious discrimination in allocating council housing.

The man was married with children, had been on the council waiting list for eight years, been proposed for a Dungannon council house by the opposition councillors 16 times in the previous two years and rejected each time. Several newly-wed Protestant couples – some of them not on the waiting list, some of them from 40 miles away – had, during this period, been given houses. The CSJ sought funds under the Legal Aid scheme (introduced to Northern Ireland in 1965, 17 years after the rest of the UK) to fight the case. The authorities in Northern Ireland refused to allow Legal Aid funds for the case, and the CSJ, intimidated by the prospect of having to pay enormous costs, was forced to drop the case.

Whereas American blacks campaigning against discrimination could always cite that the law was, in theory, on their side, the CSJ could not. As Bernadette Devlin McAliskey, a student at Queen's in the mid-1960s and later a leading figure in the civil rights movement in Northern Ireland, suggested:

> We didn't have the fall-back position of a constitution, which people often forget. That whole dimension of the American civil rights movement which at least allowed you [to] create some space for other battles – so that according to the constitution I can sit at this bar and I can hold this line here non-violently and get thrown out ... because I also know that somebody somewhere else is going to push this and I am right and am going to be proved right ... we didn't have that.[50]

Richard Rose, in his comparative study of Northern Ireland and America's Deep South, echoed the point:

> Ulster Catholics have not had the choice of strategies available to Southern blacks, for the United Kingdom enumerates no justiciable civil or political rights. The 'rights' that an Englishman may believe that he enjoys are simply cultural norms, generalizations from customary behaviour.[51]

Special laws governed Northern Ireland. The Civil Authorities (Special Powers) Act was passed in 1922. Originally intended to last for a year, it was renewed until 1933, and then made to last indefinitely. It permitted the authorities various powers, including the right to search and arrest without warrant, imprison without trial, and to allow punishment by flogging. While citizens of Northern Ireland could lawfully be whipped with a cat o' nine tails, those in the rest of the United Kingdom could not, as the Act only applied to the six counties ruled by the Stormont parliament.[52]

Confronted with a local government that was, in many ways, a law unto itself, the anti-discrimination campaigners looked to the British parliament in London for help. In July 1965, some sympathetic MPs in the British House of Commons formed the Campaign for Democracy in Ulster (CDU), which called for an enquiry into the administration of government in Northern Ireland. Just as the US Congress turned a blind eye to racist laws passed by state legislatures in the South, so too successive governments in London had hidden behind 'The Convention', a parliamentary understanding that issues delegated to the Stormont parliament could not be raised in Westminster. The Convention dated from 1922, when a question about attacks on people in Belfast was ruled out of order by the Speaker in Westminster.

An early member of the CDU was Labour MP Kevin McNamara, who explained:

> The Convention was that once a country was given its own self-government ... questions would not be asked about it because they were the responsibility of the local legislature, which meant in fact that we were left here [in London] with responsibilities for foreign affairs, trade and defence and payroll/taxation, because all other powers had been transferred to Stormont.[53]

Armed with *The Plain Truth* and other evidence supplied by the CSJ, CDU members attempted to persuade the London parliament to override The Convention and act against discrimination in Northern Ireland, but with little success. In 1965, the Labour Government introduced the first two bills outlawing racial discrimination in Britain. For the next three years the CDU tried to amend the bills to have religious discrimination outlawed as well as racial discrimination, and to have the law extended to include Northern Ireland (the province was to be exempted from legislation on racial discrimination). These attempts also failed. Between 1964 and the outbreak of large-scale violence in Northern Ireland in

1969, the House of Commons devoted less than one-sixth of 1per cent of its time to discussion of Northern Ireland questions, and most of those were on matters of trade.[54] While dozens of Labour MPs joined the CDU and urged Prime Minister Harold Wilson to take action over discrimination in Northern Ireland, Wilson did not regard the matter as a priority. 'Some things are more urgent than others', explained Wilson's secretary, Sir Oliver Wright.[55] The Prime Minister's response to an appeal made directly to him in a letter from the CSJ is typical of the British Government's hands-off attitude at the time. 'The matters about which you allege discrimination are falling within the field of responsibility of the Northern Ireland Government and Parliament. This being so, he thinks it would be wrong for him to seek to intervene', wrote Wilson's secretary in August 1965.[56]

Frustrated by the courts and parliament, the CSJ looked to the London-based pressure group, The National Council for Civil Liberties (NCCL) for support. Founded in 1934, the NCCL was a voluntary organisation dedicated to protecting individual civil liberties and minority rights, and it seemed logical to the campaigners in Northern Ireland to try and enlist its help. In March 1965, the NCCL organised a conference on civil liberties in Northern Ireland, where representatives from the CSJ and from the Working Committee on Civil Rights at Queen's, among others, gave evidence on discrimination. Eamonn McCann suggests that one of the aims of the students' project was to persuade the NCCL to open an office in Northern Ireland, where they had no presence.[57] Others, like Betty Sinclair, had been trying to interest the NCCL in Northern Ireland for much longer. Sinclair was a communist who had studied at the Lenin School in Moscow in the 1930s. She had been imprisoned in Armagh jail in 1940 for printing a 'subversive' (that is, Republican) article in the local communist newspaper, and stood as a Communist Party candidate for the Cromac constituency in Northern Ireland in the 1945 general election and won 4,000 votes, against the winning Unionist's 8,000. She became secretary to the Belfast Trades Council (BTC) in 1947. Due to Sinclair's interest in international affairs, the BTC became widely known outside Northern Ireland for its anti-apartheid campaign and its work for black American singer and political activist Paul Robeson, whose American citizenship had been withdrawn due to his socialist activities.[58]

Sinclair, through her international links, had contacts with the NCCL as far back as 1949, and had organised a meeting between NCCL and BTC representatives in 1965. When she became chairperson of the Northern Ireland Civil Rights Association (NICRA) in 1967, she hoped the organisation would operate along the lines of the NCCL. But while the NCCL continued to produce reports on the situation in Northern Ireland during the 1960s and after, it refused to establish a permanent base in the province.[59]

Representatives of older political traditions were also beginning to explore the idea of a civil rights campaign. Republicanism had been a powerful force in Irish history for almost 200 years, and had provided the ideological framework for the struggle for Irish independence in the early part of the twentieth century. By the 1950s, however, the Irish Republican Army still rejected the validity of the Treaty signed by Michael Collins in the early 1920s, and therefore the legitimacy of the Irish government and, of course, British rule in Northern Ireland.

The three decades following the Irish Civil War saw support for the defeated IRA drop dramatically, and its military activity was minimal.[60] By the mid-1950s there were only a few hundred members in the whole of Ireland. An ill-fated military campaign aimed at British installations along the border dividing the Irish Republic from Northern Ireland failed to capture much popular support. The Border Campaign, which started in 1956, resulted in 500 incidents, and included the deaths of eight IRA volunteers, four supporters, six members of the RUC, and 32 members of the British security forces before it was finally called off in 1962.[61] It had been disastrous for the IRA, and had completely failed to ignite popular support. In the Irish Republic's elections of 1961, Sinn Fein's share of first preference votes fell from its 1957 total of 5 per cent to 3 per cent.

At the end of the campaign, several key figures inside the Republican movement urged a radical rethink in strategy. One of these was Tomas MacGiolla, president of the IRA's political wing, Sinn Fein:

Some of us had made up our minds that the military road was totally wrong ... the American civil rights movement had an influence naturally ... [where] the black people were having their marches and doing political agitations for their rights, so we began to think of this civil rights, and that was the first time we talked of civil rights which would have been about 1964/1965.[62]

Cathal Goulding, the new IRA chief of staff, supported the plans:

We wanted to clear the ground for political action. In other words to gain freedom for political manoeuvrability, the first thing we needed was civil rights. There was a kind of Mickey Mouse movement which wrote letters to the government about prisoners in South Africa ... and so we decided to revive that. We told Republicans to join the civil rights movement and to develop it with the idea of gaining civil rights in the north.[63]

The decision to steer the Republican movement away from military action and towards community politics and agitation for civil rights was to prove a difficult manoeuvre. Left-wing Republicans joined the Wolfe Tone Society, set up in October 1964, to discuss new approaches to Republicanism, and to replace the traditional approach of guerrilla warfare. In August 1966, the Wolfe Tone Society's newsletter, *Tuairisc*, praised the anti-discrimination work of the McCluskeys and urged Republican support for 'a widespread and vigorous civil right movement in the Six Counties putting the maximum pressure on [Northern Ireland Prime Minister Terence] O'Neill and on the Westminster Government and Members of Parliament to secure greater democracy for the area'.[64]

That same month, leading Republicans, including Goulding, met at Maghera in Northern Ireland to discuss the feasibility of a mass civil rights campaign. Another meeting was held in November 1966 in Belfast, where guest speaker Ciaran Mac an Aili, president of the Irish Pacifist Association, urged that the Republican movement emulate the civil disobedience tactics of Martin Luther King.[65] MacGiolla explained:

We decided that the civil rights campaign as they were doing in America was the proper road for us and those of us who were against the idea of another military campaign decided that if we got this strong powerful campaign going, it would take our own people's minds off it – they would see victories being achieved this way that had never been achieved by militarism.[66]

Other Republicans also drew on the example of the American civil rights movement. During the mid-1960s, O Dochartaigh in Derry received a magazine produced by black Americans in the US South. The magazines influenced O Dochartaigh's thinking about the local situation in Derry, and the arguments he made in Republican circles about the need for a civil rights struggle in Ireland: 'I used some of that [black American] stuff in my early documents in the

Republican movement [like my] *Ballot or Bullet* document arguing that constitutionally we could bring it forward.'[67]

The extent of Republican involvement in the civil rights movement has proved a highly charged question since the Maghera meeting, and would be used by Unionists – with some success – to discredit the movement. No doubt Republicans were significantly involved in the movement from its earliest stages, and Ian Paisley and many more moderate Protestants repeatedly insisted that the civil rights campaign was nothing more than an IRA front, a suggestion supported by Tomas MacGiolla:

> Of course it was! I mean we were organising it. And the funny thing about it was, the ones who were organising it were organising it in order to stop any further IRA campaigns. One of our purposes in all our agitations was to be winning struggles without military activities and confrontation.[68]

Although the distinction between Irish Republicanism and the aims of NICRA was clear, with NICRA happy to establish civil rights within a British state, and the Republicans working for the eventual overthrow of British rule in Northern Ireland, for a while the two aims converged. This convergence confuses attempts to measure Republican influence on the civil rights movement in any scientific way. Many people were both civil rights campaigners and Republicans throughout. Many started out campaigning for civil rights and ended up joining the IRA, and would have difficulty defining when they 'stopped' being civil righters and 'started' being Republicans. So it is impossible to judge how many strings in the civil rights movement were actually being pulled by Republicans, although charges that well-meaning individuals were being manipulated by revolutionaries was one echoed across the Atlantic. While there were undoubtedly communists in the American civil rights movement, and revolutionary Republicans in the Northern Ireland movement, in neither case were they strong enough to dominate. Gerry Adams, who joined the Republican movement in the mid-1960s and later became president of Sinn Fein, insists that 'we were there from the very beginning. Republicans were actually central to the formation of NICRA' but insists that 'far from using it as a front organisation those of us who attended the first meeting were directed to elect only two of our membership to the executive.'[69]

That first meeting of what later became NICRA was held on 29 January 1967 at a hotel in Belfast. About 80 people turned up, from various strands of political tradition. Apart from the Republicans, there were representatives from Northern Ireland's trade union movement and the left-leaning political parties, including the Northern Ireland Labour Party and the Communist Party, a few liberal Protestants, some students, Betty Sinclair of the BTC and Conn McCluskey of the CSJ. 'Five of our Campaign members were there, and I must confess I knew very few others present,' remembered McCluskey.[70] A steering committee of 13 was elected and five broad objectives agreed.[71] The objectives did not mention the Border, and it was repeatedly emphasised that the civil rights group took no position on the partition of Ireland and would not try to subvert the state. Of the 13-member steering group, only four had straightforward Republican affiliations.[72]

Some of the headstrong Republican elements in the movement were frustrated by its pedestrian approach. Gerry Adams remembers that at the inaugural meeting 'my fellow young Republicans and I were frankly bored by the ponderous proceedings', while Fred Heatley, elected as treasurer on the new committee, described the first 18 months of NICRA as 'a time of frustration ... the most annoying aspect of the early period was the lack of real interest shown by our first council members – at times we couldn't muster up the required six members for a quorum at the monthly meetings.'[73]

Despite NICRA's condemnation of the government ban on Republican clubs (which had been set up to get round the ban on Sinn Fein introduced in 1964), and its call for a repeal of the Special Powers Act, by early 1968 some of its more radical members thought its NCCL-type tactics of highlighting individual cases should be developed into more direct action, as practised by the American civil rights movement. Fred Heatley recalled:

> ... the tactics of Martin Luther King in America had been absorbed inasmuch as that it was felt by some that only by public marches could we really draw world attention to what we were trying to achieve by normal democratic means. But we had members who either didn't relish the trouble this could create or were too constitutional in their thinking.[74]

O Dochartaigh also cited the American experience in urging for a more radical approach:

> The ironic thing was that most of the old Communist Party people like Betty Sinclair were taking a very NCCL line in dealing with individual cases, but we were arguing that the blacks in

America tried that for years but it didn't do anything – you have to get on the streets, you have to make it a major issue. That struggle [within NICRA] went on for the best part of 18 months until [we said] the state has to be confronted publicly ... we were very influenced by the whole American thing, because Martin Luther King, Jesse Jackson, these people had tried all that – we knew they had tried doing it through individual cases.[75]

It wasn't just Republicans who pushed for direct action. Austin Currie had been elected as a Nationalist MP to Stormont in June 1964 at the age of 24. Currie was one of the working-class Catholics who benefited from the post-war education reforms, and had been to university, where he had studied American history and the American Constitution. By the mid-1960s, he was familiar with the political struggles of the American civil rights movement 'and very much aware of the constitutional and legal background to it'. In October 1967, Currie warned Stormont that if social reforms weren't forthcoming extra-parliamentary activity would be introduced within a year.[76]

While Currie's perception of the US civil rights movement was based on his formal studies and through the media, for other activists the influence was more direct. Derry radicals O Dochartaigh and Eamonn McCann both spent time working in London in the mid-1960s. For McCann, this meant exposure to the international left, joining the anti-nuclear Aldermaston march, and involvement in the beginnings of the anti-Vietnam War movement. By 1966, he says, he 'would have known quite a lot about [black American radical] Stokely Carmichael and political splits between the Student Non-Violent Co-ordinating Committee and the NAACP'. In fact, McCann met Carmichael at a conference in London in the mid-1960s, where McCann spoke about discrimination in Northern Ireland.[77]

O Dochartaigh, meanwhile, was encountering the US civil rights movement via his membership of the Connolly Association, a London-based socialist Republican organisation dedicated to the ideals of Irish revolutionary James Connolly, executed for his part in the 1916 Easter Rising. The Connolly Association's membership base was drawn from the Irish community living in England, Scotland and Wales, and it produced a newspaper, the *Irish Democrat*, which reported on the struggle for civil rights in Northern Ireland and in the US. As early as February 1964, the *Irish Democrat* produced an editorial which declared that discrimination in Northern Ireland 'is the exact parallel of the Negro question in the United States, for in that country the freedom of the people as a whole is dependent entirely on the emancipation of the coloured people.'[78]

The following year, the *Democrat* reminded readers of Cromwell's part in shipping thousands of Irish to plantations in the Caribbean, and suggested that the Irish living in Britain had much in common with their West Indian neighbours, and featured a photograph of Catholic nuns from the New York archdiocese taking part in a civil rights march in Harlem.[79] O Dochartaigh became a correspondent for the *Irish Democrat* on his return to Derry in 1966, and remembers the influence of the paper's international page in comparing American blacks with the position of Catholics in Northern Ireland. The international page carried a long piece in February 1967 expanding on the similarities between Northern Ireland and the American South:

> ... there is regional discrimination siting industry away from coloured areas – just as industries are kept to the Lagan valley of Ulster, while [Catholic areas like] Newry, Derry and Strabane do without. There are negroes' jobs and white man's jobs – just as there are Catholic and Protestant jobs in the six counties ... there are whole trades where negroes do not work and are not encouraged to work. This goes for Catholics in the six counties also. ... Irish people should take an interest in and support the struggle for negro rights in the U.S.A.[80]

The experience of the American civil rights movement and its increasingly apparent similarities with the situation in Northern Ireland meant that some sort of direct action was likely. In June 1968, Austin Currie suggested to the Nationalist Party's annual conference that a campaign of civil disobedience should be adopted. On 20 June, he took action himself in an incident which drew more attention to the issue of discrimination than anything that had happened before. Currie, who had been looking for an opportunity for some time to make a dramatic gesture, heard of a house being allocated to Emily Beattie, a 19-year-old unmarried Protestant woman in an area where 269 people were on a housing waiting list. 'This was the perfect symbol. I said at the time that if I live to be a hundred I'll never get a better case to symbolise the situation in Northern Ireland,' he said.[81]

Currie went to the house in Caledon on the morning of the day the woman was due to move in and, with two others

> ... broke a back window with a poker and got into the house and barricaded ourselves in ... we continued to be barricaded in the house for a number of hours. Eventually the RUC arrived and

they and Emily Beattie's brother battered down the front door and ejected us straight into the cameras.[82]

The incident was carried on the BBC evening television news. For many people in Britain, it was the first they heard of religious discrimination in Northern Ireland, and it made a bigger impact on the British public than all of the CSJ documents of the previous four years. Currie recalled that he wanted to maintain the momentum in the media with a civil rights march.

> I put the proposal [to Conn McCluskey] that it was time to get away from just disseminating facts and figures, time to get away from the civil liberty group in Britain upon which they had based the civil rights association up to then and to take it to the streets.[83]

Two days after the squatting incident at Caledon, the Derry Housing Action Committee (DHAC) also made a dramatic gesture. After heckling the monthly meetings of the Derry Housing Corporation to protest at the city's woefully inadequate and discriminatory housing practices, the DHAC decided it needed to stage a high-profile stunt. On 22 June, some of its members lugged a caravan – which, despite having no running water or lavatory was home to a family of four – into the road at a busy junction to highlight the poor quality of housing. When the action was repeated the following week, leading DHAC activists – including O Dochartaigh and McCann – were summoned to court, but claimed victory when the family who lived in the caravan were rehoused in much healthier accommodation.[84]

The day of the court hearings in July coincided with the official opening of the lower deck of Derry's Craigavon Bridge to traffic. As the VIP cars trundled ceremoniously across the bridge, a group of protestors sat down in front of the motorcade. As they were hauled away, fellow protestors on the pavement – including, inevitably, O Dochartaigh and McCann – began to sing 'We Shall Overcome'. While most had heard the song in snatches from the television, O Dochartaigh had learned the words from the song page of the *Irish Democrat*, and so 'stepped forward to assume the role of conductor and prompter ... most people were singing about three or four words after me, because they didn't know it', he remembered.[85] Within months, tens of thousands of people who had never been on a protest of any kind would be marching across Northern Ireland, demanding civil rights and singing 'We Shall Overcome'.

3

On the March

After the Craigavon Bridge incident, the American influence on Irish civil rights activists became increasingly obvious. Previous studies have minimised the role of the American influence on the Northern Ireland civil rights movement, suggesting that ties were superficial and that tactics borrowed from America were learned largely via the media.[1] However, during the years between 1968 and 1972, there is significant evidence of direct, important links between the two movements. Leading civil rights activists in Northern Ireland studied the literature of their American counterparts, imitated some of their initiatives, and established contacts with key black leaders in America.

Austin Currie's idea for a civil rights march was borrowed from America, and was no less ambitious than those organised in the Deep South. Following some haggling over a date (Currie wanted to press ahead immediately after the squatting incident to maintain momentum), the march was eventually set for the last Saturday in August 1968, exactly five years since both the March on Washington and the Dungannon families' takeover of the pre-fabs.[2]

A march in Northern Ireland required pulling together several disparate political strands for the same disciplined purpose. Republicans, students, anti-discrimination activists and the generally curious assembled in Coalisland on the designated evening to march along the few miles of country road to Dungannon. Bernadette Devlin, a student at Queen's University in Belfast, was home on holiday near Coalisland when she read about plans for the march.

'Civil rights march! Excellent idea! It's about time somebody did something about the situation in Northern Ireland', she thought, and set off for the march with her little brother and a friend.[3] Devlin was not involved in the student politics at Queen's. After a brief dalliance with the Republican Club, she decided

... there was more real politics in the Folk Music Society than in any of the parties. They sang black civil rights songs in the folk music society before anybody at Queen's was interested in the race problem. ...That was a good society. It had a strong American influence in it ... We sang Irish non-controversial folk music and were allowed to sing black songs because they didn't apply to us. But they did, and in some ways that was also our closet expression before '68.[4]

Devlin was a psychology student from a working-class family, another of the Catholics who was the first in her family to make university. A relative newcomer to protest, and disdainful of those students engrossed in political theory – 'they used to piss me off because I thought what a bunch of trendy middle-class wasters; they've read all the books and they don't know the price of a pound of butter, or how the welfare system works' – Devlin would soon become the best-known civil rights activist in Northern Ireland, the key figure in relations with black America and the most prominent Irish politician since Daniel O'Connell to challenge Irish-Americans on their attitude towards black civil rights.[5]

Michael Farrell, on the other hand, was already very politically active at Queen's by 1968. He had set up a group called the Young Socialist Alliance (YSA) at the university, modelled on the Young Socialist Alliance in the US. Farrell's group received political literature from the American YSA, which was heavily involved in the civil rights movement there.[6] Farrell and a handful of supporters arrived at the march with the flag of the Vietnamese Liberation Front, left over from their regular Saturday afternoon anti-Vietnam War protests. The flag led to an immediate clash with the march's stewards – Republicans who had been recruited to keep order and ensure a non-violent protest. Tomas MacGiolla travelled up from Dublin for the march to join the local contingent of Republicans, who had also organised a lorry for the march. With such a pronounced Republican presence in the march's organisation, protestors had to be reminded it was a civil rights march, not a Republican event. In fact, just before the march, when the IRA's director of information, Roy Johnston, tried to have a message read from the platform, NICRA's Fred Heatley 'tore it up in front of his eyes'.[7] Devlin described the march as having a sort of good-natured, holiday atmosphere:

We had stewards marshalling us who thought we were in the army, and kept singing out 'Pick up your feet! March in fours! One, two; one, two!' and everybody was just roaring at them

... we all jogged along happily, eating oranges and smoking cigarettes and people came out of their houses to join the fun.[8]

Several thousand people turned up for that first civil rights march, but when the procession reached the outskirts of Dungannon they found the road ahead blocked by a police cordon, behind which stood several dozen counter-demonstrators, led by Rev. Ian Paisley. A request to reroute the protest and the presence of the police threw the civil rights marchers into some confusion. MacGiolla remembered 'an actual fistfight between our people – the ones saying "No, this is a peaceful march, this is a civil rights march, we're not here to fight the police" and the ones saying "Get the bastards!"'[9]

It was during this confrontation between the police and the march leaders that Nationalist MP Gerry Fitt made his way to the front of the protestors and warned 'If one of those black bastards of the Northern Ireland Gestapo puts a hand on any man here, I'll lead you through!'[10] Betty Sinclair intervened in an attempt to prevent any violence, called an end to the protest and suggested that before they disperse, those in the crowd should sing the civil rights anthem. She began 'We Shall Overcome', but few of the protestors knew the words, and many sang the nationalist 'A Nation Once Again' instead. For most of those on the demonstration, the march was their first act of protest for civil rights, and as the protest had passed off peacefully and relatively successfully, the organisers were pleased. Another march was scheduled for Derry six weeks later.

NICRA representatives met the local activists who had proposed the Derry march. A route was agreed – from Duke St in the predominantly Protestant Waterside area, across Craigavon Bridge, scene of the July sit-down and song-singing protest, through the city walls and into an area called The Diamond. The march was due to take place on Saturday 5 October. Organisational responsibilities fell to local radicals like Eamonn McCann, who were careful to promote the march as a socialist demonstration. 'None of the placards demanded "civil rights". We were anxious to assert socialist ideas, whether or not the [NI]CRA approved', he said.[11] Such pre-publicity gave the march a more radical tone than the August protest at Coalisland, and despite the city's recent peaceful history – in 1966, Derry's crime rate was proportionately lower than any city in Ireland or Britain – some expected confrontation with the police.[12] Fionnbarra O'Dochartaigh, believing that the state's response to the civil rights protest would be violent 'like in America', arrived at the march wearing a crash helmet.[13]

Tension increased in the days before the protest. On 3 October, the *Belfast Telegraph* carried a feature story on how the civil rights movement in the US had fallen into the hands of militants. The newly-formed Black Panther Party 'have already joined with the militant negro organisation "Student non-violent Co-ordinating Committee",' warned the story, as it explained how the American civil rights movement had started out advocating non-violence but had soon fallen into the grip of radical militants.[14] The Derry radicals organising the march were delighted when Home Affairs Minister William Craig banned it, prompting NICRA to arrange a meeting with McCann and the other locals the night before the march was due to take place. After much haggling, it was decided to go ahead with the protest. McCann expected at least as many marchers as had been at Coalisland, and hoped for 5,000. In fact, less than a tenth of that number showed up.

A few hundred yards after the protestors began their march, they were blocked by a police cordon. Another police cordon drew up behind the marchers, sandwiching them on Duke Street. Betty Sinclair, Austin Currie, Eamonn McCann and others took turns to address the marchers. Then both police lines closed in on the protestors, batoning the marchers and pursuing them up the alleys that lead off Duke St. A police watercannon – the first ever used in Northern Ireland – appeared, to general astonishment. A police officer in the cordon which stopped the marchers knew the water cannon was in reserve, but recalled 'being surprised when it was used'.[15] The first demonstrator arrested was NICRA treasurer Fred Heatley, who raced to the front of the march when he saw it had been halted:

> When but a few paces from the police lines in Duke St I reached the front ranks of the marchers, was almost immediately kneed in the groin by a constable, was dragged behind the RUC lines and was ordered into a Black Maria.[16]

First to join Heatley in the police car was Belfast Republican Martin Meehan, who had gone to the march hoping for confrontation. Meehan would later become a leading figure in the Provisional IRA. Mayhem ensued in Duke St, and over 100 people needed hospital treatment. The official British government report into the incident acknowledged the police brutality: '... the police broke ranks and used their batons indiscriminately on people in Duke Street. ... the District Inspector in charge used his blackthorn [stick] with needless violence.'[17] The television pictures of police violently breaking up the Derry march gave the civil rights movement in Northern Ireland its highest profile yet. Parallels with the US were obvious, and frequently noted. Brigid Makowski, a Derry woman who had emigrated to the US, moved back to Derry the day before the protest and filmed the march. 'I was reminded of news reports I had seen of confrontations between civil rights marchers and police in Selma, Alabama,' she wrote.[19]

The afternoon's events sparked riots throughout the weekend in Derry. When the Queen's University new academic term began on Tuesday 8 October, 2000 students marched to Belfast City Hall to protest about the events in Derry. That night, the students established a new organisation, People's Democracy (PD), which – under the influence of Michael Farrell – would consciously model itself on the US student-based civil rights organisation the Student Non-Violent Coordinating Committee (SNCC). Like the Black Panther Party (BPP) in America, which had been founded two years earlier in Oakland, California, PD was formed by students, many of whom retained a strong identification with their working-class origins. Like Huey Newton, Bobby Seale and Dave Hilliard, the founding members of the BPP, many students in PD were from the first generation in their families to go on to higher education.

In November 1969, Eilis McDermott of People's Democracy was invited to meet the BPP in Boston. After updating the local Panther leadership on the situation in Northern Ireland, she was made an 'honorary Black Panther sister'.[20] A few years later, PD's most prominent member, Bernadette Devlin, would strengthen links with black radicals by briefing Huey Newton on the struggle in Northern Ireland and visiting leading black activist Angela Davis in jail, where she was waiting to be tried for murder. Northern Ireland was of some interest to black American radicals. Angela Davis recalled the Northern Ireland political situation being discussed in black political circles in the late 1960s:

I can remember a number of very interesting conversations and meetings around the situation in Northern Ireland. The question that was posed was that whether or not in fact Northern Ireland belonged politically to the Third World because of the situation of colonisation, because of the continued repression and because of the similarities and the way people – Catholics – were treated in Northern Ireland.[21]

The Black Panthers were associated with some of the more radical elements in SNCC, and looked to the writings of Frantz Fanon, Chairman Mao and Malcolm X for their political ideology. There was also a strong identification with the legacy of Marcus Garvey's black nationalism, which itself had been influenced by the Irish Republicanism of the 1920s. The BPP's core document was its Ten-point Program, which included demands like the exemption of black men from military service, and 'the power to determine the destiny of the black community'.[22] The programme echoed Garvey's earlier Eight-point Platform, which had also sought to 'advocate self-determination'.[23] The Panther symbol came from a logo used by SNCC in May 1966 in Lowndes County, Alabama, a notoriously segregated district which had been on the route between Selma and Montgomery walked by civil rights activists in March 1965. Michael Farrell of PD saw the student movement in Northern Ireland as analogous to SNCC, and tried to model PD in its likeness. In the most blatant example of the Northern Ireland civil rights movement copying tactics from its American counterparts, Farrell organised a Selma to Montgomery-style march in January 1969 to go from Belfast to Derry.

The weeks following the Derry incident in October 1968 saw several more civil rights marches as many people in Northern Ireland joined the protests to demand fair housing allocations and one man, one vote. On 16 November, 15,000 people gathered on Craigavon Bridge in Derry, asserting the right of assembly denied to a few hundred in the same place six weeks before. The scene was reminiscent of the Selma protest in the US where, on 7 March 1965, 400 people had set off to cross the Edmund Pettus Bridge and walk to Montgomery. The protestors were beaten back by the police with such ferocity that 7 March went down in American civil rights history as 'Bloody Sunday'. A few weeks later 35,000 gathered to march across the Edmund Pettus Bridge. As in Selma, a huge number of Northern Ireland civil rights protestors returned to the scene of an earlier march broken up by the police to restage the protest. When 15,000 civil rights marchers massed on Craigavon Bridge on 16 November, a policeman who had been part of the cordon which stopped the original Derry march on 5 October was again on duty. 'It was an awesome sight, this mass of people coming across the Craigavon Bridge. It was quite frightening, actually ... it was a victory for them ... there was no way we could stop them that day,' he recalled.[24] Civil rights protests broke out all over the country. 'For a brief period we had gone marching mad' said

McCann, as people took to the streets singing 'We Shall Overcome' in Strabane, Armagh, Belfast, Dungannon and elsewhere.[25]

By the middle of December, the situation had become so tense that the Northern Ireland Prime Minister Captain Terence O'Neill, made a television appeal for the acceptance of reform and an end to civil disorder and agitation. He also sacked Home Affairs Minister William Craig, who had banned the Derry march of 5 October. NICRA responded to O'Neill's appeal by calling for a period of 'truce' without marches or demonstrations. The more radical PD, however, announced it would march from Belfast to Derry, starting on 1 January 1969. Michael Farrell, more politically savvy than most in PD, argued that a protest modelled on the American civil rights march from Selma to Montgomery was the best way forward:

> As I saw it the Selma–Montgomery march forced the federal government to intervene in Alabama: that you had the local law enforcement agency that was completely biased against the blacks, and you could not achieve any sort of justice within the legal institutional or political structures within Alabama, so they staged a dramatic march across Alabama which was attacked by white racists. The drama of that forced the federal government to intervene, and that was in my mind and I think in that of most of the marchers what we were trying to do, that we were trying to force the issue onto the political stage and to force the British government to intervene over the head of the Northern Ireland government, because we had assessed that the Northern Ireland government and the local security authorities were fundamentally biased and so you couldn't achieve anything within that structure.[26]

Farrell's study of the American civil rights movement was to have a dramatic impact on Northern Irish history. 'I certainly for the first year or so of the [Northern Ireland] civil rights movement saw the People's Democracy as performing a similar role *vis-à-vis* the NICRA as SNCC did with the Southern Leadership Conference [sic]', he noted.[27] Farrell says he was also heavily influenced by a pamphlet written by American Trotskyist George Breitman, 'How a Minority Can Change Society'. Breitman was a biographer of Malcolm X, and a prominent theoretician of black nationalism in the US. The march was to take several days, and required overnight stops at friendly towns en route. In direct imitation of the Selma march, PD described the Belfast to Derry protest as a civil rights and anti-poverty march, just as SNCC had done. Farrell recalled:

We had two banners, one saying 'Civil Rights' and the other saying 'Anti-Poverty', and we planned to give out leaflets on the way – we actually did research on poverty in the areas we were going through. The thing we went on about in those days was dry toilets ... that was an index of poverty and backwardness, and we drew up the figures for the different towns and villages we went through in order to produce leaflets.[28]

Not all those on the march grasped the political sophistication of Farrell's SNCC-based techniques. 'Farrell was the key proposer, instigator and organiser of the long march to Derry which he very clearly modelled in terms of effect, slogans and everything on the Selma march', said Bernadette Devlin. She had no clear idea of the ultimate objective of the march:

Personally I hadn't a clue ... and was there because I'd signed for a demonstration that nobody else would sign for and I'd done that really because I was pissed off with these serious-minded revolutionaries who still had one eye on their degrees and their middle-class parents ... Farrell and McCann were the only people to my knowledge who were thinking strategically but the general plan seemed to be to draw into conflict the British and the Unionists.[29]

Handouts given to the marchers suggest they were unprepared to cope with the violent attack they would encounter. Although they copied the political methods of SNNC, apparently no one had stopped to think through what to do to defend themselves against assault. The tips for marchers contained the telephone numbers of local doctors and hospitals, but did not offer advice on how to best protect one's head against a baton. In fact, the handout confined itself to suggesting that

... in the event of the march being attacked or faced with a hostile crowd or police cordon marchers are reminded that PD is committed to a policy of non-violence and marchers are asked under the circumstances to conduct themselves with the maximum possible restraint and calmness.[30]

The handout also suggested that those on the march 'should endeavour to provide themselves with sweets, chocolates, fruit etc. which they may wish to eat along the route'.[31]

Part political demonstration, part student parade, the marchers set off from Belfast, inevitably slightly late, on the morning of 1 January. Some supporters – including Gerry Adams – who would not be walking all the way to Derry joined the march for a few miles as it left Belfast. Devlin recalled:

> Groups of people as we went past either cheered or shouted abuse, depending on the colour of their principles. Outside Belfast Major Bunting [a prominent supporter of Rev. Ian Paisley] dropped out of the procession – just at the entrance to Bellevue Zoo, which made everybody feel pretty witty – and we hollered remarks at the good Major who, stone-faced, stood trooping his colour as we went past.[32]

The lone anarchist among the marchers held up one pole of his banner while the other dragged along the ground behind him. Robust singing added to the light-hearted atmosphere on the hike, recalled Devlin: 'Orange songs, Green songs, red, black and white songs, and just general pub-crawling and rugby songs, to keep us marching, and the whole tone of the thing at this stage was very good-natured.'[33] The marchers faced 75 miles and four days before they reached Derry, which they dubbed 'Selma' for the duration of the march. 'On to Selma' they chanted as they trudged along the country roads – although the American civil rights protestors had actually left from Selma, and had marched to Montgomery.

If the students' aim had been to draw the state into direct confrontation with the march, they succeeded. After several days of encountering small bands of counter-demonstrators, which often resulted in the police diverting the march around potential flashpoints, the marchers set off on the final leg of the journey to Derry. By now, the march had swelled to about 800 as locals joined those who had come from Belfast for the last few miles. As the protestors approached Burntollet Bridge, they were ambushed by a mob, who were helped in their attack by police supposedly there to protect the marchers. 'What had been a march was a shambles', said Devlin:

> The attackers were beating marchers into the ditches, and across the ditches and into the river. People were being dragged half-conscious out of the river. Others were being pursued across the fields into the woods. Others had been trapped on the road and were being given a good hiding where they stood.[34]

Given the level of violence, it was incredible that no one was killed, although 87 were taken to hospital for treatment. What was left of the march regrouped and made its way into Derry.

Andrew Young, an organiser of the Selma protest, has written that Montgomery was chosen as their destination because it was 'the capital of Southern racism and bigotry'.[35] When Bernadette Devlin arrived in Derry from Burntollet, she called it 'the capital city of injustice', a phrase immediately picked up by the press and flashed all over the country.[36]

The days following the march saw serious rioting in Derry, particularly in the mainly Catholic neighbourhood of the Bogside. For a while a no-go area was set up with barricades, keeping the police out. McCann and his radical friends even found a radio transmitter and broadcast to the area, calling themselves 'Radio Free Derry, the Voice of Liberation'. The radio broadcasted suggestions for a civil disobedience campaign which cited the Montgomery Bus Boycott: 'There can, for instance, be total boycott as was done in one city in America with the result that the local Transport Company, brought to near-bankruptcy, was forced to yield to the demands of the protesting negro population.'[37] Listeners were also treated to regular harangues from McCann and co., and bursts of revolutionary music ('Reception was good, the listening audience vast', claimed McCann).[38]

While McCann was a relatively old hand in local politics, Devlin was not. The Belfast to Derry march (or the Burntollet March, as it became more commonly known) helped project her to a more public role in the civil rights movement. The month after the Burntollet march, Devlin was chosen as a PD candidate in the British general election. The students had decided to stand in the election without any serious hope of winning, but to take advantage of the British electoral system which would pay for PD to mail its manifesto to every home in every constituency where it fielded candidates. Devlin stood for election in South Derry, and lost to James Chichester-Clark, soon to be Prime Minister of Northern Ireland. Two months later, a by-election was scheduled for the Mid-Ulster constituency caused by the death of Unionist MP George Forrest. Mid-Ulster was one of those constituencies where, in theory, a non-Unionist candidate could win if all the non-Unionists – Nationalists, Republicans and others – could unite behind a single candidate. There were three or four constituencies which regularly sent Unionist MPs to Westminster because the Catholic vote was split between two or more candidates. Patricia

McCluskey sought to find a candidate in Mid-Ulster acceptable to enough non-Unionists to win the seat:

> We called meetings in every little town, and we asked the people if they wanted somebody to represent them, so we got in touch with various members of the IRA or what passed for the IRA ... the Republicans, to see if we could agree on a candidate. ... I chaired all the local meetings and the people who thought they could represent us got up and they were all given about ten minutes to make their speech and to let the people see them, and amongst them Bernadette presented herself and now she just stole the show all up through Mid-Ulster at every meeting.[39]

Although only 21 years old, and with just a few months' political experience, which largely consisted of late-night discussions at university, participation in several civil rights marches, and some reading – including Black Panther Bobby Seale's *Seize the Time* – Devlin was a genuinely compelling speaker, and made an impressive candidate. 'People identified with me for some reason – perhaps because I looked like their daughter or because I came from Mid-Ulster,' she said.[40] Devlin agreed to be the unity candidate partly to prevent Austin Currie from standing, as she and others in PD believed him to be too nationalistic, and feared he would win simply by appealing to Catholics. Devlin hoped to attract a class-based support, which would include working-class Protestants. Currie and the Republicans agreed to step aside and allow Devlin to stand against the Unionist candidate, Anna Forrest, the former MP's widow. The election attracted sizeable national press coverage, and Devlin's victory on a civil rights manifesto became international news.

The rejoicing which accompanied Devlin's win masked serious fractures within the civil rights movement. The students controlling PD were moving increasingly leftward, bringing them into conflict with the main body of NICRA and the older civil rights activists. Some, like Conn McCluskey, felt Devlin had been led astray by the radicals: 'She had wonderful capabilities which of course she threw away ... associated with a crowd of extreme left-wingers.'[41] The splits in the Northern Ireland civil rights movement mirrored the American experience almost exactly. SNCC was more radical than other major civil rights organisations like the Southern Christian Leadership Conference (SCLC), whose members, it often felt, were too middle-class and too cautious in their demands. The students in SNCC, like those in PD, tended to see the issue as one of class, and often pushed for a more confrontational style of protest. During the early to mid-'60s, John Lewis was chairman of SNCC. Lewis called the SCLC the 'tea and cookie set', with much the same attitude as PD regarded many in NICRA ('they felt we were too old and fuddy-duddy', said the McCluskeys).[42] The similarities were not coincidental, of course, as Farrell had deliberately tried to steer PD along the path pioneered by SNCC, and on some occasions the students' experiences were near-identical. 'I had a feeling that the position of John Lewis was quite similar to ours', said Farrell:

> When John Lewis spoke at the Lincoln Memorial during the August 1963 March on Washington, there was tremendous haggling over his speech which had to be vetted by the leadership beforehand and so on and I certainly had exactly that situation in civil rights marches, because they often allocated one speaker to the PD, and they were always scared of what we were going to say and there were attempts of varying degrees of sophistication to censor what you were going to say.[43]

In April 1969, Farrell was elected to the NICRA executive with Kevin Boyle, also from PD. Boyle suggests, 'The big conflict was with the PD over the question which had arisen in the US, too, in alliances, whether you should cooperate with any group, whether this contaminates your revolutionary socialism'.[44] Revolutionary socialism was the last thing on the minds of many in NICRA who were becoming increasingly uneasy at PD's aggressive attitude. NICRA officials, sensing they were losing control of the civil rights movement, began to resign in protest. '[The radicals] were using us, we felt, as a façade, as a cover, and I felt things were getting out of hand,' said Patricia McCluskey.[45]

The marches themselves were getting out of hand, too. A week after the violence at Burntollet, a PD march in Newry developed into a riot, and police vehicles were burned when, according to Gerry Adams, 'It was Republican stewards who took the initiative, discarded their armbands, and turned with gusto on the RUC.'[46] The police baton-charged the crowd and the protest was regarded as a fiasco by many in NICRA. The radicals in PD were also split among themselves. Three days after Devlin's election victory, the PD leaders met for a rare strategy session-cum-press interview.[47] After much theorising by Farrell and McCann (who were identified by the British press as 'the brains of the organisation'),[48] it was Devlin who hit the nail on the head:

We are totally unorganized and totally without any form of discipline within ourselves. I'd say that there are hardly two of us who really agree, and it will take a lot of discussion to get ourselves organized. The fact of the matter is that everybody knows where they don't want us to go, but nobody really knows what they do want and nobody is prepared to organize: we are all madly tearing off – nowhere.[49]

Tension, meanwhile, was steadily mounting in Northern Ireland. The political situation was becoming increasingly unstable, with civil rights marches often turning into stand-offs, or riots, between protestors and police, or demonstrators and counter-demonstrators. World media attention following the police violence at Derry and Burntollet compounded the difficulties, and Devlin's election success ensured that the British government could no longer turn a blind eye to discrimination. Explosions at a reservoir at the end of April threatened Northern Ireland's water supply. The British Army was brought in to guard key utility installations. The same day a crowd attacked a police station in Belfast after a civil rights rally. A week later another bomb wrecked the main water supply to Belfast. On 28 April 1969 Prime Minister Captain Terence O'Neill announced his resignation, and James Chichester-Clark replaced him, but the political turmoil increased. NICRA declared it would mount a campaign of civil disobedience until adequate reforms were introduced. And attacks on the police increased.

Black activists across the Atlantic were keeping a close eye on these developments. In January 1969, the NAACP leadership passed a resolution supporting 'the valorous efforts of the Catholic minority in Northern Ireland to secure political, economic and social rights equal to those enjoyed by the dominant Protestant majority'.[50] More militant voices joined the chorus of support. In the week following the deployment of British troops to guard water and electricity installations, the *Black Panther* newspaper carried a large article titled 'Ireland Oppressed Fight Back':

Apparently tired of being pushed around by reactionaries without making any retaliation, the Ulster Civil Rights Movement has started to fight back. The rank and file have given practical evidence of their ability to struggle by routing reactionaries and armed police in several battles ....[51]

The piece noted that non-violence had not worked in Northern Ireland, and predicted with some foresight that 'the introduction of

British troops into the struggle will raise some interesting problems. [British Prime Minister Harold] Wilson will want desperately to tread on "middle ground" but there is no middle ground in Ulster.'[52]

Disturbances broke out in towns across Northern Ireland in the following months, and by July serious rioting had occurred in Derry and Belfast. The possibility of large-scale violence in Derry during the middle of August looked real. The Apprentice Boys march, held by Protestants, was due to take place on 12 August as part of the 'marching season'. It was rumoured that British troops or police might be sent to Northern Ireland if the local police could not cope. When Tuesday, 12 August, arrived, the Apprentice Boys parade went off peaceably until the afternoon, when skirmishes broke out between those in the parade and Catholic youths from Derry's Bogside. The Bogside neighbourhood is an area of a few square miles, and for generations has been almost exclusively Catholic. To keep Protestant attackers and the police out of the area, the Bogsiders had thrown up street barricades. On 12 August, Bogsiders threw stones across the barricades at the police, who responded with an occasional charge. In Belfast, barricades were also put up around Catholic neighbourhoods to defend them against outside attack.

Violence escalated throughout Northern Ireland. Full-scale rioting broke out in Derry that evening, and the Bogside was besieged by Protestants and an exhausted police force. Law and order collapsed as the rioting carried on non-stop for several days. Bernadette Devlin and other civil rights activists were in the Bogside breaking paving stones for ammunition to use against the police. Petrol bombs were also used against the police, and widespread sniping was reported from Belfast.

In Armagh on 14 August a man was shot dead after taking part in a NICRA rally. Irish Prime Minister Jack Lynch made a television appeal asking for UN troops to be sent to Northern Ireland to restore order. He moved Irish soldiers to the border to set up field hospitals for the casualties. In Belfast and in Derry local defence committees were hastily arranged to coordinate defence. In some places, prominent civil rights activists took the lead in organising neighbourhoods. As far back as January, Derry civil rights leader John Hume had supported the formation of a local 'citizen's army' to defend the Bogside.[53] Locals were organised to keep the barricades properly stewarded. Known as the 'Peace Corps', they also ensured first aid posts were set up in anticipation of trouble. Republicans – whether involved in the civil rights movement or not – became central to the defence of Catholic neighbourhoods, often with material support from the Dublin government.

Samuel Dowling, chairman of Newry and District Civil Rights Association, said he was supplied with gelignite, submachine guns and other arms by the Irish government to use for defending the Catholic population.[54] Catholics under attack looked to their traditional defenders – the IRA – for support, but the demilitarisation of the IRA in the early 1960s had left them short of arms. In Belfast, Catholic streets were defenceless against attacks from Loyalist mobs. The police proved unable or unwilling to prevent the violence, and so on 15 August the British government sent in soldiers to stop the rioting.

From this point on, it was difficult to distinguish those in the civil rights movement from those in defence organisations or from Republican groups. These allegiances were far from mutually exclusive, and it was common for people to be involved in all three. What was clear, however, was that the Republicans had lost ground in some Catholic neighbourhoods which had expected the Irish Republican Army – rather than the British Army – to protect them from the police and from Loyalist gangs. The perceived failure of the IRA to defend Catholic enclaves caused a split in the Republican movement over the IRA's role. Those involved in the IRA at the time had conflicting views about what they were supposed to do. Francie Donnelly rejected the idea that the IRA was there to protect northern Catholics against Protestants: 'That's something that should be nailed, that the IRA existed solely to defend the Catholics in the north ... the whole history of Republicanism ... was not just as defenders of nationalists.'[55] Other Republicans like Sean MacStiofan rejected such political theory: 'That was a looney attitude – the first function of any IRA unit in the north is to defend its people from attacks.'[56] In June 1969, NICRA Chairman Frank Gogarty had visited IRA headquarters in Dublin seeking assurances that civil rights activists would be protected by the IRA if the violence escalated, but he left unconvinced. Republican strategists like Tomas MacGiolla saw the way forward for Republicanism best served by a withdrawal of the IRA, rather than its resurgence. 'The objective was ... to try and help the people defend the areas rather than have the IRA come out and start a new campaign. We never wanted the role of the defender of the Catholics,' he claimed.[57]

Politicians in Dublin, apparently alarmed at the leftward lurch of the IRA, encouraged the split, and supplied the northern Republican dissenters with arms, training and money. How much material support the Irish government delivered to the northern IRA units is hotly disputed; in 1970 the Irish Agriculture Minister, Neil Blaney, the Finance Minister (and later Prime Minster) Charlie Haughey, and an intelligence officer in the Irish Army, Captain James Kelly, stood trial in the Republic of Ireland for conspiracy to smuggle arms and ammunition to the North. Although they were all acquitted, there is no doubt that the IRA in the North received substantial help from the Dublin government to protect Catholic neighbourhoods from attack, and to bolster the northern units in their argument with the leftist philosophy of IRA leaders in Dublin.[58]

In boosting the northern IRA dissenters, the Irish government helped to weaken the influence of Republicans like MacGiolla, who had organised civil rights agitation in southern Ireland in 1965 and 1966 in protest at housing conditions. '[There were] fierce slums and we started the housing action group who were bringing people out on the streets in Dublin and they were actually being batoned off the streets by the Gardai [Irish police force]', he said.[59] As the IRA units in the North became less dependent on their southern leadership for arms, and more frustrated at its reluctance to sanction military action, units in Belfast and elsewhere became increasingly autonomous. An ideological division became apparent between the 'traditionalists', who emphasised the IRA's Catholic, military heritage, and the 'reformers', who wanted to make the IRA a revolutionary organisation. The formal split came in October 1969, when the Republican leadership voted to drop its abstentionist policy, declaring that it would take up seats it won in the British and Irish parliaments. Hitherto, it had refused to recognise the legitimacy of either parliament. The traditionalists, outraged at what they regarded as a betrayal of 50 years of struggle, elected a Provisional Army Council headed by MacStiofan. When the new policy of abstentionism was formally embraced by Sinn Fein at a convention in January 1970, the Republican movement split between the 'Official IRA' – those who accepted the new leftist political direction – and MacStiofan's 'Provisional IRA'.

The Provisionals would soon dominate Republicanism in the North, but the split proved confusing for many IRA sympathisers uncertain about which faction was most legitimate. Republicans in the civil rights movement fell either side of the divide. Belfast activists like Gerry Adams and Martin Meehan were Provisionals; Tomas MacGiolla and Cathal Goulding remained at the head of the Official movement. American supporters, eager to fund Republicanism, were often unsure about which side they should be on. Eventually, each group found separate sources of funds from America, with the Official IRA being supported by the Irish

Republican Clubs, who were sympathetic to the Officials' leftist politics, and who supported the black civil rights movement in the US. A similar group to the Irish Republican Clubs was the National Association for Irish Freedom (NAIF), which had links with the Republican Clubs but had a more formal association with NICRA.[60] NAIF's sponsors included Rev. Ralph Abernathy, successor to Martin Luther King as head of the SCLC, and black comedian and civil rights activist Dick Gregory.[61] Kathleen Cleaver, a leader of the Black Panther Party's International Section, recalled that 'All our sympathies were with the IRA – even with the Provisionals – because they took such a clear-cut position on armed struggle.'[62]

Back in Northern Ireland, the introduction of British troops brought short-term stability – even joy – to some Catholic areas, but territory which had been defended by youths in the Bogside would not be surrendered easily to the new force of law and order. The barricades stayed up, and a mini-government was established to administer the new 'Free Derry', with its own 'police force'. A few months later, when the political heat had cooled and violence largely subsided, the British government promised a series of reforms and the barricades once again came down. Resistance to the political order was largely funnelled into the resurgence of Republicanism, and although NICRA continued to function and to organise protests, it had largely lost its momentum of the previous 18 months. Many civil rights activists were confused by the new political situation. Minutes from a meeting of the local PD branch in Coalisland reveal a common problem of the time: 'A long, confused discussion took place [on self-defence] with some members unable to distinguish between defence and attack.'[63] By 1970 NICRA was concentrating on trying to establish a 'Bill of Rights' for the UK, for which it sought the support of Rev. Ralph Abernathy.[64]

PD, for its part, became more radical, and increasingly expressed support for black militants in the US. The bond between the PD and the Black Panthers was cemented during the early 1970s by Bernadette Devlin's growing reputation among the left in the US, and in November 1970 PD recommended Black Panther Bobby Seale's *Seize The Time* to its members (describing it as 'repetitive but instructive').[65] When Devlin was imprisoned for six months in 1970 for her part in the previous year's rioting, PD mounted a 'Release Bernadette' campaign with posters and stickers which imitated the 'Free Huey' slogans orchestrated by the Black Panthers to have Huey Newton released from prison. In September 1971 the PD newspaper carried an article on the death of leading Black Panther George Jackson, who had been shot by guards in San Quentin Prison, and quoted Jackson as saying 'our problems are historically and strategically tied to the problems of all colonial people'.[66]

On her first trip to the US in August 1969, fresh from the Bogside riots, Devlin visited Operation Bootstrap in Watts, the Los Angeles district torn apart by riots a few years earlier. Although the local black activists appeared unprepared for Devlin's visit and the media which accompanied her ('No one was hippin' us that this chick was coming,' said one), the visit strengthened her reputation as an unusual politician, an MP from Northern Ireland interested in more than the Northern Ireland situation.[67] By the early 1970s, Devlin was in personal contact with several black radical leaders, including Huey Newton, Angela Davis and Stokely Carmichael. The Black Panther archives include a telegram from Bernadette Devlin dated 25 May 1971 congratulating Panthers Bobby Seale and Erika Huggins on their acquittal on murder-conspiracy charges: 'JUST HEARD THE NEWS ABOUT BOBBY AND ERIKA STOP WE HAVE NOT FORGOTTEN THOSE WHO STILL REMAIN IN PRISON STOP LOVE BERNADETTE DEVLIN.'[68] Devlin was something of an oddity to the black Americans, who were generally unused to support from Irish-Americans. Devlin recalled their astonishment towards her: '"We didn't know they made white people like you" they'd say to me – "Are you sure you're not black?" I'd say no, there was no question of my being black.'[69]

When Devlin was presented with the keys of New York City by Mayor John Lindsay in 1969, she promptly passed them to Eamonn McCann to present to the Black Panther Party, causing a fair-sized stir in the media. The *New York Times* reported on 3 March 1970 that McCann handed over 'a golden key to the city given by Mayor Lindsay to Bernadette Devlin, the Irish civil rights leader "as a gesture of solidarity with the black liberation and revolutionary movements in America"' to Black Panther Robert Bay, and quoted a statement sent by Devlin and read at the ceremony declaring 'I return what is rightfully theirs [America's poor], this symbol of the freedom of New York.'[70]

The meeting with Angela Davis in 1971 was even more controversial. Davis had been on the FBI's 'Ten Most Wanted' list, been described by President Richard Nixon as a 'terrorist', and was in jail awaiting trial for murder and kidnapping when Devlin visited her in February 1971.[71] 'Angela Davis and I are involved in the same struggle ... for the liberation of our own people,' said Devlin, and described the prison visit somewhat improbably as 'like meeting McCann in the tube ... there was someone you knew you had an affinity with and you knew were essentially on the same tracks.'[72] On her return to Ireland, Devlin suggested that the split in the Black Panther Party between Huey P. Newton and Eldridge Cleaver was akin to the split in the IRA. Cleaver emphasised race over class as the most important political dynamic for the Panthers, and Newton the opposite. The Provisional IRA seemed to emphasise religion over class as the dominant theme, whereas the Official IRA favoured the class-based approach.[73]

PD's newspaper covered Davis's case regularly, repeatedly calling for her release and describing her as 'a symbol of all political prisoners, from [black militant] Ruchell Magee to [Irish Republican] Billy McKee'.[74] The introduction of internment without trial in Northern Ireland on 10 August 1971 led to hundreds of Catholic men being detained in prisons, and an increased identification with black political prisoners in the US. The following month *Unfree Citizen* carried a piece on prisoner George Jackson, a field marshal in the Black Panther Party shot dead by guards a few weeks earlier.[75] In June 1972, the PD paper carried a detailed chronology of the case of the Soledad Brothers, friends and fellow inmates of Jackson who were charged with killing prison guards, and it compared the black political prisoners with internees in Northern Ireland.[76]

While the strongest links between the civil rights activists in Northern Ireland and the US were on the radical wings of each movement, there was also significant contact between the relatively moderate factions. The NAACP magazine *Crisis* protested in 1969 that the 'Protestant majority has systematically deprived the Roman Catholic minority of basic civil rights in much the same manner that white people in this country have suppressed the rights of Negro citizens.' It also noted that the

> violence which has flared in Ulster in recent months has moved the government to institute some belated reforms but not enough to meet the demands of some of the Catholic civil rights activists, again a parallel with what happens in America'.[77]

It was the killings of Bloody Sunday in Derry in January 1972 which caused the most outrage in black America, however. On 30 January, 13 unarmed protestors were shot dead by British soldiers at a march organised by the Derry Civil Rights Association. 'Can it be that Britain does not mind shooting down Irishmen ostensibly on behalf of other Irishmen ... but is alarmed at the prospect of using force against white Rhodesians who hold their black fellow citizens in cruel subjugation?' thundered *Crisis*.[78]

Two weeks after the massacre the SCLC despatched senior officials to Belfast to take part in protest marches and to speak at a NICRA meeting. Bernard Lee, a veteran of the Atlanta sit-ins and a close associate of Martin Luther King, was part of the group which included Juanita Abernathy, wife of Rev. Ralph Abernathy. Juanita Abernathy told the NICRA conference that 'the struggle for Irish freedom is the same struggle as that going on in the United States'.[79] Juanita Williams was also part of the delegation of black American civil rights activists, and remembered the tension of the civil rights marches she joined in Northern Ireland, when 'you never knew when a bomb was coming'.[80] The Belfast hotel where the Americans were staying was bombed twice during the three days they were there.[81] Other black moderates offered support to the Northern Ireland civil rights movement in the aftermath of the massacre. Black Republican Senator Edward Brooke protested in Congress about the killings of Bloody Sunday, and called on the European Commission on Human Rights to intervene: 'The situation is similar to the one in Selma, Alabama, under Dr. Martin Luther King, when blacks and whites marched to Selma, Alabama, at that time, Mr. President, protesting oppression of minorities by majorities.'[82]

To mark the first anniversary of internment in August 1972, NICRA suggested large-scale street protests where people would turn out in the middle of the night

> ... and there everyone stands silent for a few minutes in memory of those who have died as a result of internment. Banners should be brought out. It could be really effective if either a loudspeaker system or a local radio station could play 'We Shall Overcome'.[83]

It was a nice idea, but too much had happened since Fionnbarra O Dochartaigh had first sung the song on Craigavon Bridge in the summer of 1968. The American civil rights movement had greatly influenced the civil rights movement in Northern Ireland in the previous five years, and provided support and guidance for key activists. It had influenced strategy and tactics, and sent some of its most prominent members to Belfast in a gesture of solidarity with the Northern Ireland civil rights movement. But by early 1972, political momentum had fallen to other groups in the province, and the funerals of the Bloody Sunday victims proved to be the last great civil rights marches. What was left of the civil rights movement in Northern Ireland in 1972 splintered under the pressure of internal friction, internment and exhaustion. Guns and soldiers had flooded into the country to conduct politics by other means.

4

Irish America

Nothing can compare with the brutality of the slave trade, where hundreds of thousands of people were kidnapped from Africa, crammed into ships and forcibly taken to the Americas. An unknown number died fighting off the kidnappers, in the holding stations at places like the Ile de Goree in Senegal, and on the slave ships crossing the Atlantic. The slave trade dislocated the African economy, reshaped African societies and largely defined what it means to be an African-American. The forefathers of black Americans were almost all unwilling immigrants who had not wanted to make the voyage from one continent to another. Unlike other ethnic groups, they did not choose America as their destination, but were forced there against their will.

By contrast, for some Irish immigrants, arrival in America was the culmination of years of planning and saving, the result of a conscious choice to leave Ireland for better economic and social opportunities offered by the New World. For hundreds of thousands of others, it was a desperate act of escape, as they fled from political oppression and near-certain death from starvation. The Irish who left their homeland during the mid-nineteenth century often had little choice, and many were reluctant emigrants. Their passage across the Atlantic was often as hazardous as had been the Africans' journey a century before. Thousands of Irish, fleeing the famines of the 1840s, made the trip in open lumber ships. In 1847, 84 such ships were held outside Quebec at Grosse Isle, and 10,000 Irish passengers died in the winter cold because of a delay in landing.[1] Between 1845 and 1854, starvation drove an estimated 1.5 million Irish people to America.[2]

The Irish famine years coincided with the last decades of the slave system in the US. When Irish immigrants landed in America, the debate on the future of slavery dominated American political life; by 1861 the issue had plunged the country into civil war. Newly-arrived Irish immigrants often competed with freed black Americans for jobs, and the two groups shared a similar social status. In *How the Irish Became White*, Noel Ignatiev notes that the legal position of American slaves before the Civil War was very similar to that of Catholics in Ireland a century earlier.[3] Whereas the Dred Scott judicial decision in the US in 1855 declared that 'the Negro has no rights a white man is bound to respect', so too Catholics in Ireland had, under the Penal Laws, been denied basic human rights, including the right to vote, serve as teachers, attend university, take part in the manufacture of books or newspapers, or own a horse worth more than five pounds.[4]

American employers in the middle of the nineteenth century often had their pick of Irish or black labour. In his study of the American slave system in the 1850s, Frederick Law Olmsted recorded that some preferred Irish workers, others black.[5] One Virginia landowner claimed Irish workers would perform over 50 per cent more work in a day than black slaves; another tobacco farmer from the same state explained to Olmsted that he employed Irish labourers over blacks not because they were more productive ('he thought a negro could do twice as much work, in a day, as an Irishman') but because the work could be dangerous, and 'a negro's life is too valuable to be risked at it. If a negro dies, it's a considerable loss, you know', Olmsted was told.[6] Olmsted himself owned a farm in New York, where there was no slavery, and he chose to employ Irish workers, as he believed they produced more and cost less than black labourers.[7]

Whatever their relative merits, black and Irish workers were commonly regarded as comprising the lowest social strata of American society. An English historian visiting the US wrote home in 1881:

> This would be a grand land if only every Irishman would kill a Negro, and be hanged for it. I find this sentiment generally approved – sometimes with the qualification that they want Irish and Negroes for servants, not being able to get any other.[8]

Similar socioeconomic positions rarely strengthened bonds between black Americans and recently-arrived Irish immigrants in the 1840s and 1850s. Even Frederick Douglass, so sympathetic to Ireland's political aspirations, begrudged the opportunities offered to Irish immigrants. In 1853 he complained:

> Every hour sees us elbowed out of some employment to make room for some newly-arrived emigrant from the Emerald Isle, whose hunger and color entitle him to special favor. These white men are becoming house servants, cooks, stewards, waiters, and

flunkies ... If they cannot rise to the dignity of white men, they
show that they can fall to the degradation of black men.[9]

Irish America, for its part, had rejected O'Connell's pleas to support
the abolition of slavery, and although many Irish-Americans fought
on the Union side in the Civil War which ended American slavery,
relations between blacks and Irish-Americans were often tense. The
situation was not relieved by the gradual Irish climb up the social
ladder. Many Irish immigrants concentrated on building political
organisations as a means of access to local government jobs. By
delivering blocs of votes to a political party (usually the Democratic
Party), local Irish political leaders were granted patronage powers,
with which they could reward faithful voters with jobs in, typically,
the police or fire departments.

The impressive Irish political gains often left black Americans
behind on the bottom rung of the ladder, and by the middle of the
twentieth century, when the black civil rights movement began to
challenge the American law directly through sit-ins and marches, it
often found itself in direct confrontation with Irish law enforcers,
exacerbating the tension between the Irish-American and black
communities. A black civil rights demonstration would often be
met with a hostile reaction from police, and the chances were good
that the police would be Irish-Americans. For example, the police
commissioner in Birmingham, Alabama was the notorious Eugene
'Bull' Connor; the Cook County State's Attorney who directed
operations against the Black Panthers in Chicago was Edward
V. Hanrahan, and the FBI agent tracking SNCC in Mississippi
was Thomas Fitzpatrick. There were 'too many Irish policemen
who conveyed racist attitudes', said top Panther official Kathleen
Cleaver.[10] This heavy representation of Irish-Americans in police
forces has contributed to an exaggerated notion of Irish-Americans
as racist.

Not all Irish-Americans were against civil rights for blacks
in the US, of course, and Irish America's response to the civil
rights movement was neither uniform nor simple. It has been
suggested that the Irish-Americans' struggle for sociopolitical
respectability left them unsympathetic towards black efforts for
advancement. According to this theory, the Irish knew they had
not been responsible for the slave trade, had nothing to feel guilty
about in terms of the position of blacks in American society, and
believed that blacks ought to raise themselves up, as the Irish had
done, without any special favours. Some black leaders appeared
to advocate the Irish example for blacks. Stokely Carmichael and

Charles V. Hamilton wrote in their 1966 work, *Black Power*, 'Irish Catholics took care of their own first without a lot of apology for doing so, without any dubious language from timid leadership about guarding against "backlash". Everyone understood it to be a perfectly legitimate procedure.'[11] One study of the Boston Irish suggested that many Irish-Americans also thought that blacks ought to follow their example rather than base their case on a moral argument:

> [Irish-Americans] were not inclined to give anything away to the black civil rights leaders who seemed to be seeking leverage by assuming for their group a special moral status based on white guilt. Yankees or Jews might have been susceptible to such an appeal – most Irish were not.[12]

Nevertheless, the most famous Irish-Americans (also from Boston) were the Kennedy brothers, who enjoyed enormous popularity among black Americans. John Kennedy was elected US president in 1960 with a large percentage of the black vote (68 per cent), although his voting record in Congress on the issue had been rather unspectacular.[13] After a disappointingly slow start to civil rights reform, President Kennedy eventually responded to civil rights demands with some effective action, desegregated interstate bus terminals, faced down segregationist Governor George Wallace and forced the integration of the University of Alabama. Through television addresses to the nation, Kennedy increasingly identified with the black struggle for civil rights.

Although sometimes more reactive than proactive, and inevitably more cautious than many black leaders wished, the Kennedy brothers were none the less generally popular in the black community. The national mourning which followed President Kennedy's assassination in November 1963 helped pass the Civil Rights Act of 1964, and many black Americans came to regard him as the most helpful president since Lincoln. Much of this affection was transferred to Robert Kennedy, who, as attorney general in his brother's administration, had supported voter registration drives for blacks in the South. Walter Fauntroy, a lieutenant of Martin Luther King during the 1960s and later congressman for Washington DC, suggested that within the black community there was a

> feeling that his brother [President John Kennedy] was assassinated for the forthright stand he was moved to take in 1963 around the Birmingham [civil rights] movement ... and at a subliminal level,

blacks felt that for whatever reasons he was killed, among them was his forthrightness on the question of civil rights. ... There was a desire to reward [Robert Kennedy] with what the people would've rewarded his brother had he lived.[14]

Robert Kennedy became senator for New York in 1965, and ran for president in 1968. During these three years he became closely identified with the black civil rights movement and proved a remarkably popular candidate with black voters. He set up a ghetto renewal scheme in the Bedford Stuyvesant ghetto of New York, met militant black leader Floyd McKissick and continually gave him money, and was one of the first major American (or foreign) politicians to go to South Africa to attack apartheid.[15]

President John Kennedy had halted loans to the South African government, and forbidden any weapons deals with the Pretoria regime in protest at its policies, but Robert Kennedy's trip in 1966, which included stinging attacks on the Pretoria regime and a highly-publicised visit to 'banned' Nobel Prize winner Zulu chief Albert Luthuli, helped cement his credentials with leading black American civil rights leaders. At a press conference on his return from South Africa, Kennedy compared the position of American blacks with Irish-Americans:

> Everything that is now being said about the Negro was said about the Irish Catholics. They were useless, they were worthless, they couldn't learn anything. Why did they have to settle here? Why don't we see if we can't get boats and send them back to Ireland?[16]

In 1961, while attorney general in President Kennedy's administration, Robert Kennedy noted that just as America had an Irish Catholic for a president, 'in the next forty years a Negro can achieve the same position that my brother has.'[17] Robert Kennedy's own bid for the presidency relied heavily on black support. Martin Luther King suggested Kennedy would 'make a great President' and in the presidential primaries he entered he won the overwhelming support of black voters.[18] Kennedy was so popular with black voters that his candidacy, though welcomed by most blacks, threatened the political leverage of some radical black leaders. SNCC Chairman Stokely Carmichael had complained to a Kennedy aide in 1966: 'I would not want to see your man run for president because he can get the votes of my people without coming to me. With the other candidates, I'll have bargaining power.'[19] Kennedy's

assassination in June 1968, only hours after winning the California
presidential primary election, had a tremendous impact on the
black community in America and on its leaders. NAACP leader
Roy Wilkins recalled:

When Sirhan Sirhan shot Bobby Kennedy in Los Angeles, I came
as close as I ever have come to losing faith in the workings of
democracy. I had always felt a degree of distance from Bobby
Kennedy, partly because he had become senator in New York by
defeating Kenneth Keating, a Republican who had always been
a very good friend of the NAACP. But the older Bobby grew, the
more clear matters of race relations became to him. By 1968 he
obviously felt the problem deeply, and he was poised to offer
considerable help.[20]

A poll taken in Harlem following Robert Kennedy's death showed
that 92 per cent of local residents felt at least as affected, if not
more, by his murder than that of John Kennedy.[21]

It was widely believed in police and army circles that Kennedy's
death could provoke the sort of large-scale violence which had
broken out after the assassination of Martin Luther King two
months before. In Washington DC, all police leave was cancelled.
The city's black mayor, Walter Washington, explained that the
police were 'trying to be at the ready'.[22] The Pentagon announced
it was taking 'certain prudent actions' in case Kennedy's death
provoked a new outburst of rioting. 'The action consists in ensuring
that contingency plans, in which troops are detailed for duty in
civil disturbances in various parts of the country, are all in order,'
said a Pentagon spokesman.[23] 'The country is preparing for what
could be called a state of siege,' one reporter noted two days after
Kennedy's murder:

The Army's Directorate for Civil Disturbances Planning and
Operations has been in a state of alert since yesterday morning,
the California National Guard has 26,800 men ready for
deployment in the streets, and 10,000 regular troops are standing
by outside Washington.[24]

Widespread violence never materialised, but it is an indication of
the perceived level of anger about Kennedy's death in the black
community that such steps were taken, and in the months and years
following his assassination Robert Kennedy joined the pantheon of
black heroes which also included his brother John. A Motown song,
'Abraham, Martin and John' – which reached number four in the

US charts of November 1968 – grouped Bobby Kennedy with fallen heroes Presidents Lincoln and Kennedy, and Martin Luther King. Diana Ross and The Supremes played a $1,000 a plate fundraiser/ concert in April 1969, the proceeds of which went towards paying off Kennedy's campaign debts.[25] In June 1971, Motown subsidiary Mowest released 'What The World Needs Now Is Love' by DJ Tom Clancy where the lyrics were interspersed with extracts of speeches from King and John and Robert Kennedy.

The exalted position given to John and Robert Kennedy in black popular culture clearly denies any attempt to dismiss all Irish-Americans as racist, and the Kennedy brothers were not the only Irish-Americans to respond positively to the black civil rights movement. Other significant examples include Paul O'Dwyer, a prominent Irish-born lawyer with close links to Irish Republicans who represented American blacks in civil rights cases and was also involved with black political campaigns in Mississippi. O'Dwyer suggested in an article for the NAACP magazine *Crisis* that blacks should concentrate on highlighting the positive contribution made by their culture to American society, as the Irish had done.

'Negro Americans have not been the sole victims of neglect in the history popularly taught in the nation's elementary and secondary schools,' wrote O'Dwyer, and reminded *Crisis* readers that among the first ethnic groups to take action to redress the situation were the Irish-Americans, who in 1897 had established the American Irish Historical Society in Boston in order, among other things, 'To promote and further Human Freedom which has no concern for any man's race, color or creed'. O'Dwyer noted that one of the first projects undertaken by the society was the publication of a biography of Ulsterman Hercules Mulligan, who had served as a 'top secret agent for George Washington', and who had become for Irish-Americans 'what Crispus Attucks is to Negro Americans'. (Crispus Attucks was the first fatality of the American Revolution. He was killed trying to rally Americans against the British during the Boston Massacre of 1770.) O'Dwyer also mentioned that at the time of the biography's publication, Irish-Americans were 'emerging from a period of ethnic and religious prejudice, discrimination and harassment [and] were still regarded as second-class citizens'. O'Dwyer added:

The Irish struggle continues in Ulster where Mulligan was born. There his kinsmen are losing their lives for the very same rights for which he fought – the right of a citizen to employment ... regardless of his ethnic background – rights still denied the

Catholic minority in that colony by the same forces which Mulligan resisted two centuries ago.[26]

Other Irish-Americans also offered support for the black struggle. Fr Eugene Boyle, an Irish priest in San Francisco, had been the first person to open his doors to the Black Panthers' free breakfast programme when it began in 1969. According to the *Black Panther* newspaper, Boyle allowed his Sacred Heart parish facilities to be used by the Panthers for the programme despite being 'subjected to police intimidation and racist epithets and slurs, some even calling him a "nigger-lover"'.[27] Boyle also allowed the Sacred Heart Church to be used for Panther memorial services and even Panther political meetings. In May 1971, he flew 3,000 miles from California to New Haven, Connecticut to appear as a witness for Panther leader Bobby Seale, who was being tried for murder.[28]

Irish America had a mixed, sometimes confused, record of response to the demands for black civil rights in the 1960s, and its reputation as uniformly hostile to the black struggle is wholly undeserved. Many Irish-American acts of support for the black civil rights struggle were less celebrated than Kennedy making a televised address, or Fr Boyle appearing in court. During one leg of the march from Selma to Montgomery, for example, the number of marchers was limited to 300. Many more wanted to stay with the march to say they had walked for the entire five days. After much discussion about who would be awarded the coveted 300 places, Rev. Ralph Abernathy recalled one of those 'chosen was a red-headed Irishman named Murphy, who spoke with a brogue of his belief in freedom and equality for all men'.[29] Quite apart from the individual exceptions, a study by the National Opinion Research Center in the 1970s found that Irish-Americans were more sympathetic to racial integration than any other ethnic group apart from Jews.[30] Moreover, a high percentage of Irish-American neighbourhoods were found to be racially integrated, with 18 per cent of Irish Catholics living on the same block as blacks, and 89 per cent of Irish Catholics saying they were willing to vote for a black President.[31]

None the less, there were plenty of Irish-Americans unhappy at black claims for civil rights. In Boston, school integration, and particularly the issue of busing, sparked violent confrontations between Irish-Americans and civil rights activists. The chant of 'Niggers out of Boston, Brits out of Belfast' was frequently used by some Irish-Americans during the busing demonstrations.[32] In 1963, President John Kennedy made personal appeals to those leading the white backlash against integration in the city, and in 1975 his brother, Senator Edward Kennedy, was physically assaulted by his Irish-American constituents in Boston for his support of busing.[33] According to one commentator, 'the rage against [Edward] Kennedy reached a torrent because of the feeling, especially among Irish Catholics, that Kennedy, one of theirs, had betrayed them.'[34] The *Belfast News Letter* reported in April 1968 on a religious service for Martin Luther King in Dublin where Catholic priest Fr Michael Hurley urged Irish Catholics to become more involved with the struggle for black civil rights. 'What had shocked and saddened him most during his visit to a Chicago ghetto last year had been the anti-negro prejudice of so many Irish-American priests and people', noted the paper.[35]

If Irish America had an ambiguous response to civil rights in America, its reaction to demands for civil rights in Northern Ireland was no less confused. Many Irish-Americans had difficulty understanding the difference between claims for civil rights and claims for an end to partition and the expulsion of the British. America traditionally harboured the most virulent strain of Irish Republicanism. Many Irish-Americans had been forced to emigrate out of fear of retribution for their Republican activities, first by the British and, after the early 1920s, from the Irish government which hounded them into exile with just as much enthusiasm. Irish America's contribution to the cause of Irish independence had been primarily, though not exclusively, financial. Daniel O'Connell had relied on American dollars (until they were withheld over the slavery controversy), as had the Fenians, the Irish Republican Brotherhood and, in the 1960s, the IRA. Several prominent Irish revolutionaries had spent time raising financial and political capital in the US.[36] Eamon de Valera had even been born in New York, and in 1921 returned to raise $5.5 million in a bond certificate drive, which helped finance the IRA's war against the British.

Occasionally, Irish America also applied direct political pressure on the British and American governments on Irish issues. Soon after the First World War ended, for example, 134 members of the US House of Representatives cabled the British Prime Minister, Lloyd George, urging him to 'free Ireland', and voted 216 to 45 that the Versailles peace conference should consider Ireland's right to self-determination.[37] The US Senate endorsed de Valera's unsuccessful claims to represent Ireland at Versailles. During the 1950s, there were repeated resolutions filed in the US House of Representatives for a plebiscite in all of Ireland on its political future.[38]

By the 1960s, there were over 13 million Americans claiming Irish ancestry – over 6 per cent of the total population.[39] Although some pressured their elected representatives to push for a united Ireland, few – at least initially – were enthusiastic about the civil rights movement in Northern Ireland. Patricia McCluskey recalled failed attempts to interest Irish America in the anti-discrimination campaign:

> At the very beginning we had a list of all the Irish-American clubs in America – I think it was 342 – and we notified them all of the sort of work we were doing. We got a response from one, saying he would bring it up at his meeting later in the month, and that was the only response from anyone.[40]

The McCluskeys were very disappointed; they had not been looking for dollars, merely messages of support. 'Dirty things like money were never discussed ... we paid for everything ourselves,' said Patricia McCluskey.[41]

For their part, the early civil rights agitators were reluctant to invest much time or energy into eliciting Irish-American support, for a variety of reasons. Neither the McCluskeys nor anybody else thought it worth the effort to attempt to raise the issue of civil rights in Northern Ireland with President John Kennedy during his trip to Ireland in August 1963, and more radical figures like Eamonn McCann and Michael Farrell were wary of links to Irish America. McCann said:

> [There] were very edgy discussions [in the civil rights movement] about the fact that we all knew that Irish-Americans were deeply racist, or an awful lot of them were, and there was something problematical about this emotional and ideological link between black American civil rights and civil rights here [in Northern Ireland].[42]

Farrell was even more dubious: 'Those of us who were sort of politically conscious were violently anti-American, [had] no desire to go to America, didn't like Irish-Americans because we saw them all as racist bigots.'[43]

The simplistic and sometimes inaccurate view of Irish America held by some civil rights activists in Northern Ireland was often reciprocated. In a piece for the *Chicago Sun-Times* in November 1968, celebrated Irish-American journalist Jimmy Breslin reported that 'the silent understanding has been that Catholics are the

Negroes of Northern Ireland', but included the woefully misleading information that 'In Northern Ireland, Catholics are the majority of the population. Through election laws that discriminate against them, the Catholics form only a little over 10 per cent of the vote.'[44] Such exaggerations fuelled Irish America's distorted perceptions of the situation in Northern Ireland, and when civil rights activists visited the US, they often found they were asked more questions about the border and prospects for eventual reunification than about the equal rights they were claiming as British citizens.

Most Irish-Americans, however, simply weren't concerned about events in Northern Ireland in the mid-1960s. Few remembered the Anglo-Irish War, or the Irish Civil War, and overall Irish America's interest in Irish politics was weak. Ireland's neutrality in the Second World War (and de Valera's message of condolence to the German ambassador on Hitler's death) increased the political distance between Irish America and Ireland. By the time the civil rights movement took off in Northern Ireland in 1968, only the most militant Republican groups were still operating in America.[45] So when civil rights activists from Northern Ireland visited Irish-American organisations they often found them fiercely nationalistic. 'These [Irish-American] fellows, when you started talking about civil rights, were bored. We were treated well enough but they regarded us as vaguely crackpot because we weren't on the basic thing which was get the border clear,' said Conn McCluskey:

> The Irish-Americans are a group of people who left Ireland at the very bitterest time – at the time of 1916 and the ones we met there were all that type; they're very extreme and very Republican and when we saw them one of them said to me: 'You've got to say when you're speaking on the TV that the solution is a united Ireland.' Well now, that didn't please me at all. I stuck it in unwillingly because we were working on the basis that we were British citizens and we wanted British rights and even in the civil rights movement [we] were absolutely dead against talking about the border.[46]

One of the oldest and most Republican Irish-American organisations was Clann na Gael, originally established in the 1870s to support rebellion in Ireland. In the 1960s, Brigid Makowski joined the Clann na Gael branch in Philadelphia, and noted that 'the formation of NICRA received a mixed response from Clann-na-Gael members, who equated civil rights with "Black Power" in the US with which they wanted no association'.[47] When Makowski proposed a NICRA banner in the Philadelphia St Patrick's Day parade of 1969, 'the motion was finally adopted but with the provision that the banner clearly state that Clann-na-Gael was supporting civil rights in Ireland, not black civil rights in the US'.[48]

More mainstream Irish-American politicians were also slow to respond to the developing civil rights crisis in Northern Ireland. Robert Kennedy, despite his close association with the civil rights cause in the US, reportedly dismissed requests to complain about anti-Catholic discrimination in Northern Ireland on the grounds that he considered the issue to be an internal British matter.[49] When the Northern Ireland civil rights issue became an international media story, however, in late 1968, Irish-American politicians were quick to speak out, but the Nixon administration remained wary of upsetting its British ally. When Democratic Congressman James Hanley of New York urged President Nixon 'to speak out against religious hatred and discrimination practiced in Northern Ireland against Catholics', in March 1969, the State Department replied, 'The UK is a friendly country which, unlike certain other countries with civil rights problems, has a basic structure of democratic institutions and political freedom', and suggested that intervention in British affairs 'would be as difficult to justify as intervention by a foreign government in a civil rights controversy in this country'.[50] In June that year, over 100 Congressmen wrote to President Nixon to express 'concern that intolerance and discrimination are encouraged by and rooted in the laws of Northern Ireland,' but the State Department still refused to act.[51] The hands-off approach by the American government even extended to the Battle of the Bogside itself in August 1969. Brigid Makowski, caught up in the battle, feared for the safety of herself and her children – all US citizens – and applied to the US Naval Telecommunications Centre in Derry for political asylum for her family, but was rejected.[52]

It was after the deployment of British troops to the streets of Northern Ireland following that battle that Irish-American politicians really became involved in the issue. The presence of the troops framed the debate about Northern Ireland in the traditional British versus Irish context, and by the early 1970s, when the subtleties of Catholic claims for civil rights had been largely overtaken by a more straightforward nationalist agenda, Irish-American politicians began to speak out more regularly. In 1971, Senator Edward Kennedy, the only surviving Kennedy brother, presented a resolution to the US Senate calling for 'an immediate withdrawal of British troops from Northern Ireland and the establishment of a united Ireland'.[53] Kennedy suggested that the basic issue in Northern Ireland was one of civil rights, and drew a parallel with the American experience. He declared:

> Americans well know that injustice breeds bitterness, and that from this bitterness can come violence at almost any provocation. America has learned that the solution is not repression, the solution is not armed troops, the solution is not barbed wire detention camps. We have found a better way, a way of peace and reconciliation, and we believe that Northern Ireland can reach the same result. ... The crisis in Northern Ireland is a lesson to the world that religious intolerance can run just as deep and be just as cruel and violent as racial discrimination.[54]

The following year, a subcommittee of the US Congressional Committee on European Affairs held hearings on Northern Ireland. The hearings were conducted four weeks after the Bloody Sunday massacre, and heard testimony from Conn McCluskey, Fr Edward Daly (who had been in Derry during the shootings) and others. The hearings also marked the point when Senator Edward Kennedy began to compare the situation in Northern Ireland with America's involvement in Vietnam, rather than the American civil rights struggle. 'Just as Ulster is Britain's Vietnam, so Bloody Sunday is Britain's My Lai', said Kennedy at the hearings.[55]

Irish America, which had produced a hesitant response to the claims of civil rights activists in the US and in Northern Ireland, found a more certain voice in the early 1970s when the Irish question once again became centred on the legitimacy of British rule in Ulster. What still confused Irish America, however, was which Irish faction to support: the constitutional nationalists, the Dublin government, NICRA, or the Republicans, and if the Republicans which faction – the newly-formed Provisionals, or the Officials? Dozens of Irish-American organisations sprung up across the US to support and fund the various political factions emerging in Northern Ireland. At the risk of being over-schematic, within the broad spectrum of Irish-American organisations, there were two broad categories, which can be crudely characterised as left and right.

The largest group to respond to the civil rights movement in Northern Ireland was the generally conservative American Congress for Irish Freedom (ACIF). ACIF was founded and led by James Heaney, a lawyer based in upstate New York who helped the McCluskeys' Campaign for Social Justice pursue an anti-discrimination case before the European Court of Human Rights in Strasbourg in April 1968. Although ACIF was a relatively early supporter of the civil rights movement in Northern Ireland, Heaney and many of its supporters saw the ultimate objective as being Irish unification. In March 1969, ACIF sponsored Gerry Fitt and Austin Currie on a speaking tour of the US, and later that year Heaney embarked on a bizarre venture to involve the Spanish government in funding the Northern Ireland civil rights movement. The overture met with some success and Heaney managed to persuade Spanish diplomats that embarrassing Britain over its human rights record in Ulster could strengthen Spanish claims on Gibraltar. Heaney was promised $50,000 and offered Spanish broadcasting facilities to use for anti-British propaganda.[56] 'I liked Heaney even though he was a reactionary shit,' said Derry civil rights activist Fionnbarra O Dochartaigh. 'He would avoid questions about blacks in America and things like that, but at the end of the day he was on our side.'[57]

The flirtation with the Spanish government didn't come to anything, however, and although ACIF peaked to a membership of several thousand in late 1969, it collapsed soon afterwards under the pressures of reacting to the new political situation in Northern Ireland. In the early 1970s much of the old ACIF network was taken over by the Irish Northern Aid Committee (Noraid), who had close links with the newly-emerging Provisional IRA.

The largest Irish-American organisation on the left was the National Association for Irish Justice (NAIJ), which – unlike ACIF – also supported the black civil rights struggle in the US. Left-wing activist Brian Heron had co-founded NAIJ in April 1969. Heron was the grandson of socialist James Connolly, a hero of the 1916 Easter Rising, which afforded him some political capital in Irish-American Republican circles. In November 1969, NAIJ held a convention in New York, where IRA leader Cathal Goulding was guest of honour. Eilis McDermott and Kevin Boyle from PD also attended the convention during which McDermott visited Black Panther offices and was made an honourary Panther. Like ACIF, NAIJ also splintered towards the end of 1970 when confronted with a new political context in Northern Ireland, and many NAIJ members joined either the leftist Irish Republican Clubs (IRC), or the National Association of Irish Freedom (NAIF) – the organisation supported by black civil rights activists Rev. Ralph Abernathy and Dick Gregory.

The violence of the split between the Official and Provisional IRAs in the early 1970s was mirrored in America, where Provisional supporters in Noraid clashed in fights with Official supporters in the IRC and NAIF. Just as the Provisional IRA became the dominant Republican group in Northern Ireland, so too Noraid would eventually emerge as the most powerful Irish-American organisation. The left versus right antagonisms in Irish America predated the formal split in the Republican movement, however, and in the late 1960s James Heaney and ACIF were aghast at the NAIJ's links with black civil rights activists. Friction between the two groups was barely contained during the early part of 1969, but in August the focus of the dispute switched from the wisdom of alliances with the American civil rights movement to responding to the widespread violence in Northern Ireland and the deployment of British troops. Within hours of the troops' appearance on the streets of Derry and Belfast, Irish America was confronted with the most politically seismic event in several generations when Bernadette Devlin landed in New York.

Spirited out of the Battle of the Bogside, where she had helped organise ammunition for the stone throwers against the police, she was rushed out of the country and onto a plane for America. 'I didn't want to go,' she said:

> Basically I was sent to America to get me out of Derry because I opposed the acceptance of the British Army, so it was necessary to ship me out and in some way which I still don't know the [Irish] Free State Army or government or somebody [arranged it]. The first time I went to America I did not have a passport never mind a friggin' visa.[58]

Bernadette Devlin was the single most important figure in Irish-American politics of the late 1960s and early 1970s. When she arrived in New York in August 1969, many Irish-Americans expected her to heal the divisions between themselves, rouse the conscience of the nation and popularise the struggle for Irish unification among the American public. Such a trip had been planned for later in the year, but events in Northern Ireland in August had hastened her arrival by three months.

By any measure, Devlin was an extraordinary character, and she fascinated the American media. An Irish Republican, and a Member of the British Parliament, a civil rights advocate and a prominent rioter, a female political leader in the most patriarchal of societies, she appeared to be a fusion of contradictions. Her election to the House of Commons four months before she arrived in the US had received almost unanimously positive press coverage, even in the British media. 'Believe me', said one press photographer, 'she was a bloody godsend, that's what. A female in politics that didn't look like the mummified remains of Nellie Wallace.'[59] Such exposure had made her a star of the international New Left and the most famous politician in Ireland. Her prominence also made her both a despised and adored figure in Northern Ireland.

Devlin's rise in the civil rights movement was less remarkable for her youth than her sex. Fellow civil rights activist Frank McManus had also been elected to Parliament on a radical platform similar to Devlin's. Most in PD were students, and of about the same age as her, but few of the top civil rights leaders were women. There were exceptions, of course, like Betty Sinclair, and a handful of other female students, like Eilis McDermott, were prominent, but the civil rights movement, even its student wing, was male-dominated. Margaret Ward was a junior figure in PD at that time, and remembers that in early 1970:

> ... women members of People's Democracy were still unques-tioningly accepting of the fact that when we undertook a token overnight squat of a house in protest against housing policies, it was the women who would go and shop for food and make the endless sandwiches. ... I think I missed most of the political talk because I was so busy buttering bread.[60]

While some students enjoyed the more glamorous tasks of speechmaking or writing leaflets, 'for others, particularly women, the shitwork of envelope addressing or sandwich making would be ours for evermore'.[61] Interestingly, another woman in PD, Inez McCormack, cited the American civil rights movement as the inspiration for women in Northern Ireland to join in political protest:

> ... it is in [Martin Luther King's] campaigns that you first begin to see the emergence of a powerful and dangerous force – women; black women courteously declining to give up their seats in buses and restaurants and accepting the violent abuse with what looks like resignation but is not.[62]

However, the black women involved in the civil rights movment in the US also found it difficult to obtain official leadership roles. Septima Clark, for example worked for the SCLC from 1961 and became the first woman on its executive board some years later. It was a promotion, she remembered, which was resisted by some of her male colleagues. She recalled:

I can't ever forget Reverend Abernathy saying, 'Why is Mrs Clark on the executive Board?' and Dr. King saying, 'Why, she designed a whole program.' 'Well, I just can't see why you got to have her on the Board!' They just didn't feel as if a woman, you know, had any sense.[63]

The Northern Ireland political scene – even the civil rights scene, which demanded 'One Man, One Vote' – remained male-dominated. In this atmosphere, Devlin's rise to become the youngest MP for two centuries was all the more exceptional. While undoubtedly an appealing speaker and an engaging personality, there were those who appeared to believe she had almost supernatural qualities. She was often described with religious reverence. Comparisons with St Joan of Arc were common, and press reports of her career made her exploits seem near-miraculous. Devlin was in some ways a classic charismatic figure as defined by Max Weber in his study of charisma. She rose to prominence at a turbulent time, and was deemed by many to have death-defying powers, a reputation fuelled by the media. In January 1970 *Harper's* reported:

> It is part of the mystique of Bernadette that she has never been hit by a rock or bottle. Peter Cush [a law student from Belfast based in the US and part of Devlin's welcoming committee in New York] says that when she campaigned, she would walk with a bullhorn through a rain of missiles and never be touched. This increased the tendency of people to regard her as a saint.[64]

Devlin, who regarded herself less as a gifted charismatic than a lucky survivor, recalled the attack on the civil rights march in Derry on 5 October and how 'I stood there like a statue, watching people being clubbed all around me', and that at Burntollet 'I could feel stones bouncing off my head, leaving me apparently undamaged.'[65]

While Devlin rejected the aura of canonisation, declaring 'I am neither a Saint, a Martyr nor a folk hero', she regularly mentioned the possibility of assassination, which encouraged many to believe she was a martyr-in-waiting.[66] 'She is obsessed with death,' noted the *New York Times Magazine* in 1970:

> Before each demonstration, during every riot, she says: 'Today I think I'm going to die.' When friends question her about her plans for the next year she invariably replies: 'Oh I'll be pushing up daisies by then.' Any summary of her future ends with the phrase: 'I expect I'll get shot.'[67]

Just before the Battle of the Bogside, she told a reporter that 'For all I know ... tomorrow you might be writing my obituary ... I'm scared', and a month later she told *Harper's* 'Eamonn [McCann] and I will be shot while resisting arrest.'[68] There was nothing melodramatic about Devlin's fear, as there were undoubtedly elements in Northern Ireland with the motive and means to kill her. In early 1981, Loyalist gunmen broke into her house, shot her and her husband and left them for dead. Both survived.[69]

Devlin arrived in America in August 1969 to find the Irish-American community faction-ridden and confused. It seemed unsure what the civil rights struggle in Northern Ireland was about, and divided on the question of civil rights nearer home. Devlin's visit would exacerbate these tensions, as she deliberately confronted Irish-American double standards on civil rights, and repeatedly accused Irish-Americans of hypocrisy. She was not the first to point out to Irish-Americans the inconsistency of supporting civil rights in Northern Ireland while opposing them in the US, but she was the most forceful on the point. Austin Currie had visited America earlier in 1969, and with Conor Cruise O'Brien, then a professor at New York University and later a minister in the Irish government, addressed an Irish-American audience in New York. When Currie and O'Brien mentioned the similarities between the two civil rights struggles, many in the audience walked out in protest.[70]

Devlin made the comparison a major theme of her visit, and from her first moments in America she identified with the black struggle more readily than with many of her Irish-American hosts. She remembered:

> I had never been anywhere other than being elected to Parliament and I'd gone to London which was the first time I'd been there. I was now in America. I came from a welfare state background ... The first major Irish-American home I went into I mistook for a boarding house.[71]

She had been met at the airport by leftist activist Brian Heron, who declared that she was in America to raise a million dollars and was calling on the Irish-American community for support. Her first meeting with the disparate Irish-American groups took place in the Manhattan offices of the Peace and Freedom Party, a New Left political group which had endorsed Black Panther Eldridge Cleaver's presidential candidacy the year before. After much argument between the various Irish-American elements over who should organise Devlin's itinerary, and where the money she raised should go, Devlin told the group that she was going to raise money 'to build new apartments for our people that the government will never have any control over'.[72] This seemed to satisfy both left and right elements. The breach was not healed, however, and Devlin's behaviour in the following week only heightened tensions between conservative and liberal Irish-Americans. Her visit drew huge press coverage; she was interviewed and photographed receiving the keys of New York City from Mayor Lindsay which she would pass on to Eamonn McCann to hand over to the Black Panthers; she appeared on several top television talk shows, and was featured daily by the main newspapers. Her trip to the ghetto project Operation Bootstrap in Watts provoked murmurs of discontent among some Irish-Americans disappointed at her left-wing opinions, as did her repeated comparisons between the civil rights movements in the US and Northern Ireland. Many Irish-Americans refused to see any similarities between the civil rights movements in Northern Ireland and the US. 'Everybody's got freedom here,' said one Irish-American at a Devlin rally, 'You've got equal rights for anybody who wants to use their rights. A lot of 'em are too damned lazy to use them.'[73]

The distance between Devlin and many Irish-Americans existed simply because Devlin felt less comfortable with many Irish-Americans than she did with black Americans. She dutifully sang Irish songs in Irish clubs, but the lifestyles of her Irish-American hosts were alien to her experience in Northern Ireland:

> I'd never seen wealth like this but by American standards these were not wealthy people. They were comfortable middle America but I had never seen houses with two bathrooms. ... These people had two bathrooms and almost inevitably if they had children they had a black woman doing washing. ... Now there were people here [in Northern Ireland] who had women who came in. They were usually Protestant women, and the women who came in were Catholics. So when I got to America ... I'd get up to help with the dishes, and [my hosts] would say 'No, I have a woman that does that, a woman that comes in.' The women that came in at home were our mothers. The women that came in there were black women. And the women who had women who did [housework] over there were the people in whose houses I was staying.[74]

Her identification with American blacks made her relations with Irish-Americans increasingly difficult:

> ... [T]hose who were supposed to be 'my people', the Irish-Americans who knew about English misrule and the Famine and supported the civil rights movement at home ... looked and sounded to me like Orangemen. They said exactly the same things about blacks that the Loyalists said about us at home.[75]

Four days into her trip, she outraged many Irish-Americans by singing – even dancing – with a black man at a rally in Philadelphia. John Russell was a local black tenor who had been hired to sing traditional Irish songs like 'I'll Take You Home Again Kathleen' before Devlin was to speak. At the end of his set he asked Devlin, the guest of honour, what she would like him to sing for her. When she requested 'We Shall Overcome', she remembers Russell looking 'mortified'. One reporter noted that 'the mouths of half the audience dropped open,' and that many left in anger.[76] Devlin told him 'I'll stand here and sing it with you ... we'll sing it 'til they stand,' believing that the audience would eventually be shamed into standing for the civil rights anthem.[77] Many did stand, and some did not: 'The people who never rose were the front rows of dignitaries of the Irish-American communities ... There were priests and nuns and members of the Ancient Order of Hibernians who sat with faces like thunder.'[78] She recalled:

> I spoke to thousands of Irish-Americans across the country, and it was sad to see how many of them were right wing in their political and social attitudes. I deliberately made a comparison between Ulster's Catholics and America's blacks ... no doubt I lost a lot of potential contributions by doing this.[79]

When Devlin reached Detroit, several stops into her itinerary, word had spread in the black community that she used her speeches to support civil rights struggle in America. Hundreds of blacks turned up to hear her speak at an event in Detroit, which had been organised by local Irish-Americans. The organisers would not let them in, and so Devlin refused to speak until the blacks were allowed into the auditorium. The organisers relented, and she gave the audience, both black and Irish-American, a speech on Irish Republicanism:

> We weep for [Roger] Casement and his grand ideals, but we like to forget that Casement spent a great deal of his life fighting for the rights of people in the Belgian Congo ... I cannot understand the mental conflict of some of our Irish-Americans who will fight forever for the struggle for justice in Ireland, and who yet play the role of the oppressor and will not stand shoulder to shoulder with their fellow black Americans.[80]

After presenting Devlin with a cheque in front of press photographers, the organisers took the cheque back and, says Devlin, sent it to the Irish Red Cross.[81]

By the time she reached Chicago the next day, her attraction for much of Irish-America was fading fast, thanks to her insistence on linking the civil rights struggle in Northern Ireland with that in the US. Chicago was the personal fiefdom of Irish-American political boss and Mayor Richard Daley, and he held onto power partly by gerrymandering districts on the city's south side along racial lines.[82]

Daley had tussled with Martin Luther King when the civil rights leader took his campaign to Chicago three years before to highlight segregation and poverty in the city. King had hoped to draw Daley into confrontation with the civil rights movement through a campaign of civil disobedience exposing the harsh realities of the city's segregation. The tactic had worked in the South, but instead of being goaded into conflict, Daley played a more wily game, frustrating the civil rights leader by appearing to welcome King's efforts at improving living conditions in the city's ghettoes. 'The Daley machine was as powerful and delicate as a nuclear reactor,' said Rev. Ralph Abernathy, and it included various black politicians loyal to the mayor, like Congressman William Dawson.[83] Whereas politicians in the South like George Wallace had confronted the civil rights movement head-on, Daley was much more skilful, suggesting that all right-thinking Americans were against segregation and poverty.[84] One in three of Daley's constituents was black – almost a million in all – but his record on improving their living conditions was poor.

Initially, Daley appeared to respond positively to the grievances of the civil rights movement. When King moved into a dilapidated flat to expose the poor living conditions of many blacks, Daley declared, 'in the next two years we will eliminate every slum and blighted building in Chicago', puncturing the civil rights leader's publicity coup.[85] But when King continued to lead protests throughout the city, Daley lost patience. He secured a court injunction limiting civil rights marches in Chicago, and blamed

King for riots which broke out in July 1966. The two had met and struck a deal in an effort to end the unrest, but some black leaders thought King had been outwitted by the Irish-American mayor, and resentment against Daley was felt by many in the civil rights movement. 'We were unprepared for Daley's devious strategy ... like Herod, Richard Daley was a fox, too smart for us, too smart for the press,' said Abernathy.[86]

Daley was also the nemesis of the international New Left after ordering his police to use teargas and clubs to disperse demonstrators at the Democratic Party convention in Chicago the year before Devlin's arrival in the US. Daley and Devlin had little in common politically (or personally) save a common heritage. He even suggested that the money for relief in Northern Ireland should be given to the Red Cross instead of to Devlin. Devlin responded by saying that during the Battle of the Bogside, 'we saw no Red Cross coming in when the police bombarded us for forty-eight hours with tear gas, a weapon I believe not uncommon to Mayor Daley'.[87]

On her arrival in the US, Devlin had compared the conduct of the B Specials of the RUC with that of the Chicago police during the Democratic Convention. Daley had called off a planned reception for Devlin in Chicago, and the rift never came close to being healed. 'I wouldn't shake that corrupt old boss's hand for the entire US Treasury,' she told *Playboy*.[88] Her regard for Daley illustrates the broad gulf in politics between Devlin and Irish America. After the Kennedys, Daley was the most prominent and powerful Irish-American politician of the 1960s, a success story among Irish immigrants, one of the country's leadership elite. To Devlin, however, 'Mayor Daley was the enemy – we called the old Chief of Police in Derry after him.'[89]

Devlin's public spat with one of Irish America's leading figures alarmed conservatives in the Northern Ireland civil rights movement as well as Irish-Americans, straining what was becoming an already difficult trip. 'The Chicago Irish never really forgave me,' said Devlin.[90] She had become increasingly worried where the money she was raising from Irish-Americans was going to end up, and so a couple of days after leaving Chicago she called NICRA Chairman Frank Gogarty, asking him to join her in America. Devlin had specifically told audiences that she did not want the money for guns, but had overheard an NAIJ organiser of her trip suggesting that the dollars might be diverted for arms anyway. When Gogarty arrived, he declared that while he supported what Devlin had done, he was there for other purposes, to raise money for a fighting fund.

Devlin immediately made plans to return to Ireland. Believing she 'was no longer in with the in-crowd', she asked Paul O'Dwyer for help, and he arranged for her to leave America and head back for Ireland.[91] She had cut her trip short, and Gogarty made a poor substitute at scheduled appearances in Washington DC and Boston. Back in Northern Ireland, Devlin explained her hurried departure in an article in the *Observer*:

> I didn't feel I could go to Boston, where there was a hugely generous Irish-American community just waiting to be asked for money, nor to Washington, where there was a lot of sympathy for our cause, when I could no longer guarantee to people how their money might be used.[92]

She claimed she had been advised by Irish-American leaders not to meet the Black Panthers, and in Los Angeles had been told by a Catholic priest she should not talk about 'Negroes, Protestants, socialists, or James Connolly'.[93]

'I must admit,' she told *Playboy* later, 'that after two weeks in America, I was glad to get back to Ulster, even though a jail sentence awaited me.'[94] Devlin was sentenced to six months' imprisonment for her part in the Battle of the Bogside. A week after being re-elected to her seat in Parliament in June 1970, she went to Armagh Gaol to begin her sentence. Three months after her release, she was back in the US.

Her second trip was notably different from her first. She was even more controversial, more confrontational and more unpopular with more Irish-Americans than before. '[For] the '69 visit I got thrown in there. The '71 visit I knew who I wanted to see,' said Devlin.[95] Those she wanted to see included Huey P. Newton, Stokely Carmichael and Angela Davis. 'I was getting an opportunity to meet with people like the Panthers ... and the more I met them the more paranoid the Irish-American community would get,' she remembered.[96] Her trip was designed to publicise her book *The Price of My Soul*, and was planned around a series of lectures she delivered at universities across the country. During her talks, she hammered on familiar themes: 'Over 70 per cent of this city is black, yet less than 3 per cent of this audience is black,' she complained at Georgetown University, the Jesuit-founded college in Washington DC.[97]

She gave 37 speeches in three weeks, and found time to visit Angela Davis in prison in California. 'Angela Davis was very aware of the enormity of what I had done in terms of the Irish-American community ... she saw that I was putting myself out on a limb,' said Devlin.[98] Davis remembered:

I guess I was surprised to hear that she wanted to meet with me and of course extremely pleased that she had decided to visit me in jail even though there was a great deal of resistance in the Irish-American community in the Bay Area. We talked about the similarities of the situations in Northern Ireland and in the US with respect to African American people and people of colour.[99]

Devlin identified more readily with the young black radicals than with Irish-Americans: 'There is a certain comfort, or comfortableness [with the black radicals] that does not exist when you're with what are supposed to be your own people.'[100]

Devlin regularly visited the US in the following years and continued to clash with many Irish-Americans over the issue of race. During the busing controversy of the mid-70s, she criticised Irish-Americans for fighting against desegregation in Boston.[101] Devlin spoke at an anti-racist meeting with Stokely Carmichael in Boston which was interrupted by Irish-Americans from south Boston: 'The doors just burst open and this guy came down the middle of the hall with this [Irish] tricolour and then he realised it was me and he stopped.' She recalled:

I said 'If you take another step forward I'll ram that thing so far down your throat that it will come out your arse' [and] the vulgarity of it stopped them ... it changed the agenda and I always believed that we could have changed the agenda, in small ways at least, by making the Irish-Americans who picked their side on Ireland pick the same side on America by quite forcibly setting the confrontations out.[102]

Devlin confronted those Irish-Americans with an ambiguous position on civil rights more forcefully than anyone else. When nationalism replaced civil rights as the paramount political issue in Northern Ireland in the early 1970s, it became easier for Irish-Americans to duck the contradiction of opposing civil rights in the US while supporting them in Northern Ireland. The introduction of British troops to the political equation brought a certain clarity to the situation for many Irish-Americans, and cast the struggle in a more familiar light. Like several visitors on fundraising tours, Northern Ireland labour leader Paddy Devlin (no relation) found Irish-Americans in the early 1970s willing to give money for guns, but not for rebuilding houses through co-operatives.[103] It was often easier for Irish-Americans to channel their support into old-style republicanism.

5

Backlash

Just as the civil rights movements in the US and Northern Ireland often used the same tactics, they often provoked similar responses from the state, from paramilitary groups and from the media. In both situations, the British and American national governments stepped in over the heads of regional governments, supplanted local authority – at least temporarily – and dispatched their own security forces to restore order. In both Northern Ireland and in the US, 'outside agitators', usually communists, were blamed for initiating, or at least exacerbating, civil disorder. In both cases, too, when protests against the local authorities became violent, the national governments reacted by appointing high-profile commissions to examine the complaints of the aggrieved minorities, and the administrations in both London and Washington DC were eventually forced into making political reforms to accommodate the civil rights protestors.

In Northern Ireland and the US, media reactions to the protests proved unenthusiastic until the advent of television. Footage of the local governments' responses to civil rights marches, in the form of policemen attacking marchers, elicited widespread support for the demonstrators which activists had previously never enjoyed. The civil rights groups also provoked counter-groups, anti-civil rights organisations which launched violent attacks on the demonstrators. The distinction between the anti-civil rights groups and official state organisations was sometimes blurred in both the US and Northern Ireland. Civil rights activists in both countries regularly complained that police officers who were supposed to protect their rights of assembly and protest were in league with the anti-civil rights demonstrators, and collaborated in their attacks. Several local politicians in the American South and Northern Ireland were also believed by many civil rights activists to be involved with shadowy underground groups opposing civil rights. In the US, many law enforcement officers were members of the White Citizens Councils, or even the Ku Klux Klan.

However, while civil rights activists from Northern Ireland like Bernadette Devlin travelled to the US and made contact with the civil rights movement in that country, and many others in PD studied the literature and tactics of the US civil rights movement, there appears to have been no attempt by either the RUC or the British security forces, or by the anti-civil rights groups in Northern Ireland, to study the responses of their American counterparts to the civil rights protests. For example, while Michael Farrell modelled the Belfast to Derry march on the one from Selma to Montgomery, and other protestors in Northern Ireland copied the sit-down tactics of American protestors, neither the police authorities nor the British Army sought advice or training from the American police in dealing with civil disobedience or riot control.

Of course, the British security forces had a wealth of experience to draw on elsewhere on the globe. From Cairo to Cape Town to Calcutta, British authority had encountered violent and non-violent challenges to its power. However, there was something different about the nature of the Northern Ireland protests. Previous campaigns against British laws had not been conducted on television. By 1968 the British police had no real experience of dealing with televised protests, whereas the American police did. Nevertheless, it seems as though no one from the British security forces asked them for help when disturbances broke out. 'We had on-the-job training,' said an RUC officer who policed the first few civil rights marches, '... we were totally ill-prepared.'[1]

There was one important exception to the general lack of formal contacts between those either policing or opposing the civil rights movements in the US and Northern Ireland. Rev. Ian Paisley spoke out against the civil rights movements in Northern Ireland and in the US from both shores of the Atlantic. He cemented a political alliance in the US with a prominent segregationist, and repeatedly compared the situation in the US with that in Northern Ireland. Paisley's links with America dated back to 1954, when he obtained the first of his academic degrees by mail order from the Pioneer Theological Seminary in Illinois, described by the US Department of Higher Education as a 'bogus degree mill'.[2] Four years later he sent off for a master's degree from Burton College in Colorado, which the US government described as 'perhaps the most infamous of all the degree mills'.[3] In 1966, he was awarded an honorary degree from Bob Jones University in Greenville, South Carolina which, like the other educational institutions, had no official accreditation, although Paisley described it as 'the greatest fundamentalist university in the world'.[4] Paisley's ties with Bob

Jones Jr, son of the university's founder, went back to 1962 when the two met at a conference in Amsterdam organised to protest about the moderation of most of the world's Protestant churches. They met again when Paisley visited the university two years later, and by the late 1960s had become close friends and political allies.

Jones Jr said he admired Paisley because 'he stands for constitutional rights and religious liberties in Northern Ireland'.[5] Jones Jr was based at the university, which was known for its right-wing leanings. Apart from Paisley it also awarded honorary degrees to conservative politicians like Republican Senator Barry Goldwater of Arizona and George Wallace, the notorious segregationist governor of Alabama. 'They're all fellas with strong convictions. Everybody today has either no belief at all or else is a liberal. If you've got strong feeling about something they think you're a lunatic. This is a permissive age, son,' Bob Jones Jr told a Press Association reporter in Belfast in 1969.[6] Among Jones Jr's convictions was the belief that average plantation slaves in the Deep South before the American Civil War were better off than unemployed blacks in urban ghettos of the 1960s.[7] The university fought a series of expensive court actions over several years to keep out black students and Bob Jones Sr believed the separation of the races was ordained by the Bible.[8] The university was far from typical of American campuses of the 1960s. According to one contemporary profile, its rules forbade students from watching any Hollywood movies, playing cards or wearing tight pants. It also insisted that 'Whether sitting or standing, couples must always keep a six-inch space between their bodies.'[9]

Paisley made several trips to the university during the 1960s. By that time, he was already established as a minor political figure in Northern Ireland. A series of high-profile demonstrations, including an incident in which he organised a march objecting to the lowering of the British Union flag at Belfast City Hall on the death of Pope John XXIII in 1963, and another when he led protests against the display of an Irish tricolour in West Belfast in 1964, resulted in a flurry of publicity for the Free Presbyterian Church minister.

Within a couple of years, he had set up two organisations – the Ulster Constitution Defence Committee and the Ulster Protestant Volunteers; these would provide vigorous counter-demonstrators during the civil rights era. In 1966, he established a newspaper, the *Protestant Telegraph*, which carried ferociously anti-Catholic articles. It also featured regular updates from what it called 'The World's Most Unusual University' – Bob Jones in South Carolina – 'where the students are known not only for their culture and intellectual and artistic attainments, but also for evangelistic zeal and uncompromising orthodoxy'.[10]

The university's extreme Protestantism had few supporters, Paisley excepted. Figures like evangelical preacher Billy Graham were criticised by Jones Jr and Paisley for being too moderate. 'The church which has Billy Graham in its pulpit will have the curse of the Almighty on it,' said Paisley.[11] Even militant Protestant figures like American Presbyterian Carl McIntyre were too compromising for Paisley and Jones Jr. Although once admirers of McIntyre's anti-communism (in 1953 he planned to float bibles attached to balloons across the Iron Curtain), Paisley and Jones Jr fell out with McIntyre when he signalled his acceptance to join with right-wing Catholics in the crusade against international Marxism.[12]

Willingly separated from mainstream, even fundamentalist, Protestantism, Paisley and Jones Jr became increasingly dependent on each other for support. Paisley relied on the university for his academic credibility, and was a regular visitor to South Carolina. In April 1968, he was on a tour of a dozen southern American states when Martin Luther King was assassinated. The *Belfast News Letter* promised that on his return Paisley would give a first-hand report of the racial troubles he had witnessed, and although the piece never appeared, Paisley's *Protestant Telegraph* had plenty to say about Martin Luther King and the American civil rights movement.[13]

While mainstream media in the US and Britain eulogised the assassinated Nobel Peace Prize laureate in the week after his murder, the *Protestant Telegraph* suggested that although King

> had the name of the Protestant champion [Martin Luther], the Negro leader, alas, had not the same gospel to proclaim. ... He chose liberal theology rather than fundamentalism ... he chose pacifism, looking to Ghandi as his guru and to the Pope as his friend, but his pacifism could not be adequately transmitted to his followers. The people that he led have now taken to riot, arson, looting and murder. The smouldering racial tensions have once again been rekindled.[14]

Paisley's newspaper blamed 'Communist agitators' for the violence which followed King's death in many American cities, and suggested that the US was 'on the brink of civil war'. It also revealed an interesting attitude towards King's work. 'There can be no integration or equality of the races ... until and when nations and men submit to Christ – the Prince of Peace.'[15]

The next edition of the paper was even more critical of King. Alongside articles praising South Africa and Rhodesia for their progress in fighting communism, the *Protestant Telegraph* attacked the American civil rights leader:

> Martin Luther King Jr loaded the gun of his own destruction by making himself the symbol of resistance to law and order. ... Only the brainwashed or deluded really believe there is such a thing as 'non-violent' or 'passive' resistance to law and order.[16]

The message was clear – civil rights protestors, whether in the US or in Northern Ireland, were 'brainwashed'. By the end of 1968, in the weeks following the civil rights march in Derry, the *Protestant Telegraph* was eager to dismiss the civil rights movement in Northern Ireland as a Republican front organisation. In an article headlined 'CRA = IRA', it declared that 'It is hypocritical for any Roman Catholic, or Communist, to march for "Civil Rights". The whole movement is obviously for the advancement of Republicanism.'[17]

Although there were undoubtedly Republicans who agreed with that last proposition, the piece expressed the fears of many Loyalists fearful that the IRA would launch a sneak attack while camouflaged by the civil rights movement. As early as 1966, when the civil rights movement was still largely a collection of anti-discrimination activists, Protestant paramilitaries began to organise themselves. Alarmed at growing Catholic self-assertion, notably during the commemoration of the 50th anniversary of the Easter Rising in 1966, several Protestant groups emerged, including the Ulster Volunteer Force (UVF), which took its name from the organisation first formed in 1912 to fight Home Rule for Ireland. Although most of the original UVF volunteers – who at their peak numbered 90,000 – were to be killed in the Battle of the Somme in 1916 fighting for Britain, the UVF legend had lived on, if largely in Protestant folklore, for the next half-century.

In May 1966 a group from the Protestant Shankill area of Belfast launched a number of sectarian attacks on Catholics in the name of the UVF. When civil rights demonstrations began in the following years, other Loyalist paramilitary groups became active in counter-demonstrations. Loyalist paramilitary groups attracted those who felt the security forces couldn't sufficiently protect Protestant neighbourhoods from IRA attacks. One study of Loyalist paramilitaries concluded that they were generally less well-organised than their Republican counterparts, partly because they drew from a smaller base of recruits. Whereas the IRA could enlist virtually all of those Republicans prepared to use force to fight the state, Loyalist paramilitary organisations could only draw on those who were unwilling – or unable – to join the state's security forces.[18]

Whatever the truth about the calibre of Loyalist paramilitaries, those who threatened civil rights activists were often dismissed as Northern Irish versions of the Ku Klux Klan. The PD newspaper referred to 'The masked and hooded Ku Klux Klansmen of the UDA [Ulster Defence Association]', and the newsbulletin of NICRA called the government's undercover squads 'Britain's Ku Klux Klan'.[19] Other civil rights activists in Northern Ireland who identified with the civil rights movement in the US also identified their enemies with the enemies of American civil rights. 'We viewed [the Orange Order] as similar to the KKK – so bare-faced and confident enough in the bigoted status quo that they wore bowler hats and sashes rather than white robes and pointed hoods', wrote Fionnbarra O Dochartaigh.[20]

While it would be grossly inaccurate to suggest that the Orange Order mirrored the Ku Klux Klan, the two organisations shared obvious similarities, not least an active hostility to Catholicism. Members of both organisations also paraded in bizarre costumes, the Klan in its trademark white hoods and sheets, the Orange Order in bowler hats and flamboyantly-coloured sashes. While Klan leaders went by names like Imperial Wizard or Grand Goblin, Orange Order leaders were known by the slightly less exotic title of Worshipful Master, or were elevated to become members of the elite Royal Black Preceptory. However, the Klan and the Orange Order shared a very similar perception of the Catholic Church as a dangerous threat. Both organisations appeared to be more concerned in attacking the foreign nature of the Catholic Church than in concentrating on its theology. In Wyn Craig Wade's classic history of the Klan, he noted that during the 1920s the Klan targeted the Catholic Church because it filled 'an emotional need for a concrete, foreign-based enemy ... the Pope', and that opposition to Catholicism proved an important unifying force in cementing support for the Klan among Protestant churches.[21]

Typically, too, militant objections to Catholicism in Northern Ireland focused on the Pope or the Vatican, and concentrated on the religion's headquarters in Rome rather than disputing its ideological tenets. For example, some of the Catholic Church's teachings which proved most controversial elsewhere in the world, like those on abortion or homosexuality, were never major areas of dispute between Catholic and Protestant religious leaders in

Northern Ireland, who generally shared a social conservatism. It was the foreignness of the Catholicism which was more likely to arouse militant Protestants. So while 'No Pope Here' was for generations a favourite slogan on walls throughout Loyalist neighbourhoods, 'No Transubstantiation Here' was not. Militant Protestants in Northern Ireland also used similar language to the Klan in their attacks on the Catholic Church. Whereas the Klan urged its members during the 1920s to 'save our Protestant institutions from the "Scarlet Mother" [the Catholic Church]', 40 years later Paisley told the BBC that the Pope was the 'Roman anti-Christ', and the Catholic Church the 'harlot of Babylon'.[22]

Paisley's relationship with Bob Jones Jr apart, however, there is no evidence of any links or co-ordination between anti-civil rights elements in the US and Northern Ireland. Indeed, civil rights leaders like Eamonn McCann and Michael Farrell tried to shift the focus of civil rights anger from Loyalist counter-demonstrators, with whom they sought some degree of class solidarity, to the more formal apparatus of the state's security forces. During the Belfast to Derry march of January 1969, for example, just hours before the marchers were to be violently attacked at Burntollet by Loyalists, Eamonn McCann told the protestors that the Loyalist counter-demonstrators

> are not our enemies in any sense. They are not exploiters dressed in thirty guinea suits. ... They are the men in overalls who are on our side, though they do not know it yet. The protestant poor have been bullied and bribed to the stupid belief that they are in some way privileged beyond other people, beyond Catholic people.[23]

Even after the beatings, Farrell stuck to the same line, insisting that those who attacked the marchers were not the enemies of civil rights activists: 'Largely they are the Protestant people who are impoverished under the same predatory system. Impoverished they are, and wholly misled.'[24]

The Burntollet episode was one of many where civil rights activists alleged that policemen colluded with paramilitaries to attack demonstrations, and there were often indistinct lines between activities which were sanctioned by the state and carried out by its police, activities which were not sanctioned by the state but carried out by its police anyway, and activities which were neither sanctioned by the state nor carried out by its police but to which the police turned a blind eye. The situation was not dissimilar to that in the US. In May 1961, when a group of black and white civil rights activists set out to challenge the desegregation of transport facilities in the South, Alabama police allowed local Klan members to attack the 'Freedom Riders' for 15 minutes before intervening.[25] 'A detective on the [Birmingham] force had told [the local Klan] they had exactly fifteen minutes "to beat them, bomb them, burn them, shoot them, do anything they wanted to with absolutely no intervention whatsoever by the police"', noted one report.[26] Asked why the police had only arrived 15 minutes after the trouble started, Alabama Governor George Wallace explained that as it was Mother's Day many of his men were at home sharing quality time with their families and so could not be easily summoned.

In the summer of 1964, three civil rights workers – Jim Chaney, Mickey Schwerner and Andy Goodman – were murdered in Mississippi, and the FBI investigation concluded that 21 local Klan members, including Sheriff Lawrence Rainey and his Deputy Cecil Price, were responsible.[27] Elsewhere, the involvement of law-enforcement officials in anti-civil rights organisations was also common. During the Montgomery Bus Boycott, for example, the city's police commissioner Clyde Sellers openly joined the local White Citizens Council. The Citizens Councils had sprung up throughout the American South in the wake of the Supreme Court decision insisting on school desegregation in 1954 and its subsequent enforcement at Little Rock, Arkansas, in 1957. Like many Protestants who joined the Orange Order, white southerners joined the Councils 'to protect their way of life', which they believed was threatened by the rise of the civil rights movement.

Although deeply racist, the Citizens Councils fancied themselves as the respectable face of white resistance, a civilised alternative to the Klan. Members prided themselves that Council activities stayed within the law, and many members regarded themselves as respectable middle-class people. The Councils drew enthusiastic support from the South's white business community who thought that Klan violence was bad for trade, and so preferred to oppose the civil rights movement through other means. In Montgomery, for instance, the local Citizens Council planted misleading newspaper ads to break the Bus Boycott. When the civil rights protestors in Montgomery eventually won the tussle over bus seating, some members of the city's Citizens Council left to join the Klan, disenchanted with the legal, 'respectable' approach.

Police involvement in the Klan and the Citizens Councils was not uncommon, but there were other ways for US law enforcement officers to oppose the civil rights movement. Governor George

Wallace of Alabama, for example, refused to allow his police to patrol the Selma–Montgomery march, and so President Lyndon Johnson federalised the Alabama National Guard and sent US troops to police the protest. A belief that the police in the South were either collaborators, or at least sympathisers, with the Klan was widespread among civil rights activists in the US. Protestors in Northern Ireland believed the RUC to be guilty of similar collusion with anti-civil rights elements.

At the first civil rights march from Coalisland to Dungannon, for example, it was widely believed among the protestors that the police were in cahoots with the counter-demonstrators led by Paisley. Conn McCluskey described how, when the march reached Dungannon, it was stopped by a police blockade dividing the marchers from the counter-demonstrators. 'Many [counter-demonstrators] carried clubs and staves but the police in the area did nothing but exchange greetings with them.'[28] Recalled Tomas MacGiolla: 'We didn't believe it but we saw it, and we knew we were going to have this collaboration between the RUC and the Loyalist groups.'[29]

The RUC appears to have had a fairly casual approach towards counter-demonstrators on the street level, at least initially, and the police and the governments of both Northern Ireland and Britain were caught wholly unprepared for the widespread civil rights demonstrations and the violent reactions they provoked. Before the media coverage of the Derry march of 1968, both governments appeared to be content to disregard complaints of discrimination. The CSJ was repeatedly fobbed off at Stormont and Westminster, although someone seems to have been sufficiently worried by the McCluskeys to have tapped their telephone and stolen their passports.[30]

For their part, the RUC would later claim that they were completely understaffed to cope with a full-scale civil rights campaign of civil disobedience, let alone widespread rioting throughout the province. In 1968 there were about 3000 policemen in Northern Ireland, backed up by about 8000 part-time reservists, or B Specials. Such numbers were adequate for a place the size of Northern Ireland in peaceful times, and Northern Ireland enjoyed one of the lowest crime rates in Ireland or Britain.[31] Moreover, until 1968 there appeared to be little hint of large-scale trouble erupting. RUC officers were still trained along paramilitary lines up to the early 1960s, and differed considerably from their colleagues in the rest of Britain in that they carried guns and referred to their police stations as 'barracks'; however, by 1967 things had apparently reached such a level of normality that many RUC officers had stopped wearing their firearms on patrol.

Even the 1966 Easter Rising commemorations passed off without any notable incidents of disorder. One RUC officer on duty at an Easter Rising commemoration in nationalist Coalisland remembered a 'carnival atmosphere' at the parade:

> There were thousands of people there ... everybody running about waving tricolours, but we walked about and there was no animosity or hostility towards the police, it was policed just as we would have policed an Orange parade in those days.[32]

When the civil rights protests began two years later, the police were completely unprepared for the change in tone of the demonstrations, and appeared to have learned little from the American experience. While American police forces had realised that hosing demonstrators or attacking them in full view of television cameras could be counter-productive, the RUC repeated many of the mistakes made by their American counterparts in the early 1960s. In the first years of civil rights protests in Northern Ireland, RUC officers appear to have been given little or no training in crowd control, or how to deal with sit-down demonstrations. 'We were very disciplined along paramilitary lines' said one RUC officer on duty in Duke St on 5 October 1968, 'If the head constable said "I want this street cleared", then you cleared the street as best you could.'[33] In Duke St that day, this included hosing demonstrators with water cannon, the first time the weapon had been used in Northern Ireland. Although the water cannon tactic was presumably inspired by the American model of crowd control from the early 1960s, it was a primitive response, and looked bad on television. A government-commissioned report later concluded 'There was no justification for the use of the water wagons on the bridge, while the evidence which we heard and saw on film did not convince us of the necessity of their use in Duke Street.'[34]

Bernadette Devlin McAliskey remembered: 'Quite deliberately they hosed in upstairs windows and shop-fronts, and they went right across Craigavon Bridge, hosing all the onlookers. The police just went mad.' The ill-judged police reaction presented the protestors with a marvellous publicity coup. 'Without the police, it would have taken much longer to get off the ground', said Devlin.[35] A year later, CS gas would be used for the first time in Britain during the Battle of the Bogside, a decision which also damaged the RUC's public image.

The RUC appeared to have failed to have sought training or advice from American security experts on more sophisticated techniques in dealing with protestors, and it took many years of trial and error before a protest could be dispersed without risking an instant riot, or triggering a public relations disaster. Simple, efficient ways of removing sit-down protestors which did not look brutal in front of media lenses took time to perfect, although they were already in use in the US. For example, in the early days of civil rights protests, four RUC officers would approach a demonstrator, grab an arm or a leg each, and drag the demonstrator off. Later they learned that only two officers, marching the protestor backwards, could do the job in a much more efficient manner which did not look so dramatic in front of media cameras.

Training in crowd control for most RUC officers did not begin until 1969, and the force was desperately ill-equipped to deal with the violence which broke out that year. Officers regularly worked 16 hours a day in the summer of 1969, shuttling from town to town as incidents flared. Some were reduced to using dustbin lids to protect themselves during the Battle of the Bogside. Police barracks were regularly left understaffed as officers were called away on duty. One incident at a police station in the largely Catholic Falls Rd in Belfast illustrated how the local population turned from the police to vigilantes for protection. During the rioting of 1970, Catholics called at the RUC barracks on the Falls Rd to ask for help as their houses were being attacked by a Protestant mob. There were only two officers left in the station, who explained they were so short-staffed that they could offer no help.[36] In desperation, people turned towards groups like the Provisional IRA who were offering protection where the police were not.

The rise of paramilitary vigilante groups was the result, at least in part, of a failure by the governments of Northern Ireland and Britain to properly train and equip the RUC. Expertise in dealing with civil rights agitators was presumably available across the Atlantic, but was apparently never sought. Successive British governments did adopt the American tactic of commissioning high-profile investigations into civil rights disturbances which, as in the US, brought a greater understanding of minority grievances to the general population. In July 1967, following a series of urban riots across the US, President Lyndon Johnson established a commission to investigate what happened and why, and to suggest ways to avoid the recurrence of 'racial disorders' in the future.[37] The commission, chaired by Governor Otto Kerner of Illinois, was made up of eleven moderates (including New York Mayor John

Lindsay, who presented Bernadette Devlin with the keys of the city in 1969); it delved into various areas of ghetto life, including the history of the ghettoes, community policing and the media's response to the riots.

The Kerner Commission's exhaustive report included recommendations for reform. Its strategy was 'neither blind repression nor capitulation to lawlessness. Rather it is the affirmation of common possibilities, for all, within a single society.'[38] Specifically, the programmes suggested overhauls in the areas of employment, education, welfare and housing. The report recommended that the government 'enact a comprehensive and enforceable open-occupancy law making it an offense to discriminate in the sale or rental of any housing ... on the basis of race, creed, color, or national origin'.[39] The Cameron Commission, appointed by Northern Ireland Prime Minister Terence O'Neill in January 1969 to investigate the violence occurring after 5 October 1968, made many similar observations to those which appeared in the Kerner Commission. Cameron, for example, also cited 'unfair methods of housing allocation' as a major cause of the disorders. The Cameron Commission even suggested that in Northern Ireland, quite apart from religion, 'There is division also in the segregation of race, real or imagined as it may be.'[40]

Both commissions also blamed segregated educational facilities, the low proportion of minority policemen in the forces and police indiscipline itself as causes of violence.[41] The Cameron Commission also noted that

> the events of last Autumn [1968] occurred at a time when throughout Europe, as well as in America, a wave of reaction against constituted authority in all its aspects ... was making itself manifest in violent protests. ... The psychological effect of this example in other countries and other circumstances cannot be discounted.[42]

The Cameron Commission's report was published in September 1969, but as the violence continued, another commission, headed by Justice Leslie Scarman, was appointed. Its findings were made public in April 1972, and although it too severely criticised the RUC, it concluded that the police was not a partisan force siding with Protestants against Catholics.[43]

In August 1969, two weeks after British troops were deployed on the streets of Northern Ireland to restore order and a month before the Cameron Commission was published, British Home Secretary

James Callaghan made high-profile visits to Belfast and Derry and promised to speed up the implementation of reforms announced the week before. These included fairer housing allocations, an end to discrimination in employment and an acknowledgment of equal rights.[44] The reforms angered Unionists, as did the announcement of yet another enquiry, this time to investigate the RUC.[45] Paisley sent Callaghan a 20-point memo suggesting that the problems of housing and unemployment 'can be attributed exclusively to the Papist population. These people breed like rabbits and multiply like vermin.'[46]

Although the reforms represented the most positive steps the British government had ever taken to address discrimination in Northern Ireland, and were in effect a vindication of much of the effort made by civil rights activists, the civil rights movement was still regarded with some suspicion. PD was attacked by the Cameron Commission for its political extremism and interpretation of what constituted 'non-violence'. The commission noted that 'In their vocabulary it is not violence to link arms and by sheer weight and pressure of numbers and bodies to press through and break an opposing cordon of police,' and that some of the PD leaders ultimately hoped for a 'Worker's Socialist Republic'.[47]

Raising the spectre of communist agitation was a classic American tactic which the British government appears to have borrowed in an attempt to discredit the radical elements in the Northern Ireland civil rights movement. US government officials had used the ploy to smear civil rights activists throughout the 1960s, although anti-communism had been a powerful force in the US for some time before that. A 'Red Scare' had followed the First World War in America, while in the early 1950s, the country had been temporarily mesmerised by the allegations of Republican Senator Joe McCarthy, who claimed communists riddled the American government, particularly the State Department.

Although McCarthy's bullying tactics and wild accusations had been largely discredited by the late 1960s, Britain and the US were still fighting the Cold War. Indeed, the US was fighting a real and expensive war to stop communism in south-east Asia. Suggesting that a politician was under the influence of communists was a serious charge in the 1960s, and was used by both American and British politicians in attempts to discredit the civil rights movements. Stanley Levison, a close aide to Martin Luther King, was believed by the FBI to be a communist. After the FBI tapped King's phones and relayed its suspicions to President Kennedy,

Kennedy told King in June 1963 that Levison was a communist, and that King should fire him.[48]

In 1965, Irish-American Mayor Richard Daley of Chicago alleged that communists had infiltrated the civil rights movement in his city, a theme echoed by some members of the Derry City Council three years later.[49] Interestingly, it was a Nationalist alderman, not a Unionist, who accused a Derry civil rights agitator of being 'a card-carrying member of the Communist Party'.[50] In 1969, Paisley deftly tied both civil rights movements to the same conspiracy:

> What is happening in Ulster today will happen in America tomorrow. Make no mistake about it. O may God open our eyes to see the conspiracy, the international conspiracy, that is amongst us! May He help us to see that there is a deliberate association of attacks against law and order and for revolution and anarchy and Marxism in the land![51]

In fact, some of the student activists in PD did describe themselves as some sort of Marxists, and there is no doubt that there were some communists in the American civil rights movement. However, there is no evidence that the Soviet Union had any hand in stirring up civil rights agitation in either country. Indeed, there were those in PD who regarded the old-style communism of the Soviet bloc as outmoded. Betty Sinclair, who had chaired NICRA and helped found the civil rights movement, had communist links with the Soviet Union dating back to the 1930s, but was regarded by many of the young students as outdated, even conservative. When Eamonn McCann was challenged by journalists who asked if he was a card-carrying member of the Communist Party of Ireland, he told them he had never been that far to the right.[52]

After the Battle of the Bogside broke out in August 1969, a few leftist students from Britain and mainland Europe offered help, and some even made the trip to Derry to join the effort. Bernadette Devlin remembered 'getting all these crazy instructions' from left-wing organisations in Europe:

> They were telling us about how to deal with CS gas and all sorts of things which led the police to believe that we were part of an international conspiracy, but these were obviously people who, looking at us, figured out that [we] hadn't a clue.[53]

When two students – one French, the other German – were arrested for throwing petrol bombs during the disturbances in Derry, British politicians smelt a conspiracy. Conservative MP Enoch Powell, who would later become a Unionist MP in Northern Ireland, suggested the disturbances were part of a wider New Left masterplan:

> The thing which has happened in Ulster these last two or three weeks has little kinship with the Irish troubles of the 1920s and before. It has great kinship with what has been happening in the universities and cities in the United States.[54]

One of the most prominent leaders of the student left in America was Tom Hayden, who spent much of the 1960s protesting against the war in Vietnam and organising a black community union in Newark. Hayden traced Irish roots to County Monaghan, and in December 1971 flew from Los Angeles to Ireland 'to experience a Catholic version of the American civil rights movement'.[55] An FBI memo cited an informant who suggested 'HAYDEN PLANS ON GOING TO NORTHERN IRELAND THROUGH SOUTHERN IRELAND AND ANTICIPATES TAKING PART IN PRESENT REVOLUTION ...'.[56] Hayden didn't make it past Shannon Airport in the Irish Republic, as he was ordered off the plane and sent back to America. 'The US intelligence community had informed the Dublin government of my coming. ... I couldn't believe it. The "outside agitator" theory even extended here', he said.[57]

The leftist masterplan theory was far-fetched, however. As McCann explained:

> People afterwards said 'look, German students with petrol bombs, this proves it's an international conspiracy', and we sort of played that up a bit because it sounded good – you know, international solidarity, but there was no conspiracy. Would that there had been![58]

Bernadette Devlin was a particularly favourite target for those alleging that the civil rights movement in Northern Ireland was influenced by communists. She was called 'Fidel Castro in a mini-skirt', by Unionist politician Stratton Mills, and 'International Socialist Playgirl of the Year' by Paisley.[59] During her first trip to the US in 1969, the *Detroit News* called her a 'mini-skirted Danny the Red', and during her second in 1971 right-wing American politician Barry Goldwater described her as an 'undesirable alien'.[60] In February 1971, a piece in the *Columbus Dispatch* went as far as to claim that Devlin was stoking a race war in Britain. It suggested she was in the US

... hoping to cement her relationship with the black power factions around the world, looking forward to the day when any racial conflagration between British blacks and whites will pave the way for a Castro-type Socialist dictatorship. ... Miss Devlin is fanatical enough to believe she can bring down both the Northern Ireland and the British governments in an eventual race war.[61]

Earlier American coverage of Devlin, and of the Northern Ireland civil rights movement, had been much more positive. When the movement appeared to be adopting the non-violent methods of Martin Luther King, and television footage from Northern Ireland showed the police reacting with baton charges and water cannons, American media reaction was generally sympathetic to the demonstrators. Although it is difficult to compare the impact of television coverage over newspaper or magazine reports, television coverage of civil rights protests in the US and Northern Ireland appears to have had several important effects. Television cameras afforded demonstrators a level of publicity never experienced in the days when media coverage meant only printed words.

After the 5 October 1968 march in Derry, Michael Farrell said, 'Later we would learn that marches had been batoned off the streets of Derry regularly in the 1950s, but there had been no TV there then.'[62] Attempts to organise marches in the city in 1950, 1951 and 1952 had also been met with physical resistance by the police, but had never made international news. The October 1968 march was the second civil rights march that year, but as there had been no widespread television coverage of the larger march from Coalisland to Dungannon six weeks before, it was not until October that the international media became interested. 'Everybody thinks civil rights marches started in Derry – they've all forgotten about the Coalisland one,' said Tomas MacGiolla. [63] Another major difference between the August and October marches had been the levels of violence, and it was undoubtedly the pictures of police brutality which made the October incident more newsworthy. The Cameron Commission noted that 'One of the consequences of the break up of the demonstration in Duke Street was that press and television reports ensured that some very damaging pictures of police violence were seen throughout the United Kingdom and abroad.'[64]

The footage proved so devastating to the RUC that Northern Ireland Minister for Home Affairs William Craig claimed that the BBC had taken footage 'quite clearly showing the civil righters led by Gerry Fitt attacking the police', but that when Craig asked the BBC for a copy, they told him it had been destroyed.[65] The film footage of the march severely damaged the credibility of the police and the Northern Ireland government, and neither were well prepared for the media assault which followed. RUC officers in the 1960s received no training in dealing with the press; the force didn't even have a press office. Although the civil rights activists were also largely unskilled in maximising sympathetic coverage, and often just imitated what they had seen on television of American tactics, the media was generally more sympathetic to them.

'We saw the civil rights [protests] in America and they sat down, and so did we, but they didn't show you on the television all the debate and planning and organising of the non-violent approach, [so] we didn't do any of it,' said Bernadette Devlin.[66] Belfast writer Brian Moore noted in the *Atlantic* in 1970 that coverage of the Watts riots and televised clashes between students and police at Berkeley 'could be absorbed as an educational visual aid by the students at Queen's University, Belfast', and that 'the IRA was our Black Panthers'.[67]

Television footage of civil rights protests was carried in both directions across the Atlantic, and while the coverage of American protests appears to have had some impact in Northern Ireland in the mid-1960s, footage of demonstrations in Northern Ireland shown on American television a few years later was no less powerful. In a detailed study of news coverage by the American television networks of Northern Ireland between 1968 and 1979, Ken Ward analysed the broadcasts that reached an estimated American viewing public, in 1969, of 57.5 million.[68]

Following the breakup of the civil rights march in Derry on 5 October 1968, the American television network NBC sent a camera crew to the city to film a 'civil rights story'.[69] In 1969, before live satellite link-ups were common, filmed reports from foreign countries were sent back to the US to be edited, and often took several weeks to appear on air. The NBC piece was not shown until 7 November 1968, and suggested that the violence of 5 October was the result of Catholics wanting a greater voice in the local government, and emphasised the legitimacy of the Catholic demands. It also described a demonstration by Paisley supporters as 'patriotic antics'.[70] An ABC report in January 1969 was even more sympathetic to the civil rights movement, and made an explicit comparison with the civil rights movement in the US. The piece included the singing of 'We Shall Overcome' behind the voice of reporter Bill Beutel, who noted that 'some observers have compared the plight of ghetto residents in Northern Ireland to ghetto residents in this country'.[71] The comparison was not a new one for American journalists, and *Newsweek* in December 1968 had featured an article on Northern Ireland Catholics called 'The White Negroes'.[72]

American television reports of the Battle of the Bogside in August 1969 were also generally sympathetic to the Catholic community, and presented images of a neighbourhood under attack from outside aggressors. In a brilliant PR stroke, one Bogside resident had put up an American flag, and a Stars and Stripes was shown fluttering in the middle of the besieged Catholic ghetto on NBC's *Nightly News* on 14 August 1972.[73] The following night, NBC carried an interview with Bernadette Devlin as she cleared up rubble from the rioting, followed by an analysis of the problem by anchorman Chet Huntley:

> The white Catholics in Ulster are the same as the blacks in the United States; they've been deprived of their rights, hurried into slums, and denied jobs, hurt and slashed ... And like the blacks they've revolted ... and like the blacks they're burning down the very ghettos that were built to contain them, and like the blacks they're being shot down.[74]

Huntley's speech that night presented the demands of the civil rights activists in Northern Ireland positively, and in a context easily understood by his American audience. His approach was used by other American journalists. In reporting the welcome of British troops in some Catholic neighbourhoods, Russell Stetler told *Monthly Review* readers in 1970:

> At first, the troops were welcomed in the Catholic communities in much the same way as Federal marshals were welcomed by SNCC workers in Mississippi in the summers of 1963 and 1964 ... accepted as impartial guardians of a law and order that would redress the grievances which had developed under the repressive rule of the Ulster Protestants, whose police consistently behaved with the decorum of Southern sheriffs.[75]

The rise of the Provisional IRA, and its attacks on civilians, made the issue more difficult for American reports to contextualise for their audiences, and within five years the black American/Ulster Catholic comparison had been substituted with another easily understood example. 'Just as Americans grew weary of war in Vietnam the

British today are getting tired of their costly commitment to Northern Ireland,' suggested ABC reporter George Watson in June 1974.[76]

If the American media's lack of interest in discrimination in Northern Ireland before 1968 was understandable, the collective blind eye turned by British print and broadcast journalists was less excusable. With a few notable exceptions, the British press displayed little enthusiasm for highlighting the unfair housing allocations, gerrymandering, or the McCluskeys' anti-discrimination campaign. In the early decades of the Northern Ireland state, before the Second World War, local BBC radio in the province reflected Unionist domination. For instance, only the results of those sports played mainly by Protestants were broadcast, whereas the results of Gaelic games, played by those from the Catholic minority, were not.[77]

In 1959, British television journalist Alan Whicker went to Northern Ireland to prepare some reports for the BBC's current affairs programme *Tonight*. The first ten-minute report, intended to be part of a series of eight, was about betting shops, which were legal in Northern Ireland and about to be introduced to the rest of Britain. During the report, Whicker mentioned – as asides – some of the differences between Northern Ireland and the rest of the UK. His commentary reminded viewers that the province had armed police but no military conscription, and the footage included brief shots of graffiti with the slogans 'No Pope Here' and 'Vote Sinn Fein'.[78] The programme sparked outrage from Unionist politicians sensitive to the implication that there was anything abnormal about Northern Ireland. Prime Minister Lord Brookeborough intervened, the Stormont parliament threatened to prevent the BBC from broadcasting, and a BBC sports crew filming a local football match was attacked by spectators.[79] Cowed by the protests, the BBC never screened Whicker's seven other reports.

In the early 1960s, the mainstream British print press displayed some sporadic interest in discrimination in Northern Ireland. Prompted by the CSJ, the *People* newspaper on 2 October 1963 carried a piece on discrimination in Dungannon housing allocation, and in June 1964 the Catholic newspaper the *Universe* featured a similar article, as did the *Sunday Times* two years later. But, as Conn McCluskey noted, 'Not until the violence started did the British press generally begin to interest itself in our doings.'[80]

The Irish newspapers based in Dublin were little better, although there was a sprinkling of reports from 1963 to 1968 describing the anti-Catholic discrimination. The press north of the border was predictably divided about the CSJ campaign. Papers like the *Dungannon Observer*, and the *Irish News*, with mainly Catholic readerships, were supportive of the McCluskeys' efforts, whereas those which had mostly Protestant readers, like the *Belfast News Letter*, generally ignored the CSJ campaign, although the relatively liberal Unionist *Belfast Telegraph* produced several editorials supporting the calls for reform. Before 1968, however, the outside world – even the rest of Britain – was largely unaware of the discrimination, or the campaign against it. In 1966, a BBC television journalist reportedly quit when he was not allowed to produce a programme on gerrymandering in Northern Ireland.[81]

Austin Currie's act of civil disobedience in June 1968 was designed to provoke media coverage, and his removal from the house in Caledon provided television pictures dramatic enough to be shown throughout Britain on news programmes. Currie's act was at least partly staged for the media, and he had carefully arranged for television crews to be in place to film his ejection. Currie's wife gave him a lift to Caledon, where with two others he broke a window in the house chosen for the symbolic squat and waited to be ejected. '[After] my wife dropped me off she drove home and informed the media', said Currie.[82]

Suggestions from television reporters for a follow-up feature programme on the background to Currie's squatting incident were rejected by the BBC hierarchy, however, and it was not until the 5 October march in Derry that serious media interest was sparked.[83] Had more thought been given to how best to stage protests for television exposure, the civil rights activists might have been able to generate more media coverage for their campaign. Currie's success in having his squat recorded by camera crews was unusual; the CSJ had never managed to stage anything so filmworthy, and there was no television coverage of the Coalisland march.

For all their study of the tactics of the American civil rights movement, activists in Northern Ireland appeared to learn the lessons of media manipulation relatively late. Although PD activist Ed Moloney recalled learning an important lesson in media manipulation in November 1968, that is, that demonstrations staged on a Sunday afternoon would get coverage more easily than those which competed with weekday news, it was a lesson which could have been learned earlier from a closer study of the American model.[84]

Five years before the Coalisland march, US civil rights organisers in Birmingham had been framing their protests with media coverage in mind. 'It was important to us that the demonstrations be understood by the media, for the television networks allowed only two to three minutes on the evening news to tell the story,' said organiser Andrew Young:

> I had impressed upon Martin [Luther King] the importance of crafting a message that could be conveyed in just sixty seconds for the television cameras. ... That sixty seconds was what we were demonstrating for – that sixty-second message to the world. ... That was our media strategy.[85]

The sophisticated strategy of the American civil rights organisers – which included timing demonstrations to end by noon so film could be flown to New York two hours later to be edited to make the nightly news – was in sharp contrast to that of Northern Ireland civil rights activists before 5 October 1968. However, the news reports of the violence that day ensured that the protest generated more media attention than all previous demonstrations combined. Local newspapers carried a photograph of a protestor being manhandled by the RUC with a police officer about to club the demonstrator with a baton. The demonstrator, unnamed in the photograph, was in fact Belfast Republican Martin Meehan, who would later become a leading figure in the Provisional IRA. An RUC officer who policed the march that day noted:

> That picture of a policeman with his baton raised showed a brilliant picture of the violence of the RUC – just a godsend for whoever took it ... that picture did us a lot of harm in PR terms. [After that] the world's press descended on us. [86]

'The Bogside was deluged with journalists,' said McCann. 'A lady journalist from the *Daily Mail* came to my front door asking for the name and address of an articulate, Catholic, unemployed slum-dweller she could talk to,' he said.[87]

If the protestors were caught unprepared for the invasion of journalists, so were the police. The RUC, without a press office, found it difficult to counter the version of events presented by the civil rights activists. For a while, the civil rights movement in Northern Ireland enjoyed a media honeymoon, as stories criticising the police and supporting the protests appeared on both sides of the Atlantic. British press reaction to Devlin's election to Parliament in

April 1969 was also generally favourable, but within a few months became critical of Devlin and the civil rights 'radicals'.

When violence erupted in August 1969 and the British troops were sent in to restore order, the British press response was to swing back behind the security forces. While the civil rights movement had been associated with the tactic of non-violence, it had been supported. When it became associated with neighbourhood defence committees and the IRA, it was suspect. By January 1972, the time of the civil rights march protesting against internment without trial, most of the British media seemed to be firmly on the side of the security forces. When British paratroopers shot and killed 13 unarmed civilians at the demonstration, much of the British press was willing to swallow the army's line that the soldiers were acting in self-defence. A *Daily Express* editorial attacked the civil rights movement and claimed that 'many members of this organisation are neither civil nor right. They simply promote the aims of the IRA', while the *Daily Mail* suggested that while 'British bullets will be found in most of the bodies ... the blood is on the conscience of irresponsible political leaders and the fanatical IRA.'[88]

The British press's tendency to blame the victims was one which had also been prevalent in the US. Although initially sympathetic to the civil rights movement in its early, 'non-violent' phase, the American media began to side with the police authorities once the prospect of force was introduced. 'The television media really played a very provocative role in exaggerating particular episodes,' suggested Angela Davis:

Hoover and the FBI, in collaboration with local police departments across the country, staged a number of assaults on Black Panther offices – we're talking about Los Angeles, Philadelphia, New York, New Orleans – these confrontations were actually staged but ... television invariably portrayed the BPP [Black Panther Party] as having attacked the police when in fact the members of the organisation were attempting to defend their lives.[89]

The official US government investigation into ghetto riots noted the residents' disillusionment with the media. It suggested:

Distrust and dislike of the media among ghetto Negroes encompasses all the media, though in general, the newspapers are mistrusted more than the television. ... Even so, many Negroes, particularly teenagers, told researchers that they noted a pronounced discrepancy between what they saw in the riots and what television broadcast.[90]

The British press was also hesitant in investigating allegations of torture which began to surface with increasing frequency in the summer of 1971. Although the Irish papers reported statements in August 1971 from internees claiming they had been tortured in custody by security forces in Northern Ireland, the allegations were not covered in the British press until October.[91] Some of the victims were later awarded compensation by the British government, and in 1978 the European Commission of Human Rights ruled that the interrogation techniques constituted inhuman and degrading treatment. None the less, when the allegations were being made in 1971, the media largely ignored them. A television interview recorded with Michael Farrell on his release from detention was scheduled to be broadcast in September 1971, but was never screened because, according to a BBC official, it was 'an item of marginal importance, being a description by an admitted extremist of conditions in the Crumlin Road prison'.[92]

While both the British and the American media were initially sympathetic to the claims of the civil rights movement in Northern Ireland and were suspicious of the police during the period from late 1968 to the summer of 1969, the British media soon began to side with the police and the army against the IRA. As long as the American media could make direct comparisons with its own civil rights movement, it was supportive of activists in Northern Ireland, but it too became less comfortable criticising the British security forces once large-scale street violence broke out. From about 1970 the American media identified with the British Army's position, suggesting it was like the US Army's situation in Vietnam. The change in the media's sympathy in Northern Ireland and the US coincided with a shift in the civil rights movements' demands from protection of constitutional rights to wholesale reform of the economic and political systems.

Official government responses from Britain and America were also similar. Both appeared sympathetic to the non-violent phase of activism, but were capable of ruthless aggression. During the early and mid-1960s, moderate civil rights leaders like Martin Luther King were feted at the White House by Presidents Kennedy and Johnson.[93] By the late 1960s, the FBI had mounted a massive Counterintelligence Program – known as COINTELPRO – against the Black Panther Party which included the assassination of leading black figures.[94] In 1969, the British government announced a series of reforms to end discrimination in Northern Ireland, but in 1971 introduced internment – indefinite detention without trial – a device used exclusively against Catholic suspects.[95] Codenamed

Operation Demetrius, the first swoop of suspects was a public relations and tactical disaster for the British Army. Soldiers dragged off scores of completely innocent men – often brutally – in the middle of the night and so helped unite the Catholic community against the British troops.

Internal criticism of the operation was led by Brigadier Frank Kitson, who thought the operation had been badly executed. He was the British military's leading expert on counter-insurgency and a veteran of Kenya, Malaya and Cyprus. Kitson would become a major strategist in countering the IRA, and also acted as a consultant on counter-insurgency to the Pentagon. That same year, 1971, he suggested that 'The law should be used as just another weapon in the government's arsenal, and in this case it becomes little more than a propaganda cover for the disposal of unwanted members of the public.'[96] Kitson advocated gathering as much intelligence information on the IRA as possible, and maintained that wars such as those in Northern Ireland were fought mainly in people's minds. He advocated the extensive use of psychological operations against the IRA rather than full-pitched battles. Rumours were spread, disinformation encouraged. The methods were very similar to some of those used by the FBI's COINTELPRO operation. The American agency also favoured spreading rumours about leading black figures in the black community. 'Bad jacketing [creating suspicion about key figures in an organisation] was a very commonly used technique,' noted one study of FBI methods.[97] Those bad-jacketed included Stokely Carmichael, who was the victim of a rumour spread by the agency that he was a CIA informer.

Many leading figures in the Black Panther Party were killed, including Fred Hampton, Jon Huggins and Alprentice 'Bunchy' Carter, the victims of alleged political assassination. Hampton was shot dead in Chicago in December 1969 by police who claimed they were acting in self-defence. However, many blacks believed Hampton had been executed while lying wounded on his bed. The controversy was similar to many later 'shoot-to-kill' incidents in Northern Ireland, where Republicans were killed by security forces in disputed circumstances.

'I remember looking in later years at "shoot-to-kill" [tactics] here', said Bernadette Devlin:

> That was the experience of the Panthers and even when people like myself and McCann and others who at that time were political enough to know the experience of the Panthers, it never entered ... our strategy that it could happen to us. Those were the links we weren't making.[98]

6

Heirs Apparent

No official date marks the end of the civil rights movement in Northern Ireland. Some put it in August 1969, when the British troops arrived on the streets of Belfast and Derry and the confrontation with the state became more violent, others when Britain assumed direct rule of Northern Ireland in 1972, and the Stormont parliament was dissolved. For others, the civil rights movement ended on Bloody Sunday in January 1972, when 13 civilians were shot dead by British soldiers on the anti-internment protest in Derry at the 'last civil rights march', and there are those who regard the civil rights struggle as never having ended, and believe it is still ongoing, albeit in a violent phase.

Since the mid-1970s, the various political strands which made up the civil rights movement have each laid claim to its legacy, and – perhaps in an attempt to lend themselve some political credibility – have emphasised the influence of the American civil rights experience as an important inspiration.

As Eamonn McCann noted in an article on the twentieth anniversary of the October 1968 march in Derry: 'Everybody says it was a good thing and everybody wants to lay title to the mantle of 1968.'[1] In 1988, a pamphlet was circulated in Northern Ireland claiming that Rosa Parks, heroine of the Montgomery Bus Boycott of 1955, would appear as a guest speaker in Derry at a commemorative event to mark the Duke St march. 'It's not unknown, false billing', said McCann.[2]

John Hume, in a 1985 speech at the University of Massachusetts, declared 'The American civil rights movement gave birth to ours. The songs of your movement were ours also.'[3] Two years later a long article on Hume in the *Chicago Tribune* suggested he was the Irish Martin Luther King, and noted that 'he frequently sings "We Shall Overcome" at the end of his lectures and speeches.'[4] Indeed, Hume's party, the SDLP, still sings the civil rights anthem at its annual conferences, and in a 1996 book Hume suggested that he 'read a huge amount of the writings of Martin Luther King in those days ... it was no accident that the civil rights movement began here in the sixties, directly inspired ... by the American movement.'[5]

Old tensions resurface within the civil rights movement when civil rights commemorations are organised, as conflicting elements each claim to be the rightful heirs of the movement. 'I was very annoyed the other day to discover the Provos setting up a march from Duke St ...' said Tomas MacGiolla in 1996, 'they had a march from Duke St the other day asserting civil rights. Now the biggest opposition we had to the civil rights campaign was the hardline Republicans ... their slogan was "damn your concessions England we want our country".'[6] But those hardline Republicans who lay claim to the civil rights legacy today do so with some justification. Many members of the IRA and INLA, prominent and minor, were involved in the early push for civil rights. Shane O'Doherty, for example, who carried out countless IRA bombings in Northern Ireland and England, took part in civil rights marches as a teenager. 'The experience of sitting in defiant pacifist gesture among thousands of Catholics singing "We Shall Overcome", filled me with the belief that we were united in an almost mystical, religious unity and cause', he recalled.[7] The early agitation for housing rights in Derry was helped by 14-year-old Mickey Devine, who helped paint placards for protests. Devine joined the IRA, and then the INLA, and in 1981 was one of ten prisoners who died on hunger strike in the Maze Prison while attempting to win special category status.

For some Republicans, the present conflict is about the original civil rights demands, a natural outgrowth from the non-violent protests. In the late 1970s, a leading Provisional suggested:

> Look, there wouldn't be any trouble or IRA if the Catholics hadn't been denied civil rights. This is a civil rights war: what's different is that we reckon we can only get these rights through national liberation, so it's a national liberation war, the two go together.[8]

The IRA Green Book (the IRA's Code of Conduct for its members), issued in 1987, alludes to 'the attempted repression of the Civil Rights Movement, and from then until now the struggle has taken on a steady momentum of its own'.[9] (The book also includes a provision outlining the IRA's commitment to anti-racism.[10]) In the early 1990s the sister of an IRA member said 'It's a war, isn't it? It is for me. They shouldn't have treated Catholics like second-class citizens.'[11]

During the 1981 hunger strikes, when Northern Ireland again became the focus of international attention, the prisoners' protest was repeatedly described in the context of civil rights. Unionist MP Harold McCusker complained that media coverage was 'so concerned about the civil rights of [IRA hunger striker Bobby] Sands'.[12] Church of Ireland Primate Dr Robert Eames interpreted Protestants' view of the protest as: 'Here they're at it again [the Protestants were saying]. They're getting America on their side. They're getting the civil rights thing all stirred up again ...'.[13]

In fact, the 1981 hunger strikes did spark enormous interest in the Northern Ireland situation in America, and led to a visit by prominent American civil rights activists to Belfast. Threatening to undertake hunger strikes in prison is not a tactic exclusive to Irish Republicans. Many others, including Martin Luther King, used the strategy. However, hunger striking to secure non-criminal status is an old tradition in Republican politics, and many leading Republicans have died on hunger strike either by starving themselves or by being force-fed by prison authorities. Tomas Ashe, a prominent figure in the 1916 Rising, died on hunger strike after being force-fed in 1917. Terence MacSwiney, on whose behalf Marcus Garvey had appealed to the British government, died on hunger strike in a London prison in 1920, and in the following decades the tactic was used to gain political, or special category, status with varying degrees of success by Republicans in British and Irish jails.

In June 1972, forty Republican prisoners, led by IRA chief Billy McKee, went on hunger strike in support of their demand to be treated as prisoners of war. The British government conceded to their demands, and for several years paramilitary prisoners wore their own clothes, conducted their own education classes (which even included lectures in explosives and weapons training using wooden replicas), and organised military parades and drills. Then the British government announced that anyone found guilty of any crime after 1 March 1976 would be treated as an ordinary criminal, thereby revoking the special category status for future paramilitary prisoners. A new prison, the Maze, was built to replace the old Second World War base at Long Kesh, which had been converted into a jail. The new prison was characterised by a series of buildings shaped like the letter 'H', and soon became known as the 'H-Blocks'.

Under the new rules in the new jail, prisoners would not be allowed to wear their own clothes and would be required to do prison work. Republican Ciaran Nugent, convicted of possessing weapons and hijacking a car, was the first prisoner who refused to comply, and so wore only a blanket instead of the prison uniform. In 1978 the prisoners began to refuse to leave their cells, claiming they were beaten by warders when they left their cells to use the toilet facilities. The warders would not clean the cells unless they were empty, so the protest escalated as the prisoners were left in the cells with their own excreta, and began to smear it on the walls to reduce the stench. By the end of the decade hundreds of prisoners had joined the 'dirty protest', and in October 1980 seven leading Republicans in the H-Blocks began a hunger strike for special category status. Almost two months later, with one of the prisoners nearing death, the strike was called off by the prisoners in the belief that the British government had conceded their central demands. When it became clear in the following weeks that the concessions the prisoners believed had been agreed were not to be granted, another hunger strike was planned.

On 1 March 1981, IRA prisoner Bobby Sands refused to eat, and continued to refuse until he died more than two months later. His election to the British parliament while on hunger strike, his death, his funeral and the deaths of nine more Republican hunger strikers in the following months focused an unprecedented amount of media attention on Northern Ireland from the international press. Sands' protest revived American interest in Irish Republicanism. His cause seemed entirely reasonable to many Americans – he was serving a 14-year sentence for being in a car which had an unloaded gun in it, an act which was not even illegal in many parts of the US. New Left icon Abbie Hoffman, in jail in New York for possessing drugs, went on short-term hunger strike in solidarity with Sands.[14]

To publicise the prisoners' campaign in international fora, a number of National H-Block/Armagh Committees were set up. Bernadette Devlin McAliskey was a prominent spokesperson for the committees, and in September 1981 was expelled from Spain when she tried to address an H-Block meeting in the Basque Country (but slipped back into the country and addressed the meeting anyway). It was through the New York-based committee that six black American civil rights activists visited Belfast in December 1981.

The group met with relatives of the dead hunger strikers, visited the Maze prison and compared their experience with that of nationalists in Northern Ireland. At a Belfast community centre they sang 'We Shall Overcome' with 200 locals whom, one of the Americans noted, 'sing passionately and with less solemnity than we used to sing this anthem in the days of lunch-counter sit-ins and freedom rides and Bull Connor's dogs'.[15] The visit was the subject of a film, *The Black and the Green*, produced by black American St

Clair Bourne. 'Once we said we were black Americans making a film [the locals] really got into it,' he recalled:

> They started telling us how the British were like white Southerners during the American civil rights era; 'They hate us for no reason, they're racist, they treat us worse than you were treated.' We were the standard of oppression both heroically and as victims.[16]

Other Belfast locals told the black civil rights activists that 'Theirs is a "Third World" struggle. ... Their allies ... are the Black people of South Africa, the Palestinians, Afro-Americans.'[17]

One of the delegation, Rev Fred Kirkpatrick, said he wanted to visit Northern Ireland because Martin Luther King had told the Kennedys that blacks and Irish were natural allies, and because he had worked with King for a long time, he wanted 'to pick up that part of the struggle'.[18] Another of the black Americans on the visit, Matt Jones, was a former SNCC field secretary, and a strong advocate of non-violence. 'It seemed they [the people he'd spoken to in Belfast] had exhausted all non-violent methods they could find,' he said. 'I don't think I have a right to tell them how to struggle ... however, violence has a way of turning back on you', he warned.[19] Black activist Rev Herbert Daughtrey interviewed leading Republican Paddy Laughrin and told him:

> I hope we can firm up the solidarity between blacks and the Irish. There is a reluctance on the part of some of our people, and rightly so. After all, the Irish in New York are often policemen, or we think of the Irish in south Boston. They have not been our friends.[20]

The film of the trip records the black Americans encountering army patrols, meeting nationalists in Belfast and offering their impressions of the situation ('to see white people oppressing white people ... is a mindblower for me,' said one[21]).The security forces appear to have made little attempt to interfere with the Americans, although 'There was a British major who came over and addressed me by name. I had never met him before', recalled Bourne.[22]

Although welcomed in Irish-American circles, the film was attacked by some black Americans. 'The criticism that I got was from the cultural nationalist black people', said Bourne. 'Their exposure to white Irish was in the Bronx or in Boston. The whole thing was "why are you making a film about them? They're white people, they're racist ... you must be a dupe."' *The Black and the*

Green was used by black and Irish groups in the US to organise anti-apartheid campaigns, and its creator, St Clair Bourne, was honoured by various Irish-American groups for his work. The Brehon Law Society in Philadelphia arranged a screening of the film and presented Bourne with a Brehon Achievement Award.[23]

Elsewhere, political ties between Northern Ireland and America have remained just as strong. The Irish Republican Socialist Committees of North America have worked closely with radical black groups since the mid-1980s, including the All-African People's Revolutionary Party, whose prominent members include Kwame Ture, formerly Stokely Carmichael. A 1988 IRSC newsletter suggested:

Irish and African people, spread throughout the world by their colonial oppressors, must look to the struggles being waged in the lands of their ancestors, with the understanding that their continued oppression and degradation is made possible in part through maintaining their homelands as 'Third World'.[24]

Contacts between the two organisations in the 1990s have remained close, with the Irish Republicans and the black Americans regularly exchanging literature and speaking at each others' rallies.

By the late 1980s, Jesse Jackson, former lieutenant of Martin Luther King, was running for president and visited prominent Irish Republican Joe Doherty in detention in New York, where Doherty was awaiting extradition. Doherty had escaped from prison in Northern Ireland in 1981 and made his way to the US. He was arrested several years later, and after a series of legal battles was returned to prison in Northern Ireland in 1993.

In the early 1990s, links between the American and Northern Ireland civil rights movements were drawn with increasing frequency by Republican activists in Northern Ireland. When Californian police were caught on videotape violently kicking and beating Rodney King, a black man, young Republicans in nationalist Coalisland painted 'Justice for Rodney King' on the town's walls when local people 'didn't know who Rodney King was', said Bernadette Devlin McAliskey.[25]

The Republican newspaper, *An Phoblacht*, prominently highlighted black American issues in the mid-1990s. In June 1995, it carried an article on the celebrated case of former Black Panther spokesperson Mumia Abu-Jamal, an alleged victim of the FBI's COINTELPRO operation who was convicted of killing a white police officer in 1981 and sentenced to death. While on death row, Abu-Jamal 'has consistently protested his innocence and there is enough reasonable doubt to make his conviction seem extremely dubious', noted *An Phoblacht*, which suggested that 'we in Ireland have had too much experience of corrupt legal systems in the past to watch quietly from the sidelines as Abu-Jamal goes to his death.'[26]

The visit of Donald Payne to Northern Ireland in August 1995 was also covered prominently by the Republican paper. Payne had, in 1988, become the first black to be elected to the US Congress from New Jersey and had been a vigorous supporter of the MacBride Principles. The principles were adopted by many in the Irish-American lobby to campaign for fair employment in Northern Ireland, and were modelled on the Sullivan Principles, which had applied to the 1977 anti-apartheid campaign in South Africa. The MacBride Principles, issued in 1984, were named after their chief architect, Sean MacBride, one-time chief of staff of the IRA, later a minister in the Irish government, co-founder of Amnesty International and a Nobel Peace Prize laureate. The MacBride Principles included provisions for an increase in the number of Catholics in supervisory positions, and training programmes for Catholic employees. By 1993, 13 US states had endorsed the principles, and they became something of a litmus test for American politicians.[27]

Payne had been at the forefront of supporting the principles, and his reception in the Nationalist areas of Belfast was enthusiastic. 'I think there are definitely parallels between the African-American experience and that of nationalists [in Northern Ireland],' he said during the trip:

> What I have heard and seen here about the discrimination of Catholics is the same kind of thing that I see at home. High unemployment rates, high school drop-out rates and the sense of alienation from and resentment towards the authorities.[28]

In 1997, Payne introduced a bill in the US Congress to ban the RUC from using plastic bullets.[29]

Republican activists perceived benefits in associating themselves with the black American struggle, which enjoyed an enviable international credibility. *An Phoblacht* used the black American comparison in 1996 to protest about Sinn Fein being excluded from a series of peace talks to which all other political parties in Northern Ireland were admitted:

Imagine 100 MPs being excluded from the British House of Commons or the representatives of the African Americans – 12% of people in the USA – being shut out of the US Congress. There would be worldwide scorn for any such blatant discrimination.[30]

When Sinn Fein President Gerry Adams made a highly controversial visit to the US in September 1994, he called on veteran civil rights activist Rosa Parks and presented her with a bowl of Waterford crystal. In a much-publicised encounter, the Republican leader said 'I never thought I'd meet you ... when you sat in the bus and refused to move, that sent a signal that one person can initiate a whole movement,' and told how he had joined marches in the streets of Belfast singing 'We Shall Overcome'.[31]

Adams's visa to the US had been vigorously opposed by the British government, and it had urged President Clinton not to meet Adams or to offer him a high-level meeting with White House officials. Adams's access, or non-access, to the White House became a highly charged issue, with Adams pushing for the symbolic admittance and a meeting with a senior White House figure, as had been afforded to Unionist politicians. In Adams's eyes, no invitation from the White House would mean being treated as second-class, and he told Niall O'Dowd, who was acting as intermediary between Adams and the White House, that he 'would not accept a place at the back of the bus'.[32] Adams was not granted an audience at the executive mansion during that trip, although he was admitted a few months later.

Adams's political journey from his early days in the civil rights movement to his acceptance at the White House in 1994 and 1995 was remarkable, and came about not least because US President Bill Clinton displayed a greater personal interest in Northern Ireland than any of his predecessors. Clinton had been a student in England when the civil rights movement gained prominence in Northern Ireland. 'I could see it [the troubles] coming,' said Clinton, 'that religious differences were likely to lead to the same kind of problems that racial differences had in my childhood. And I lived in a place that had some pretty tough racial problems.'[33] He also told Irish-American journalist Jimmy Breslin how, when he was at university in Oxford, he spent time 'following Bernadette Devlin around and reading everything about her'.[34]

Bernadette Devlin McAliskey worked at keeping her political contacts with America very strong. A frequent visitor to the US throughout the 1970s, 1980s and 1990s, she has been a regular speaker at black political gatherings, and a less frequent guest at conservative Irish-American ones. In 1988 she wrote:

> Irish America has taken 15 years to forgive me my trespasses, as they saw them. I had defied them in the cities they owned. ... I confess that I derive most satisfaction now from the knowledge that the mayors of Chicago, San Francisco and Detroit are black, that the most outspoken candidate in defence of the Irish in the recent presidential primaries, Jesse Jackson, is black, and that almost 20 years ago my cardinal sin in the eyes of many Irish Americans, and Irish at home, was refusing to accommodate Irish-American prejudice against the black community in the US.[35]

In 1996, she suggested that her first visit to America, in 1969, 'goes down in history for screwing the Hibernian agenda ... the Chicago Irish never really forgave me.'[36]

While remaining politically active in Northern Ireland in the decades since the first civil rights marches, Devlin McAliskey also became increasingly involved with black politics in America, and she travelled throughout the US highlighting the cause of Irish Republican and black American prisoners. In 1996 she spoke at fundraisers for the black churches which had been destroyed in a series of racist arson attacks across the American South. In 1997, several prominent black politicians joined the campaign to have Devlin McAliskey's daughter, Roisin, released from prison in London where she was awaiting extradition to Germany on a bombing charge. Roisin McAliskey was held for some of the time at Holloway Prison in north London under maximum security conditions. She was pregnant when arrested in November 1996, and spent the final months of her pregnancy in the prison. She gave birth to a girl in May 1997 under harsh security.

New York's first black mayor, David Dinkins, spoke at a rally in the city protesting Roisin McAliskey's detention. Angela Davis addressed a meeting organised by the Roisin McAliskey campaign in California, and attacked the 'terrible mistreatment of Roisin McAliskey by her British captors ... Roisin must be freed, and Northern Ireland released from the shackles of British imperialism!' she said. In the same speech, Davis also suggested that Roisin's imprisonment was part of an ongoing campaign of repression aimed at Bernadette Devlin McAliskey by the British authorities.[37] When Davis visited Northern Ireland for the first time in 1994 to take part in some local women's political meetings, she was surprised by the level of security force activity:

> I thought immediately about the situation in apartheid South Africa because I had visited South Africa and what struck me most was the military presence ... I've known about the occupation for very many years, but it was quite another thing to come face to face with it and to be searched everywhere ... in the aftermath of that visit I made a point to include in all of my talks some comments on the situation there.[38]

While the situation in Northern Ireland reminded Davis of apartheid South Africa, many nationalists stuck with the comparison of the American South. John Hume suggested in 1996 that the Northern Ireland Unionists could never be liberated from their own prison without help, 'largely like the whites in the Southern United States. The whites would never have been liberated without the intervention of the federal government. They would never have liberated themselves.'[39] When arson attacks were launched on churches in Northern Ireland in 1996 and 1997, parallels were drawn with those which had hit the American South the previous year. 'This is Ku Klux Klan stuff and it is happening throughout Northern Ireland', said SDLP MP Seamus Mallon after a Catholic church in his constituency had been gutted by fire.[40] When Ulster Unionist MP David Trimble arrived in the US in October 1995, he was greeted with an ad in the *New York Times* placed by an Irish-American lobby group titled 'A Welcome to David Trimble, the David Duke of Ireland', in reference to former Klan leader turned elected official David Duke.[41]

The imagery proved too tempting for Irish nationalists to resist: if Northern Ireland Catholics are the blacks, then our opponents must be the racist whites, the argument went. British politician Enoch Powell, known for his extreme right-wing views on race, was an Ulster Unionist MP for South Down between 1974 and 1987; after his first visit to the US in 1966, he reportedly told an American friend:

> Integration of races of totally disparate origins and culture is one of the great myths of our time. It has never worked throughout history. The United States lost its only real opportunity of solving its racial problems when it failed after the Civil War to partition the old Confederacy into a South Africa and a Liberia.[42]

Nevertheless, there has been no evidence of any direct connection between Unionist or Loyalist organisations in the US and American racists over the last few decades. A Loyalist group called Ulster Resistance set up in 1986 was rumoured to have links with the South African government, however, when one of its most prominent members was arrested in Paris in April 1989. The meeting was reportedly arranged to discuss the possibility of the Loyalist group obtaining arms from South Africa. Those arrested were given suspended sentences, fined and released by a Paris court in 1991.

Throughout the 1970s, '80s and '90s, Ian Paisley remained the Unionists' most prominent link to the American right through his continuing association with the Bob Jones University. In April 1982, when the US State Department refused to grant Paisley a visa to enter the US on the grounds that his inflammatory speeches did not help the situation in Northern Ireland, Bob Jones Jr sprang to his defence, and urged the university's students to pray that the Lord 'smite' Secretary of State Alexander Haig and 'destroy him quickly and utterly'. At a chapel service in the university, Jones blamed the US government's 'Catholic bigotry' and called Haig 'a monster in human flesh and a demon-possessed instrument to destroy America ... I hope you'll pray that the Lord will smite him, hip and thigh, bone and marrow, heart and lungs and all there is to him.'[43]

A year later, with Paisley a member of the school's international board of trustees, the US Supreme Court ruled that the Bob Jones University's record on racial integration was so poor it did not qualify for federal tax credits.[44] In 1997, Paisley was still listed as a member of the Co-operating Board of the university, and the Bob Jones political and social ethos remained firmly on the right. Its literature proudly noted that it was founded in 1927 to combat liberalism, and that modern-day state universities employ 'godless professors, ... Satanic emissaries [who] produce first confusion, then, uncertainty; and finally, infidelity in the hearts, minds and lives of their students.'[45] The Bob Jones University still restricts which of its students are allowed to have cars, and what sort of trips they can use them for.

While the university remains defiantly conservative, Irish America appears to have softened its antagonism towards black advancement. Although not all Irish-Americans were resistant to black progress during the 1960s and 1970s, and many provided significant help to the civil rights struggle in the US, many conservative Irish-Americans were resentful of gains made by the black community. In some areas, that hostility appears to be in decline. In 1997, the glossy *Irish America* magazine named its top 100 Irish Americans for the year. These included black television journalist Paul Berry, whose great-grandfather was the son of a slave and an Irish horse farmer in Kentucky. Berry is part of the upper echelons of Washington society, has served as compere for the city's St Patrick's Day parade, and in 1997 was named 'Gael of the Year' by Washington's St Patrick's Day Committee.[46] The magazine also celebrated Ireland's contribution to the success of 1930s' black American athlete Jesse Owens, noting that Owens' coach and 'second father' was Irish-American Charles Riley.[47]

Elsewhere in Irish America, things were more problematical. The 100 top Irish-Americans for 1996 included Chicago Mayor Richard M. Daley, son of the late Mayor Richard J. Daley, famous for his clashes with Martin Luther King (and Bernadette Devlin). In March 1997, a 13-year-old black boy was savagely beaten by three white teenagers in an apparent racist attack in Chicago. The three white teenagers charged with attempted murder were products of the same Irish-Catholic school as Daley and his father, and were residents of Bridgeport, a neighbourhood which, according to the *Washington Post*, is 'the ancestral home of the Daley clan and for decades was the epicenter of Irish American political power in the city.' The incident followed another involving the city's Brother Rice Catholic High School, which had been criticised earlier in 1997 when some of its students shouted racial abuse at a visiting black basketball team.[48]

Progress made by the civil rights movements in Northern Ireland and in the US is difficult to quantify, with apparent gains being weighed against incidents like that in Chicago. Civil rights activists from the 1960s have very different interpretations of how much was achieved. Kwame Ture, formerly known as Stokely Carmichael, suggested in 1997:

> ... if in the 1960s White people had called me in and said: 'Yeah, okay, you can register to vote. Andy Young can be mayor. Marion Barry can be mayor. John Lewis can sit in Congress, that's fine. You want black sheriffs? Fine. Drink coffee, eat a hamburger where you want,' I might have signed up.[49]

But, says Ture, despite the number of black elected officials, 'Conditions for the masses of our people are worse than before.'[50] By contrast, for Conn and Patricia McCluskey, early pioneers of the Northern Ireland civil rights movement, the effort was a success.

The protests of the early 1960s by the young women of Dungannon against their housing conditions led to meaningful reform. 'We had accomplished what we set out to do ... we had plenty of houses ... we all got grants to start industry, you wouldn't know our town [from then]', said Patricia McCluskey:

> The little girl who was the leader of the [Homeless Citizens League], she lives in the equivalent of a mansion, and she has two shops on the main street ... the girls have all succeeded past their wildest dreams ... all these people are now middle class. They've got what they wanted – they've got homes and they've got jobs and they've got education, and people can go on from there.[51]

The group of women who took over the Dungannon prefabs in August 1963 committed the first act of civil disobedience in what would eventually become the civil rights campaign. In the following decades, other groups led by women would also emerge as minor and major political influences. In 1972, Margaret Dougherty of Derry organized Women for Peace after an innocent woman had been caught in crossfire between the British army and the IRA. Five women from the group met IRA Chief of Staff Sean MacStiofain that year to press for a cease-fire, and in August 1972 the Loyalist Women's Association dispatched a 90,000-signature petition to the British government calling for an end to the violence.[52]

Throughout the 1970s, '80s and '90s individual women were influential in a variety of political and paramilitary roles, but the most prominent mass movement led by women was the Peace People, which enjoyed brief international acclaim in the mid-1970s. Two Belfast women, Betty Williams and Mairead Corrigan, headed the campaign (originally known as the Women's Peace Movement) calling for an end to violence in Northern Ireland.[53] Borrowing tactics learned from the civil rights movement almost a decade before, they organised mass marches throughout Ulster, in the Republic of Ireland and in mainland Britain. One of the principal organisers, Ciaran McKeown, had been active in the civil rights movement and in 1976 was a prominent journalist in Belfast. His media skills helped attract enormous publicity for the campaign.

Although the Peace People managed to mobilise tens of thousands of Catholic and Protestant protestors at some marches, it was perceived as being more critical of the paramilitaries than of the security forces. Although Williams and Corrigan were awarded the Nobel Peace Prize in 1977, the movement faltered as many who marched were reluctant to condemn the 'defensive' actions of the UVF or the IRA, and support for the Peace People dwindled rapidly. By the end of 1977 it had lost any political initiative it had once enjoyed, and Northern Ireland politics returned to violence as usual. The Provisionals had been particularly critical of the Peace People, organisisng counter-marches and condemning the encouragement for people to 'inform' on neighbours they suspected of terrorist activities. Although no other women's political initiative has been on the scale of the Peace People, dozens of Republican women prisoners joined the 'dirty protest' in Armagh jail at the end of the 1970s.

It has been in the Republicans' interests to minimise any gains achieved by the Peace People and by the civil rights movement, as little progress means more justification for ongoing struggle. Conn McCluskey criticised the Republicans for downplaying the advances made:

> The Republicans say, 'Ah, what have we got?' They've got an awful lot. They've got all the houses they wanted, there are an awful lot of Catholic millionaires now who would've just been making the tea; two factories in Dungannon, both owned by Catholics, both millionaires.[54]

For others in the civil rights movement, an increase in the number of Catholic millionaires is not the point, and never was. Although some of NICRA's original demands were granted relatively speedily by the British government, including 'One Man, One Vote', fair housing allocation procedures and an end to the worst excesses of job discrimination, others were not fully met. NICRA agitated for the ending of the Special Powers Act, which allowed the government to rule Northern Ireland with laws different from the rest of the UK. The Special Powers Act was invoked to introduce internment without trial in the early 1970s, and a few years later juryless 'Diplock Courts' were introduced in Northern Ireland. RUC membership remains overwhelmingly Protestant (93 per cent in 1997).[55]

Socially and culturally, however, segregation is as bad as ever. 'We grow up so close together we can hear each others' voices through the walls, but we don't know each other', said former Loyalist paramilitary David Ervine in 1997. Ervine served five years in prison for possessing explosives, later became an elected offcial of the Progressive Unionist Party, and noted 'We're divided from the beginning, sent off to separate schools and we stay separate for the rest of our lives.'[56] Housing and school segregation are still the norm in Northern Ireland. The Catholic Church has been unwilling to encourage parents to send their children to 'mixed' schools, and, as veteran Northern Ireland reporter David McKittrick suggested, 'Unless you make a big effort socially, it's possible to get through life without having any close friends of the other sort.'[57]

Unlike in the US, the rise of paramilitaries made the civil rights movement in Northern Ireland largely irrelevant, and the outbreak of widespread violence makes assessing the gains of the Northern Ireland civil rights movement particularly difficult. John Hume suggests the differences in outcome between the US and Northern Ireland were due to the frailty of the Northern Ireland political system. In 1996, he wrote:

> Whereas in the United States the structures of democracy were resilient enough to encompass the challenge of civil rights, in the unstable political environment of Northern Ireland our struggle was perceived as a threat to the very survival of the society itself and as such was resisted by the institutions of the state.[58]

It is a view echoed by Austin Currie:

> I'm often asked the question 'Was violence inevitable?' and my answer is no, it wasn't inevitable. What made it inevitable was the way the government responded to the march in Derry, and the fact that sections of the Unionist Party were dogmatic in opposing the reforms we were proposing.[59]

Eamonn McCann concurred:

> Had the state been able to concede to the [civil rights] demands, it's highly unlikely we'd have gone through the last 25 years of terror and turmoil. It was all sparked as a result of the inability of a political system here to accomodate ordinary, basic democratic norms.[60]

Widespread violence radically transformed the political context, and the guidance offered by the example of the US civil rights movement could only take the Northern Ireland activists so far. Former NICRA Secretary Edwina Stewart explained: 'NICRA just petered out in the late 1970s. People stopped coming to meetings and calling meetings. None of us could see that we could do anything as a civil rights organisation, we couldn't take it any further.'[61]

The American movement had never had to cope with the rise of paramilitary forces, with an army sent by the national government which turned out to be hostile, or with sweeping internment without trial.

Whereas the civil rights movement in Northern Ireland collapsed under the threat of civil war, the American movement also lost much of its cohesion of the 1960s and 1970s. Although there are several times more elected black officials than there were 30 years ago, and an assertive black middle class has emerged as a result of gains made during the 1960s, elsewhere progress has been slow. Poverty and crime are widespread in many black communities. Incidents like the OJ Simpson trial verdict and the subsequent rioting reveal how polarised many Americans remain, and there is still a need for the NAACP and the SCLC.

In the US, however, the civil rights movement is generally regarded as having been at least partially successful; Martin Luther King is revered as a national hero, and there is a federal holiday in his name. In Northern Ireland, the civil rights movement has yet to find a similar place in history. Its leaders are not national heroes, and the British government is unlikely ever to announce a day of celebration to mark Bernadette McAliskey's birthday. While American civil rights activists often look back to the 1960s and 1970s with some sense of achievement, even triumph, most in Northern Ireland do not. Speaking of the nostalgia which accompanied the 1988 commemorations of the civil rights march in Derry 20 years before, Eamonn McCann said 'I know there are some who have in mind to run the movie through again. I've seen the movie before, and it's a very bad ending.'[62]

Thirty years after the first civil rights protests, the struggle seems to have come full circle, with some of today's Republicans emphasising the original demands of the civil rights movement as key objectives. 'What Sinn Fein seems to be settling for is very much the civil rights demands, with parity of esteem and recognition of the Irish identity', said Edwina Stewart.[63] Bernadette Devlin McAliskey concurred: '[In the 1960s] we were only looking for, as we're back to now, parity of esteem.'[64] Speaking on American television the day after the IRA announced a ceasefire in July 1997, Sinn Fein President Gerry Adams appeared to echo activists of 30 years before, suggesting that the peace process was really about the struggle for civil rights:

I would like to think that the international community and the Clinton Administration will come to the issue on the basis of rights. In this part of Ireland, people are still denied equality of treatment and jobs. The militarisation of the situation means that democratic rights barely exist, and there is a whole range of inequities, and unjust laws which need to removed.[65]

Biographies of Key Figures

Gerry Adams 1948–

Active in Republican politics and civil rights protests in the late 1960s, Adams was interned in 1971, as he was believed by the security forces to be a leading member of the Provisional IRA in West Belfast. He was released in July 1972 to take part in secret talks with the British government. He spent the rest of the 1970s in and out of jail, but rose to the top tier of Republican leadership and by the end of the decade was urging Republicans to develop an alternative political strategy. He was a leading policymaker in the 1981 H-Block hunger strike, was elected to the Westminster parliament for the constituency of West Belfast in 1983, and became president of Sinn Fein the same year. In 1984 he was shot by Loyalist paramilitaries. Talks between Adams and SDLP leader John Hume in 1988 ended unsuccessfully, but were resumed in 1993 and led to an IRA ceasefire in 1994. He visited the US several times during 1994, and met Rosa Parks, whose refusal to give up her bus seat in Montgomery in 1955 sparked the bus boycott and catapulted Martin Luther King Jr to national prominence as a civil rights leader. In 1997 Adams regained the Westminster seat he had lost in 1992.

Stokely Carmichael – see Kwame Turé

Austin Currie 1939–

Born into a working-class family in Coalisland, Northern Ireland, Currie was among the first generation of Catholics to attend university, where he studied the US Constitution. Elected the youngest-ever Stormont MP in 1964, he tried to modernise the Nationalist Party. In 1968, impatient at the lack of media attention given to the civil rights campaign, he staged a squat in a council house in Caledon, Co. Tyrone, which had been allocated to a young single Protestant woman. He helped organise the first civil rights march in August 1968 from Coalisland to Dungannon. In 1969 he spoke to an Irish-American audience in New York and urged them to support civil rights in Northern Ireland and in the US. He co-founded the Social and Democratic Labour Party (SDLP) in 1970 and remained a prominent member throughout the 1970s and 1980s. In 1989 he was elected to the Dail (Irish parliament based in Dublin) for the Fine Gael party, and was later appointed Minister for Health.

Richard Daley 1902–76

Daley grew up in an Irish-American environment in Chicago, and rose through the city's Democratic Party structure to become mayor. First elected in 1955, he remained mayor until his death over 20 years later, and became the most prominent Irish-American politician after the Kennedys. He attracted international attention when Chicago hosted the 1968 Democratic Party convention. His police department's brutality and its use of tear gas in dispersing anti-war protestors made Daley an enemy of the New Left, and Bernadette Devlin refused to meet him when she visited the US a year later.

Daley proved a more difficult opponent for Martin Luther King Jr than most southern politicians. When King made Chicago's poor housing standards the focus of the civil rights campaign in 1966, Daley appeared to welcome his efforts and tried to avoid a head-on confrontation with King. Eventually, the two met and stuck a deal on improving conditions for the city's blacks, but many felt that Daley had got the better of the civil rights leaders. Daley's son is now the mayor of Chicago.

Angela Davis 1944–

Born in Alabama, Davis took part in civil rights demonstrations in the 1950s before attending university in New York and Germany. On her return to the US, she worked with SNCC and the Black Panther Party and joined the Communist Party in 1968. She was fired from her teaching post at the University of California in Los Angeles after her party membership was revealed by the FBI to the university's authorities. In 1970, guns she had legally bought were used in a courtroom shootout and she appeared on the FBI's 'Most Wanted' list. She was captured and sent to prison, during which time she was visited by Bernadette Devlin McAliskey in February 1971. She was tried and acquitted of all charges the following year.

She has remained politically active, visited Northern Ireland in the 1990s, and was involved in the campaign to have Bernadette Devlin McAliskey's daughter, Roisin, released from prison in Britain. Davis is now a university lecturer in Santa Cruz, California.

Eamon de Valera 1882–1975

Born in New York, de Valera was sent to Limerick as an infant where he grew up with his mother's family. In 1904 he graduated from the Royal University of Ireland and became a mathematics teacher. He was active in Dublin in the Easter Rising in 1916, and was the most senior of the Irish Volunteers not to be executed. He was imprisoned for his part in the Rising, and released in the amnesty of 1917. After Sinn Fein swept the elections in 1918, he became provisional president of the Irish Republic, and travelled to America in 1919 to raise funds and political support for Ireland. Sinn Fein's political organisation was much admired by black nationalist Marcus Garvey, who sent messages of support to de Valera in the early 1920s.

He returned to Ireland in the later stages of the guerrilla war which had been masterminded by IRA chief Michael Collins, and sent Collins to London to negotiate a treaty with the British government in December 1921. De Valera denounced the treaty agreed to by Collins, a dispute which led to civil war in Ireland in 1922 and 1923, when de Valera's anti-treaty faction was defeated.

In 1926 de Valera broke with the extreme anti-treaty elements and founded a new political party, Fianna Fail, which won the election of 1932. De Valera headed a government which lasted for 16 years, during which time he prevented Ireland from joining the Second World War, pursuing a policy of strict neutrality. During the late 1940s and early 1950s, Fianna Fail won and lost a series of elections before being returned with a decisive majority in 1957. In 1959, de Valera retired from active politics but was elected president of Ireland in 1959, and re-elected in 1966, 50 years after he had taken part in the Easter Rising.

Bernadette Devlin – see Bernadette Devlin McAliskey

Frederick Douglass 1817–1895

Born into slavery in Maryland, Douglass escaped from the American South in 1838 and settled in Massachusetts. He worked in the anti-slavery movement in the early 1840s, helping fugitive slaves escape from the South. In 1845 he wrote his autobiography, and travelled to the British Isles. He gave lectures throughout Ireland to generate support for the anti-slavery movement, and spoke at a meeting in Dublin with his political hero, Daniel O'Connell. His appearances in Belfast were the most controversial, when he criticised some of the churches' record on slavery. He returned to America in 1846, and established an abolitionist newspaper, the *North Star*. He campaigned for Abraham Lincoln during the presidential election of 1860, and during the Civil War helped raise a regiment of black soldiers. During a long political career, which included a stint as Minister to Haiti (1889–1891) he regularly spoke in favour of Home Rule for Ireland. In 1883 he returned to Ireland on honeymoon.

Michael Farrell 1944–

A founder member of People's Democracy (PD), Farrell was a leading left-wing student activist in the mid-1960s. He established the Young Socialist Alliance in Northern Ireland, modelling it on the American organisation of the same name. Influenced by Trotskyist literature on the US civil rights movement, he regarded PD as performing the sort of role SNCC had in the US. He proposed and organised the Belfast–Derry march of January 1969, consciously imitating the American civil rights march from Selma to Montgomery. He was a member of the NICRA executive from 1969 to 1970. He was interned in 1971, and again in 1973, when he was released after 37 days on hunger strike. He became a noted historian of Northern Ireland politics, and is prominent in civil liberties campaigns in the Irish Republic.

Marcus Garvey 1887–1940

Born in the West Indies, Garvey travelled to South America and Britain before settling in the US in 1916 and establishing the 'Back to Africa' programme aimed at resettling black Americans in Africa. His ideas drew significant support in New York, and thousands joined his Universal Negro Improvement Association (UNIA). He established a newspaper, the *Negro World*, which promoted his doctrine of black nationalism, and he set up a black-owned and operated steamship company, the Black Star Line. Garvey's political ideas were much influenced by Irish Republicanism, and particularly Eamon de Valera. During a 31-day international conclave convened by UNIA in New York, he sent messages of support to IRA hunger-striker Terence McSwiney and announced UNIA's formal recognition of de Valera as president of Ireland.

Allegations of financial mismanagement eventually led to Garvey's imprisonment in the US, and in 1927 he was released and expelled to Jamaica. He moved to London in 1935 where he died five years later. Garvey's ideas on black capitalism and black nationalism proved immensely influential on radical black leaders and organisations of the 1960s, notably Malcolm X and the Black Panther Party.

John Hume 1937–

Among the first Catholic schoolchildren to benefit from the education reforms of 1947, Hume went to secondary school and later university. He founded the Derry Credit Union in 1960, designed to help low-income families gain access to housing. He was active in the civil rights movement in Derry in 1968, where he was vice-chairman of the Derry Citizens' Action Committee. Elected to Stormont in 1969, he was a founder member of the SDLP in 1970 and became the party's leader in 1979. In 1979, too, he was elected to the European parliament, and in 1983 became a Westminster MP. Hume repeatedly emphasised the influence of the American civil rights movement on his political thinking during the 1960s. A regular visitor to Washington in the 1980s, he lobbied for American intervention in the political debate over Northern Ireland, and became a close political ally of Senator Edward Kennedy. Hume embarked on controversial talks with Sinn Fein leader Gerry Adams in 1993, and Hume's political leverage in the US helped secure visas for Gerry Adams during 1994.

Kennedys: John F. Kennedy, 1917–1963, Robert F. Kennedy 1925–1968, Edward M. Kennedy 1931– Jean Kennedy Smith 1928–

The most prominent Irish-American family of the twentieth century, the Kennedy politicians found significant support from black voters. Although less active on civil rights issues than many black leaders had hoped, John Kennedy's presidential administration (1961–1963) did see the desegregation of interstate bus facilities, and the integration of important educational establishments like the University of Alabama. Robert Kennedy, attorney general in the Kennedy administration, and later senator for New York (1964–1968) identified more closely with civil rights issues than had John Kennedy, and relied heavily on black support during his presidential campaign of 1968. Edward Kennedy has been a senator for Massachusetts since 1962, and ran unsuccessfully for the Democratic presidential nomination in 1980. Like his brothers, he has also proved popular with black voters, and has been prominent in pushing civil rights legislation in Congress. In the mid-1970s he was attacked verbally and physically by some of his constituents for his integrationist stance during the Boston busing controversy.

He supported the civil rights movement in Northern Ireland, and during the early 1970s was a leading critic of British policy in Ulster, calling for the withdrawal of troops and an end to Irish partition. During the 1980s he became a close political ally of SDLP leader John Hume. Kennedy was very active in persuading the Clinton Administration to appoint his sister, Jean Kennedy Smith, as US Ambassador to Ireland, and to grant Gerry Adams visas to visit the US.

Martin Luther King Jr 1929–1968

Cited by virtually every leading civil rights activist in Northern Ireland as a major inspiration, King was the son of a Baptist preacher who himself studied for the ministry and became pastor of the Dexter Avenue Baptist Church, Montgomery in 1953. He became a national figure two years later for his leading role in organising a boycott of the city's segregated bus facilities, and in 1957 founded the Southern Christian Leadership Conference (SCLC) to maintain the push for civil rights. During the early 1960s, the SCLC encouraged and organised non-violent protests against segregation throughout the South and in 1963 King was the keynote speaker at the March on Washington, a televised event which gave him international prominence. He was awarded the Nobel Peace Prize in 1964.

During the mid-1960s he took his crusade to the northern cities, and in Chicago confronted Irish-American mayor Richard Daley on the issue of the city's poverty. He became increasingly radical in his political actions, and spoke out forcefully against American involvement in the Vietnam War. King was assassinated in 1968.

Tomas MacGiolla 1924–

President of Sinn Fein 1962–1970, when he pushed left-wing political programmes in an attempt to turn the Republican movement away from militarism, MacGiolla urged Republicans to agitate for civil rights north and south of the Irish border, and spoke at early civil rights marches. After the Republican split in 1969, he became president of Official Sinn Fein, and later of the Workers' Party, which he represented as a member of the Dail 1982–1992.

Bernadette Devlin McAliskey 1947–

A student at Queen's University, Belfast in 1968, she joined the early civil rights protests, and became a prominent member of PD. Elected to the Westminster parliament in April 1969, she became the best-known member of the civil rights movement in Northern Ireland. She visited the US in 1969 after the Battle of the Bogside and chided Irish-Americans for not offering stronger support to the US civil rights movement. She was presented with the keys of New York City and gave them to Eamonn McCann to hand over to the Black Panthers in the city. In 1970 she was jailed for her part in the Battle of the Bogside, and was re-elected to parliament. The following year she returned to the US and continued her public support for the civil rights movement there. She visited black radical Angela Davis in prison, and met leading black militants Stokely Carmichael and Huey P. Newton. In 1972, she was speaking at a civil rights rally in Derry on Bloody Sunday when British soldiers opened fire on the protestors, killing 13. She punched Home Secretary Reginald Maudling in parliament during the debate on the shootings, and accused him of lying about the killings.

She failed to win re-election in 1974, but remained active in politics and throughout the 1970s was a regular visitor to the US, where she urged Irish-Americans to support the black struggle. She helped establish the Irish Republican Socialist Party in the mid-1970s and became prominent in the campaign to secure political status for Republican prisoners in the late 1970s and early 1980s. She and her husband were shot and left for dead by Loyalist paramilitaries who broke into their home in February 1981. During the 1980s she was involved with the campaign against extradition of suspected Republican paramilitaries from the Republic of Ireland and from the US, and continued to lecture in the US. In 1997 her pregnant daughter Roisin was jailed in London pending extradition to Germany for allegedly taking part in an IRA attack on a British army barracks in Germany. Angela Davis and other former political colleagues of Bernadette McAliskey joined the US campaign to secure Roisin's release.

Eamonn McCann 1943–

Having studied at Queen's University, Belfast where he was involved in an anti-discrimination study in the early 1960s, McCann was active for some time in left-wing politics in London during the mid-1960s, where he met Stokely Carmichael. He returned to Northern Ireland and agitated for fair housing in Derry. He was a leading organiser of the civil rights march in Derry on 5 October 1968, and was closely associated with Michael Farrell and Bernadette Devlin McAliskey on the left of the civil rights movement. In 1970 he presented the keys of New York City, which had been awarded to Bernadette Devlin during her visit to the city the year before, to the Black Panthers. Author of *War and an Irish Town*, a classic account of growing up Catholic in Northern Ireland, he now is a prominent journalist based in Derry.

Conn and Patricia McCluskey

Both Conn and Patricia McCluskey experienced anti-Catholic discrimination in Northern Ireland during childhood. Patricia McShane left Ulster in the 1930s to work as a social worker in the slums of Glasgow, but returned, married Dr Conn McCluskey and settled in Dungannon, Co. Tyrone. Disturbed by the local housing conditions, and particularly their affects on young women and their children, Patricia McCluskey helped found The Homeless Citizens' League in the town in 1963 to agitate for better housing. The organisation gave rise to a wider anti-discrimination movement called the Campaign for Social Justice (CSJ). The CSJ produced statistics on anti-Catholic discrimination throughout Ireland, and tried to pursue legal and parliamentary remedies. Faced with little progress, the CSJ joined with other anti-discrimination groups in 1967 to form the Northern Ireland Civil Rights Association (NICRA). The McCluskeys also tried to persuade Catholic voters to unite behind a single candidate in parliamentary elections, with some success. Conn McCluskey publicised the cause of civil rights in Northern Ireland in the US, and although prominent and active in NICRA for several years, the McCluskeys became disillusioned with its leftist influence, and Conn McCluskey left the NICRA executive in 1970. They moved to Australia for some time and later returned to live near Dublin.

Huey P. Newton 1942–1989

Newton founded the Black Panther Party for Self-Defense in 1966 with Bobby Seale, whose programme included several of those enunciated by Marcus Garvey in the early 1920s. The Black Panthers set out to monitor police practices. In 1967 Newton was jailed after an incident in which a police officer was killed, but released on bail when his conviction was overturned on appeal. Newton met Bernadette Devlin McAliskey during her trip to the US in 1971. In 1974 Newton fled to Cuba, but returned to the US in 1977. Convicted again in 1978 of the policeman's death, the decision was finally reversed by the courts and he was freed. A series of charges ranging from murder to illegal gun possession kept Newton entangled with the law until he was shot dead in an apparent street fight in 1989.

Daniel O'Connell 1775–1847

Born into Catholic aristocracy, O'Connell's parents followed the tradition of their class and had their son brought up in a peasant's cottage, where he learned the language and aspirations of the Catholic masses. O'Connell finished his education at universities in France and England before being admitted to the Irish Bar in 1798. O'Connell criticised the physical force used in the 1798 Irish revolution led by Wolfe Tone, and in the early 1800s concentrated on establishing a successful law practice in Ireland. In 1823 he organised the Catholic Association, building it into a mass movement and a powerful political force. He won election to the Westminster parliament in 1828, forcing the British government to concede Catholic emancipation. During the early 1830s O'Connell led a nationalist party in the House of Commons, and began agitating against slavery in the West Indies and the US. O'Connell urged Irish-Americans not to collaborate with slavery, and he refused to accept money from those who defended the practice, causing a major rift in Irish America, and severe financial losses for O'Connell's movement. In 1845, he spoke at a Dublin meeting with former American slave Frederick Douglass, introducing him as 'the black O'Connell'.

During the 1840s, O'Connell staged a series of monster rallies throughout Ireland in a bid to win Irish independence. In 1843 one of the mass meetings near Dublin was banned by the British government, and O'Connell – reluctant to risk violence – cancelled the rally. The movement lost momentum, and O'Connell was arrested for sedition and spent some months in prison. Although eventually released on appeal O'Connell's political strength was gone, the British parliament ignoring his final pleas for famine relief for Ireland in 1847.

Ian Paisley 1926–

Ian Paisley became politically active in the early 1960s, organising a march to protest the lowering of the British flag on Belfast city hall to mark the death of Pope John XXIII. He organised protests against reforms proposed by Northern Ireland Prime Minister Terence O'Neill, and set up the Ulster Constitution Defence Committee and the Ulster Protestant Volunteers, both of which provided counter-demonstrators during civil rights marches. During the late 1960s, he travelled to the US several times, most often to the right-wing Bob Jones University in South Carolina, which had awarded him an honourary doctorate. In 1966 he founded the *Protestant Telegraph* newspaper, which attacked Catholicism and civil rights protests in Northern Ireland and in the US. In 1970 Paisley was elected to the Westminster parliament and the following year founded the Democratic Unionist Party. He opposed the Sunningdale power-sharing executive, and led Loyalist strikers against the agreement. He was elected to the European Parliament in 1979. At the urging of prominent Irish-Americans, his US visa was withdrawn in 1981. Although overall support for the DUP fell in the 1997 British general election, he retained his seat at Westminster.

Kwame Turé [formerly Stokely Carmichael] 1941–

Born in Trinidad, Carmichael moved to the US at the age of 11. In 1960 he joined the Congress of Racial Equality (CORE) and its efforts to integrate public facilities in the South. Graduating from Howard University in Washington DC in 1964, he joined the Student Non-Violent Coordinating Committee (SNCC), soon after became its leader, and helped steer the organisation towards advocating black separatism. Associated with the slogan 'Black Power', he co-authored a book of that title in 1967. He had a brief spell in the Black Panther Party before emigrating to live in Guinea, West Africa. During the 1970s, he appeared on platforms in the US with Bernadette Devlin McAliskey and in 1978 changed his name to Kwame Turé in honour of two African political leaders, Kwame Nkrumah of Ghana and Sekou Turé of Guinea. His political organisation, the All-African People's Revolutionary Party, is active in the US, and has strong links with the Irish Republican Socialist Party in California.

Malcolm X 1925–1965

Malcolm X's parents were fervent supporters of Marcus Garvey and his United Negro Improvement Association, echoes of which would be found in Malcolm X's philosophy of black separation. Malcolm X was sentenced to 10 years in prison in 1946 on burglary charges. During his time in prison, he converted to Islam and on his release became an outspoken defender of Muslim doctrines. He spoke out against the integrationist approach to black advancement, and attacked Martin Luther King Jr for his moderation. In 1963, after describing President Kennedy's death as 'Chickens coming home to roost' he was suspended from the black Muslim movement by its head, Elijah Muhammed. He soon formed his own organisation, and trips to the Middle East and Africa influenced him towards a less vengeful approach to whites. He was assassinated in New York in 1965.

Notes

Introduction

1. Kingsley, quoted in Michael MacDonald, *Children of Wrath: Political Violence in Northern Ireland* (Oxford: Polity Press, 1986) p. 3.
2. *Punch*, October 1862, quoted in John Conroy, *Belfast Diary: War as a Way of Life* (Boston: Beacon, 1987) p. 14.
3. Perry L. Curtis, *Apes and Angels: The Irishman in Victorian Caricature* (Washington DC: Smithsonian Institution, 1997) p. 100.
4. Curtis, *Apes and Angels*, p. 101.
5. Curtis, *Apes and Angels*, pp. 19–20.
6. See J. Darby, *Dressed to Kill: Cartoonists and the Northern Ireland Conflict* (Belfast: Blackstaff, 1983).
7. Lafcadio Hearn, *An American Miscellany* (New York, 1924) p. 160, quoted in Lawrence W. Levine, *Black Culture and Black Consciousness* (Oxford: Oxford University Press, 1977) p. 301.
8. Levine, *Black Culture*, p. 303.
9. J. Fauset, *Journal of American Folklore*, 40 (1928), quoted in Levine, *Black Culture*, p. 302.
10. Christine Kinealy, *A Death-Dealing Famine* (London: Pluto, 1997) p. 111. The Native American Choctaw Nation sent a donation of $170 to Ireland when they heard about the famine. The Choctaw Indians had been moved from their land in Mississippi in 1831 and had suffered terribly during their forced relocation to Oklahoma, with about half their people dying on the journey.
11. Bob Purdie, *Politics in the Streets* (Belfast: Blackstaff, 1990) p. 244.
12. See Andrew J. Wilson, *Irish America and the Ulster Conflict, 1968–1995* (Belfast: Blackstaff, 1995).
13. Michael Farrell, interview with author, July 1996; Austin Currie in *Fortnight*, no. 268, p. 19 (December 1988).
14. Fionnbarra O Dochartaigh, interview with author, September 1996.
15. Martin Meehan, interview with author, May 1996.
16. According to the definition of 'black' in the *Concise Ulster Dictionary*, it means a 'Roman Catholic devoted to the Protestant cause'. To make things even more confusing, one of the most militant Protestant organisations in Northern Ireland is called the Royal Black Preceptory.

17. Many popular Irish nationalist songs include a slavery theme. 'Boolavogue', about the 1798 Rising, warns 'King George of England' that local hero Fr Murphy will rid any land of slavery, and the 'Jolly Ploughboy' in the song of the same name goes 'off to Dublin in the green' to join the Republicans in 1916 because, he explains, 'I've always hated slavery since the day that I was born, so I'm off to join the IRA and I'm off tomorrow morn.' The Irish national anthem includes the lines 'No more our ancient sire land/ Shall shelter the despot or the slave'.
18. Harry Belafonte, interview with Brian Ward, March 1996, University of Newcastle Upon Tyne Oral History Collection.
19. David Fleming, *James Baldwin* (New York: Alfred Knopf, 1994) p. 200.
20. Fleming, *James Baldwin*, p. 85.
21. Huey P. Newton, *Revolutionary Suicide* (New York: Readers and Writers, 1995 edition) p. 58.
22. Roddy Doyle, *The Commitments* (London: Heinemann, 1988) p. 13.
23. '"White niggers" stunned by Orange victory', *Independent,* 12 July 1996.

Chapter 1 Black and White Slaves

1. Jonathan Bardon, *A History of Ulster*, (Belfast: Blackstaff, 1992) p. 15. Original quotation from St Patrick's *Confession*.
2. For an excellent brief history of St Patrick, see Thomas Cahill, *How The Irish Saved Civilization* (New York: Doubleday, 1995) pp. 101–119.
3. Goodwife Glover, who spoke only Irish, was tried and executed in Massachusetts during the Salem witchhunts. See Chadwick Hansen, *Witchcraft at Salem* (New York: George Braziller, 1969) pp. 20–23.
4. Robin Blackburn, *The Making of New World Slavery* (London: Verso, 1997) p. 316.
5. Thomas Truxes, *Irish-American Trade 1660–1783*, (Cambridge: Cambridge University Press, 1988) p. 100.
6. Robert St-Cyr, 'An Afro-Irish Christmas in the Caribbean', *Fortnight*, No. 200 (December 1983) pp. 25–26.
7. Truxes, *Irish-American Trade*, p. 101.
8. Truxes, *Irish-American Trade*, p. 121.
9. Truxes, *Irish-American Trade*, p. 121.
10. *Barbados Mercury*, 1 February 1766, quoted in Truxes, *Irish-American Trade*, p. 339.
11. Richard Rose, *Governing Without Consensus* (London: Faber & Faber, 1971) p. 457.
12. Rose, *Governing Without Consensus*, p. 457.
13. Douglas Riach, 'O'Connell and Slavery' in Donal McCartney (ed.), *The World of Daniel O'Connell* (Dublin: Mercier, 1980) p. 176.

14. Riach, 'O'Connell and Slavery', p. 177.
15. Riach, 'O'Connell and Slavery', p. 177.
16. Daniel O'Connell, 'On American Slavery', published in *Single Works: Liberty or Slavery?* (Cincinnati: 1864).
17. Colm Kerrigan, 'Irish Temperance and US Anti-Slavery: Father Mathew and the Abolitionists', *Journal of Socialist and Feminist Historians*, Issue 31 (Spring 1991) pp. 105–119.
18. Riach, 'O'Connell and Slavery', p. 179.
19. Riach, 'O'Connell and Slavery', p. 181.
20. Riach, 'O'Connell and Slavery', p. 179.
21. Kerrigan, 'Irish Temperance and US Anti-Slavery', p. 106.
22. O'Connell, *Single Works*, p. 5.
23. O'Connell, *Single Works*, p. 5.
24. O'Connell, *Single Works*, p. 7.
25. Riach, 'O'Connell and Slavery', p. 183. It was Irish Quaker Ebenezer Shackleton who made an early comparison between the Irish and black American slave conditions in the *Freeman's Journal* of 26 August 1840: 'In America the slave is called a slave – he is black, and is flogged: in Ireland he is called a labourer – he is white, and is only starved.'
26. Timothy Byrnes, *Catholic Bishops in American Politics* (New Jersey: New Jersey 1991) p. 16. Bishop England was involved in a curious episode in the history of Irish links to black American civil rights. In 1836, he ordained George Paddington to the priesthood in Haiti. Paddington, an historically elusive figure, was a black man from Dublin, and friends with Pierre Toussaint (a former slave whose charitable works in mid-nineteenth-century New York have led to recent calls for his canonisation). Paddington wrote to Toussaint that he did not like America because it was a 'cursed land of slavery'. See Cyprian Davis, *The History of Black Catholics in the United States* (New York: Crossroads, 1995) p. 94.
27. Kerrigan, 'Irish Temperance and US Anti-Slavery', p. 110.
28. Byrnes, *Catholic Bishops*, p. 17.
29. Kerrigan, 'Irish Temperance and US Anti-Slavery', p. 111.
30. Kerrigan, ' Irish Temperance and US Anti-Slavery', p. 114.
31. Irving Bartlett, *Wendell and Ann Phillips* (New York: Norton, 1979) p. 46.
32. Douglass, speaking at Hudson, Ohio, 12 July 1854 in John Blassingame, (ed.) *The Frederick Douglass Papers 1855–63, Vol. 2* (Yale: Yale University Press, 1985) p. 520.
33. *Dublin Evening Mail,* 2 October 1845.
34. Frederick Douglass, *Narrative of the Life of Frederick Douglass (An American Slave)*, Benjamin Quarles, ed. (Boston: Harvard University Press, 1967) p. 69.
35. *Waterford Freeman,* 10 September 1845; no date for *Tipperary Free Press,* quoted in *Douglass Papers,* Vol. 1, p. 454.
36. *Cork Examiner,* 20 October 1845; *Douglass Papers,* Vol. 1, p. 55.
37. *Douglass Papers,* Vol. 1, p. 85.
38. *Cork Examiner,* 20 October 1845.

39. *Cork Examiner*, 20 October 1845.
40. *Douglass Papers*, Vol. 1, p. 86.
41. *Belfast News Letter*, 9 December 1845.
42. *Belfast News Letter*, 26 December 1845.
43. *Belfast News Letter*, 26 December 1845.
44. Frederick Douglass at Rochester, NY, 26 January 1851, *Douglass Papers*, Vol. 2, p. 291. Douglass used this quote of O'Connell's dozens of times in speeches over several decades.
45. Kerrigan, 'Irish Temperance and US Anti-Slavery', p. 111.
46. Kerrigan, 'Irish Temperance and US Anti-Slavery', p. 111.
47. *Douglass Papers*, Vol. 5, p. 276.
48. *Douglass Papers*, Vol. 5, p. 276.
49. Riach, 'O'Connell and Slavery', p. 184.
50. *Douglass Papers*, Vol. 2, p. 486.
51. In 1862 Mitchel was editor of the *Richmond Enquirer*, and between 1863 and 1865 he edited the *Richmond Examiner*. Douglass's attack on Mitchel came in New York as early as 1854. *Douglass Papers*, Vol. 2, p. 486.
52. See Toby Joyce, 'The American Civil War and Irish Nationalism', *History Ireland*, Vol. 4, No. 2 (Summer 1996) pp. 36–41.
53. Jill Fergus, 'The Life and Death of Seneca Village', *Irish America* (March/April 1997) p. 15.
54. African-Americans were later allowed to enlist, but by 1863 there was still a reluctance to arm large numbers of African-Americans.
55. Andrew Wilson, *Irish America and the Ulster Conflict 1968–1995* (Belfast: Blackstaff, 1995) p. 7.
56. *Chicago Defender*, 4 May 1916.
57. *Crisis*, Vol. 12, No. 4 (August 1916) pp. 166–167.
58. *Crisis*, Vol. 13, No. 2 (December 1916) p. 63.
59. Bradford Chambers, *Chronicles of Black Protest* (New York: Mentor, 1968) p. 62.
60. Chambers, *Chronicles of Black Protest*, p. 63.
61. *The Marcus Garvey and UNIA Papers*, Robert Hill, (ed.) (Los Angeles: University of California Press, 1983), Vol. 1. p. lxx. There is no exact translation for Sinn Fein into English. It is usually translated as 'ourselves alone', although its meaning is sometimes closer to 'we ourselves'.
62. *Garvey Papers*, Vol. 1, p. lxx.
63. *Garvey Papers*, Vol. 1, p. lxx.
64. It has been suggested that de Valera's sentence was commuted because he was American by birth, having been born in New York. However, most evidence would seem to suggest that the British decided to spare his life for fear of arousing further public anger.
65. *Garvey Papers*, Vol. 2, p. 603.
66. *Garvey Papers* Vol. 2, p. 603. Coincidentally, red, black and green are the colours of the Royal Ulster Constabulary, the police force in Northern Ireland.
67. *Garvey Papers*, Vol. I, p. lxxv.
68. *Garvey Papers*, Vol. 1, p. lxxiii.

69. *Garvey Papers*, Vol. 1, p. lxxiii.
70. *Garvey Papers*, Vol. 1, p. lxxiii.
71. *Garvey Papers*, Vol. 3, p. 12.
72. *Garvey Papers*, Vol. 3, p. 12.
73. *Garvey Papers* Vol. 2, p. 649. MacSwiney, who had been elected Mayor of Cork, died on 25 October 1920 after 74 days on hunger strike in Brixton Prison, London.
74. *Garvey Papers*, Vol. 4, p. 259 and p. 567.
75. *Garvey Papers*, Vol. 4, p. 259.
76. *Garvey Papers*, Vol. I, p. lxxviii.
77. Graham Smith, *When Jim Crow Met John Bull* (London: IB Tauris, 1987) p. 221.
78. Tony Morrow, *Derry: The War Years 1939–45* (Derry: The Heritage Library, 1987).
79. *Belfast Telegraph*, 1 October 1942.
80. *Belfast Telegraph*, 5 October 1942.
81. *Belfast Telegraph*, 5 October 1942.
82. Brian Barton, *Northern Ireland in the Second World War* (Belfast: Ulster Historical Foundation, 1995) p. 103.
83. Barton, *Northern Ireland in the Second World War*, p. 103.
84. Barton, *Northern Ireland in the Second World War*, p. 103.
85. Kenneth Christie, *Political Protest in Northern Ireland: Community and Change* (Reading: Link, 1992) p. 60.
86. *Irish News*, 17 September 1949.
87. Denis Barritt, *The Northern Ireland Problem: A Study in Group Relations* (Oxford: Oxford University Press, 1962) p. 53.
88. Bardon, *A history of Ulster*, p. 610.
89. Eddie McAteer, *Irish Action: New thoughts on an old subject* (Ballyshannon: Donegal Democrat, 1948).
90. Thomas Wilson, *Ulster Under Home Rule* (Oxford: Oxford University Press, 1955) p. 208. In July 1959, the Catholic journal *Christus Rex* carried a speech delivered by US Ambassador to Ireland Scott McLeod titled 'The US, Racism and Communism', in which McLeod stated: 'The position of the Negro who in some areas and to some extent been deprived of the franchise and other civil rights is analogous to that of the Roman Catholics here in past years' (*Christus Rex*, Vol. 13. No. 3 (July 1959) p. 174).

Chapter 2 Second-class Citizens

1. Kenneth Christie, *Political Protest in Northern Ireland: Continuity and Change* (Reading: Link, 1992) p. 89. Independent Television arrived in Ulster in 1959. Until then there had been one BBC channel.
2. Richard Rose, *Governing Without Consensus* (London: Faber and Faber, 1971) p. 492. Much of Rose's research is based on his Loyalty Questionnaire, undertaken in 1968. It asked a sample of 1,291 people in Northern Ireland (757 Protestants, 534 Catholics) dozens of questions on issues ranging from levels of education to

political affiliation and beliefs to attitudes to religious questions like ecumenism. Question 30c asked: 'Generally speaking, what would you say is the best source of information about what is happening in Northern Ireland politics?' While 24 per cent answered Newspapers, 55 per cent (58 per cent Catholics and 53 per cent Protestants) said TV/Newspapers.

3. Gerry Adams, *The Politics of Irish Freedom* (Dingle: Brandon, 1988) p. 10.
4. Michael Farrell, interview with author, July 1996.
5. Eamonn McCann, interview with author, July 1996.
6. Conn McCluskey, *Up Off Their Knees* (Galway: Conn McCluskey and Associates, 1989), Appendix 1, p. 27.
7. McCluskey, *Up Off Their Knees*, p. 10.
8. David Garrow, *Bearing the Cross: Martin Luther King Jr and the Southern Christian Leadership Conference* (London: Jonathan Cape, 1988) p. 252.
9. *Dungannon Observer*, 18 May 1963.
10. *Dungannon Observer*, 18 May 1963. The incident at Little Rock, Arkansas, had taken place six years earlier, in September 1957. President Eisenhower had sent 1,000 paratroopers to Little Rock to restore order after rioting had broken out over the racial integration of a local school.
11. *Dungannon Observer*, 18 May 1963.
12. *Derry Journal*, 31 January 1964.
13. *Dungannon Observer*, 11 May 1963.
14. Patricia McCluskey, interview with author, July 1996.
15. *Dungannon Observer*, 15 June 1963.
16. Patricia McCluskey, interview with author, July 1996.
17. King quoted in Garrow, *Bearing the Cross*, p. 284.
18. Dr Conn McCluskey, interview with author, July 1996.
19. David Garrow, *The Montgomery Bus Boycott and the Women Who Started It: The Memoir of Jo Ann Gibson Robinson* (Knoxville: University of Tennessee, 1987) p. 23.
20. Garrow, *The Montgomery Bus Boycott and the Women Who Started It*, p. 78.
21. Charles Payne, 'Men Led, But Women Organized', in Vicki Crawford et al. (eds), *Women in the Civil Rights Movement* (Indianapolis: Indiana State Press, 1993) p. 2.
22. Vicki Crawford, 'Grassroots Activists in Mississippi' in Crawford et al. (eds), *Women in the Civil Rights Movement*, p. 25.
23. McCluskey, *Up Off Their Knees*, p. 14.
24. Conn McCluskey, interview with author, July 1996.
25. Christie, *Political Protest*, p. 83.
26. Gerry Adams, *Falls Memories* (Dingle: Brandon, 1993) p. 129.
27. George Drower, *John Hume – Peacemaker* (London: Gollancz, 1995) p. 23.
28. Eamonn McCann, *War and an Irish Town* (London: Pluto, 1973) p. 74.
29. Christie, *Political Protest*, p. 83.

30. Daniel C. Thompson, *The Negro Leadership Class* (New Jersey: Spectrum, 1963) p. 142.
31. An excellent account of the origins of this protest is offered by the BBC TV documentary *Wheeler on America*, broadcast on 3 March 1996.
32. W.H. Van Voris, *Ulster: An Oral Documentary* (Amherst: University of Massachusetts Press, 1975) p. 50.
33. Rose, *Governing Without Consensus*, pp. 463–470. See also Frank Wright, *Northern Ireland: A Comparative Analysis* (Dublin: Gill and Macmillan, 1987) pp. 193–200.
34. Jonathan Bardon, *A History of Ulster* (Belfast: Blackstaff, 1992) p. 501.
35. Christie, *Political Protest*, p. 48.
36. The Cameron Commission, *Disturbances in Northern Ireland* (Belfast: HMSO, 1969) p. 59.
37. Christie, *Political Protest*, p. 51.
38. Gerrymandering, or unfair drawing of constituencies, was named after Elbridge Gerry, a former Governor of Massachusetts (and later US Vice-President) who used the tactic to secure an unfair voting system in his state.
39. Howard Zinn, *SNCC: The New Abolitionists* (New York: Beacon, 1964) p. 66.
40. Zinn, *SNCC*, p. 153.
41. Fionnbarra O Dochartaigh, *Ulster's White Negroes* (Edinburgh: AK Press, 1994) p. 9.
42. O Dochartaigh, *Ulster's White Negroes*, p. 14.
43. Christie, *Political Protest*, p. 50.
44. Rose, *Governing Without Consensus*, p. 498. In answer to the question 'Do you think these [religious discrimination] complaints should be ignored or investigated?', 26 per cent of Protestants said ignored, and 49 per cent said investigated, while seven per cent of Catholics thought complaints should be ignored, and 26 per cent that they should be investigated.
45. McCluskey, *Up Off Their Knees*, p. 20.
46. McCluskey, *Up Off Their Knees*, Appendix, p. 12.
47. J. Bowyer Bell, *The Irish Troubles* (Dublin: Gill & Macmillan, 1993) p. 49.
48. McCluskey, *Up Off Their Knees*, Appendix, p. 22.
49. The NAACP was founded in 1909 and originally advocated extending industrial opportunity and greater police protection for blacks.
50. Bernadette Devlin McAliskey, interview with author, August 1996. In fact, the CSJ announced in July 1968 that it would support people with cases of discrimination who wanted to appeal to the European Court of Human Rights. The announcement generated some good publicity, but the costs of such a case were too high for it to be feasible.

51. Richard Rose, 'On the Priorities of Citizenship in the Deep South and Northern Ireland', *Journal of Politics*, Vol. 38 (1976) pp. 248–291.

52. Anna Coote and Lawrence Grant, *The NCCL Guide* (London: Penguin, 1972) pp. 276–282. In 1957, the UK government informed the Council of Europe that it was exercising its right of derogation under Article 15 in respect of the emergency existing in Northern Ireland due to the recurrence of organised terrorism 'to the extent strictly required by the exigencies of the situation'. See Leslie MacFarlane, 'Human Rights and the Fight Against Terrorism in Northern Ireland', *Terrorism and Political Violence*, Vol. 4, No. 1 (Spring 1992) pp. 89–99.

53. Kevin McNamara, interview with author, 9 May 1996.

54. Rose, *Governing Without Consensus*, p. 465.

55. Sir Oliver Wright, interviewed in *The Sparks That Lit The Bonfire*, BBC TV Timewatch, 1993. When CDU was formed in 1965, it was composed of 38 Liberal and Labour MPs, but this number grew to about 90 in early 1967. See Vincent E. Feeney, 'Westminster and the early civil rights struggle in Northern Ireland', *Eire–Ireland*, Winter 1976.

56. McCluskey, *Up Off Their Knees*, p. 32. McCluskey offers several examples of such responses received from both Downing Street and the Home Office.

57. Eamonn McCann, interview with author, 29 July 1996.

58. Hazel Morrissey, *Betty Sinclair: A Woman's Fight for Socialism* (Belfast: John Freeman, 1983). Sinclair's conviction which resulted in her jail term arose from a curious episode. The Communist Party of Ireland's northern newspaper, *Red Hand*, suggested that the IRA was turning into a pro-fascist organisation, as it had contacted the Nazi government in order to secure weapons and supplies to use against the British. When the Republican movement asked for the right of reply in *Red Hand*, it was granted, and so Sinclair and Communist Party colleague Billy McCullough were arrested under the Special Powers Act for allowing the Republican response to be printed.

   Sinclair defended the Soviet invasion of Hungary in 1956, and was regarded as a 'reactionary' by many New Leftists in the civil rights movement during the 1960s.

59. The NCCL had written a report condemning the Special Powers Act as early as 1936. See NCCL, *Report of a Commission of Inquiry Appointed to Examine the Purpose and Effect of the Civil Authorities (Special Powers) Act (Northern Ireland) 1922 and 1933* (London: Lewis Reprints, 1972).

60. While the IRA's active membership dwindled from the mid-1920s to the mid-1950s thanks to a purge by the Dublin government, including internment during the Second World War for leading IRA members, the organisation was not completely dormant. A bombing campaign in English cities in 1939 resulted in dozens of bombs exploding at power stations, cinemas, post offices and

banks. Two men were executed in Birmingham in February 1940 after being convicted of an IRA bombing in Coventry in August the year before. The two men, Peter Barnes and James McCormack, are believed not have been directly responsible for the bomb which killed five people. See J. Bowyer Bell, *The Secret Army: The IRA 1916–1979* (Dublin: Poolbeg, 1970) pp. 170–176.

61. See Padraig O'Malley, *Biting at the Grave: The Irish Hunger Strikes and the Politics of Despair* (Belfast: Blackstaff, 1990) p. 107.
62. Tomas MacGiolla, interview with author, July 1996.
63. Goulding, quoted in Rosita Sweetman, *On Our Knees* (London; Pan, 1972) p. 142. It's unclear which organisation Goulding is referring to. Amnesty International groups wrote to foreign governments on behalf of political prisoners, but refused to campaign on civil rights locally, so there would have been little point in Republicans joining it in the hope of agitating for rights in Northern Ireland. Moreover, although Amnesty International was founded in 1961, it appears that the first Amnesty International group in Northern Ireland was set up in 1978.
64. *Tuairisc*, 31 August 1966.
65. Fred Heatley, 'The Beginning 1964–Feb. 1968,' *Fortnight*, March–June 1974. pp. 10–11.
66. Tomas MacGiolla, interview with author, July 1996.
67. Fionnbarra O Dochartaigh, interview with author, September 1996. During the late 1960s O Dochartaigh was generally known by the anglicised version of his name, Finnbarr O'Doherty.
68. Tomas MacGiolla, interview with author, July 1996.
69. Gerry Adams, *The Politics of Irish Freedom*, p. 12.
70. McCluskey, *Up Off Their Knees*, p. 104.
71. The five vague aims were:

    1. To defend the basic freedom of all citizens
    2. To protect the rights of the individual
    3. To highlight all possible abuses of power
    4. To demand guarantees for freedom of speech, assembly and association
    5. To inform the public of their lawful rights.

    See Heatley, 'The Beginning'.
72. Eamonn Mallie and Patrick Bishop, *The Provisional IRA* (London: Heinemann, 1987) p. 71.
73. Gerry Adams, *Before the Dawn* (Heinemann, London 1996) p. 86, and Heatley, 'The Beginning', pp. 10–11.
74. Fred Heatley, 'The Early Marches', *Fortnight*, April 1974, pp. 9–11.
75. Fionnbarra O Dochartaigh, interview with author, September 1996.
76. Austin Currie, interview with author, July 1996.
77. Eamonn McCann, interview with author, July 1996. McCann said:

I met Stokely Carmichael in the Dialectics of Liberation Conference in the Roundhouse in 1966 ... I remember talking about Ireland at that conference. I remember Carmichael had made a – some people thought a very charismatic – I think bullshit – speech – ... just guilt-tripping the whites ... I sat round in a group of ten or twelve people sitting around having 'discussions' you know and I started talking about Ireland and he knew absolutely nothing about it and it wasn't all that serious looking back you know, it was play acting, an awful lot of English, very pleasant, very middle-class kids getting their rocks off, and basically that was your average audience, long hair, refusing to wash ... eergh oh God, a lot of hippies around ... looking back on it I suppose it was something that had to happen, that we had to go through, but it wasn't all that serious.

78. *Irish Democrat*, February 1964, no. 230, p. 3.
79. *Irish Democrat*, April 1965, no. 245 and September 1965, no. 521.
80. *Irish Democrat*, February 1967, no. 269, p. 2.
81. Austin Currie, interview with author, July 1996.
82. Austin Currie, interview with author, July 1996.
83. Austin Currie, interview with author, July 1996.
84. O Dochartaigh, *Ulster's White Negroes*, pp. 39–43.
85. O Dochartaigh, *Ulster's White Negroes*, p. 43, and interview with author, September 1996.

Chapter 3 On the March

1. See Bob Purdie, *Politics in the Streets: the origins of the civil rights movement in Northern Ireland* (Belfast: Blackstaff, 1990) p. 244, and Wilson, Andrew J. *Irish America and the Ulster Conflict, 1968–1995* (Belfast: Blackstaff, 1995) p. 19. Wilson suggests, 'there is little evidence to show there was a systematic attempt to use the African-American civil rights movement as a model.'
2. The timing was coincidental. Austin Currie was not aware of the anniversary until I pointed it out to him in 1996:

   The proposal for a civil rights march came from me and was made to Conn McCluskey. ... I put the proposal that it was time to get away from just disseminating facts and figures, time to get away from the civil liberties groups in Britain upon which they based the civil rights association until then and to take it to the streets. ... All of this was in the aftermath of the squatting incident – that had occurred on 20 June. Had it been possible to organise a civil rights march within a week or two of that, it would've kept a certain momentum going; 24 August was a wee bit longer than I'd hoped for. (Austin Currie, interview with author, July 1996)

3. Bernadette Devlin, *The Price of My Soul* (London: Andre Deutsch, 1969) p. 91.

4. Bernadette Devlin McAliskey, interview with author, August 1996, and Devlin, *Price of My Soul*, p. 76.
5. Bernadette Devlin McAliskey, interview with author, August 1996.
6. Interview with Michael Farrell, August 1996.
7. Patrick Bishop and Eamonn Mallie, *The Provisional IRA*, (London: Heinemann, 1987) p. 72.
8. Devlin, *Price of My Soul*, p. 92.
9. Interview with Tomas MacGiolla, August 1996.
10. Devlin, *Price of My Soul*, p. 93.
11. Eamonn McCann, *War and an Irish Town* (London: Pluto, 1974) p. 94.
12. Frank Curran, *Derry: Countdown to Disaster* (Dublin: Gill and Macmillan, 1986) p. 53.
13. O'Dohartaigh, interview with author, September 1996.
14. *Belfast Telegraph*, 3 October 1968.
15. RUC officer, interview with author, May 1996.
16. Fred Heatley, *Fortnight*, 5 April 1974, p. 10.
17. The Cameron Commission, *Disturbances in Northern Ireland* (Belfast: HMSO, 1969) p. 29.
18. Tomas MacGiolla, interview with author, July 1996.
19. Margie Bernard, *Daughter of Derry: The Story of Brigid Sheils Makowski* (London: Pluto, 1989) p. 58.
20. Eilis McDermot, 'Law and Disorder' in Michael Farrell (ed), *Twenty Years On* (Dingle: Brandon, 1988) p. 153.
21. Angela Davis, interview with author, April 1997.
22. Huey P. Newton, *Revolutionary Suicide* (New York: Writers and Readers, 1995) p. 116.
23. Alphonso Pinkney, *Red, black and green; Black nationalism in the United States* (Cambridge: Cambridge University Press, 1976) p. 44. Garvey's philosophy was not copied wholesale by the BPP, which regarded the advocacy of black capitalism as counter-productive to a class-based struggle. Garvey's ideas coincided more strongly with the black separatist ideology of Malcolm X, whose parents had been active Garveyites.
24. RUC Officer, interview with author, May 1996.
25. McCann, *War and an Irish Town*, p. 105.
26. Michael Farrell, interview with author, July 1996. When asked what he suggested as a solution to guarantee the marchers' safety, Farrell replied 'What about the British army?', an answer which provoked some criticism from the far left in Britain.
27. Michael Farrell, interview with author, July 1996.
28. Michael Farrell, interview with author, July 1996.
29. Bernadette Devlin McAliskey, interview with author, August 1996.
30. Document marked 'Burntollet', PD files, Linen Hall Library.
31. Document marked 'Burntollet', PD files, Linen Hall Library.
32. Devlin, *Price of My Soul*, p. 125.
33. Devlin, *Price of My Soul*, p. 126.
34. Devlin, *Price of My Soul*, p. 140.

35. Andrew Young, *An Easy Burden* (New York: HarperCollins 1996) p. 364.
36. Devlin, *Price of My Soul*, p. 143.
37. Paul Arthur, *The People's Democracy 1968–1973* (Belfast: Blackstaff, 1974) p. 9.
38. McCann, *War and an Irish Town*, p. 110.
39. Patricia McCluskey, interview with author, August 1996.
40. Devlin, *Price of My Soul*, p. 165.
41. Conn McCluskey, interview with author, August 1996.
42. Lewis quoted in Hugh Pearson, *The Shadow of the Panther: Huey Newton and the Price of Black Power in America* (New York: Addison Wesley, 1994) p. 53; McCluskeys, interview with author, August 1996.
43. Michael Farrell, interview with author, August 1996.
44. Kevin Boyle, quoted in W.H. Van Voris , *Violence in Ulster: An Oral Documentary* (Amherst: University of Massachusetts Press, 1975) p. 155.
45. Patricia McCluskey, interview with author, August 1996.
46. Gerry Adams, 'A Republican in the Civil Rights Campaign,' in Farrell, *Twenty Years On*, p. 49.
47. See *New Left Review*, No. 55 (May–June 1969) pp. 3–19.
48. *Daily Mail*, 11 September 1969.
49. 'People's Democracy: a Discussion on Strategy', *New Left Review*, No. 55 (May–June 1969) p. 8.
50. *Crisis*, Vol. 76, No. 8 (October 1969).
51. *Black Panther*, 21 June 1969.
52. *Black Panther*, 21 June 1969.
53. Richard Deutsch and Vivien Magowan, *Northern Ireland: A Chronology of Events 1968–1973* (Belfast: Blackstaff, 1973) Vol.1, p. 17.
54. Richard Rose, *Governing Without Consensus* (London: Faber and Faber, 1971) p. 109.
55. BBC TV Timewatch Documentary, *The Sparks That Lit The Bonfire*, 1993.
56. BBC TV Timewatch Documentary, *The Sparks That Lit The Bonfire*, 1993.
57. MacGiolla, quoted in Bishop and Mallie, *The Provisional IRA*, p. 94.
58. See Bishop and Mallie, *The Provisional IRA*, pp. 128–132, and J. Bowyer Bell, *The Irish Troubles: A Generation of Violence 1967–1992* (Dublin: Gill and Macmillan, 1993) pp. 157–161.
59. Tomas MacGiolla, interview with author, July 1996.
60. See Andrew J. Wilson, *Irish America and the Ulster Conflict, 1968–1995* (Belfast: Blackstaff, 1995) p. 42.
61. Albert J. Menendez, *The Bitter Harvest: Church and State in Northern Ireland* (Washington DC: Robert B. Luce, 1973) p. 42. Both Abernathy and Gregory were highly respected in the black community. In a survey of key NAACP state and branch presidents published by the NAACP's *Crisis* magazine in January 1970, both

Abernathy and Gregory were voted among the country's 25 greatest living Negroes. See *Crisis*, Vol. 77, No. 1 (January 1970).

62. Kathleen Cleaver, interview with author, January 1997.
63. Report of PD monthly conference, Coalisland, 1 March 1970; PD Box of documents, Linen Hall Library.
64. NICRA letter dated 19 August 1970, written to various personalities in the UK, Ireland and the US; NICRA Box 1, Linen Hall Library.
65. People's Democracy leaflet, November 1970; PD Papers, Linen Hall Library.
66. *Unfree Citizen*, Vol. 1, No. 10 (17 September 1971).
67. *Harper's*, Vol. 240, No. 136 (January 1970) p. 83.
68. Dr. Huey P. Newton Foundation Inc. Collection (M864); Department of Special Collections, Stanford University. On 20 May 1972 the *Black Panther* condemned John Lennon's deportation from the US for alleged marijuana possession in the UK, and noted that Lennon had recorded several political songs, 'including "Give Ireland Back to the Irish", which was an indictment of British occupation of Ireland'.
69. Bernadette Devlin McAliskey, interview with author, August 1996.
70. 'Irish Give Keys to City to Panthers as Symbol', *New York Times*, 3 March 1970.
71. Davis was later acquitted.
72. *Irish Press*, 23 February 1971; *Irish Times*, 1 April 1971.
73. *Irish Press*, 24 March 1971. Devlin interview with Rosita Sweetman.
74. *Unfree Citizen*, Vol. 1, No. 45 (9 June 1972) and Vol. 2, No. 2 (21 August 1972).
75. *Unfree Citizen*, Vol. 1, No. 10, (17 September 1971).
76. *Unfree Citizen*, Vol. 1, No. 44 (2 June 1972).
77. *Crisis*, Vol. 76, No. 8 (October 1969).
78. *Crisis*, Vol. 79, No. 5 (May 1972).
79. *Irish News*, 14 February 1972.
80. Juanita Williams, interview with author, January 1997. Juanita Williams was married to prominent civil rights leader Rev. Hosea Williams. Rev. Bernard Lee was a close personal friend of King, and had been standing next to King when the civil rights leader was assassinated in Memphis in April 1968.
81. Juanita Williams, interview with author, January 1997.
82. *Congressional Record*, 4 February 1972, p. 2695.
83. Untitled document dated August 1972 from NICRA box 1, Linen Hall Library, Belfast.

Chapter 4 Irish America

1. Peter Duignan and L.H. Gann, *The United States and Africa* (Cambridge: Cambridge University Press, 1984) p. 41.
2. Andrew Wilson, 'The American Congress for Irish Freedom and the Northern Ireland Civil Rights Movement 1967–70', *Eire–Ireland*, Spring 1994, p. 61.

3. Noel Ignatiev, *How the Irish Became White* (New York: Routledge, 1995).
4. Ignatiev, *How the Irish Became White*, p. 34 and p. 195.
5. Frederick Law Olmsted, *The Cotton Kingdom* (New York: Random House, 1984 edition), p. 74 and p. 171.
6. Olmsted, *Cotton Kingdom*, p. 70.
7. Olmsted, *Cotton Kingdom*, p. 171.
8. Edward A. Freeman, quoted in Andrew M. Greely, *The Irish Americans* (New York: Harper and Row, 1981) p. 88.
9. Douglass, quoted in Ignatiev, *How the Irish Became White*, p. 111.
10. Kathleen Cleaver, interview with author, January 1997.
11. Stokely Carmichael and Charles V. Hamilton, *Black Power* (New York: Vintage, 1967) p. 55.
12. Ronald P. Formisano, *Boston Against Busing* (Chapel Hill: University of North Carolina Press, 1991) p. 11.
13. In 1956, Democratic Presidential candidate Adlai Stevenson had won 61 per cent of the black vote.
14. Walter Fauntroy, interview with author, May 1985. See also Brian Dooley, *Robert Kennedy: The Final Years* (New York: St Martin's Press, 1996), pp. 21–43.
15. Tom Hayden, quoted in Jean Stein and George Plimpton, *American Journey* (New York: Signet, 1969) p. 221: 'Kennedy met with Floyd McKissick and continually gave him money.'
16. Robert Kennedy, quoted in *Ebony*, Vol. 23, No. 9 (July 1968).
17. Richard Lentz, *Symbols, The News Magazines and Martin Luther King* (Baton Rouge: Louisiana State University Press, 1990) p. 54.
18. David J. Garrow, *Bearing the Cross: Martin Luther King Jr and the Southern Christian Leadership Conference* (New York: Jonathan Cape, 1986) p. 576. In the Indiana presidential primary, for example, NBC television news estimated Kennedy had taken over 90 per cent of the black vote. He won similar percentages of the black vote in Washington DC and California.
19. Carmichael, quoted in Henry Fairlie, *The Kennedy Promise* (London: Eyre Methuen, 1973) p. 356.
20. Roy Wilkins, *Standing Fast* (New York: Viking, 1982) p. 330.
21. *New York* magazine, July 1968.
22. *The Times*, 6 June 1968.
23. *The Times*, 6 June 1968.
24. *The Times*, 8 June 1968.
25. Mary Wilson, *Dream Girl – My Life as a Supreme* (London: Sidgwick & Jackson, 1987) p. 217.
26. Paul O'Dwyer, 'Correcting Ethnic History', *Crisis*, Vol. 79, No. 2 (February 1972) pp. 59–60.
27. *Black Panther*, 15 January 1972.
28. *Black Panther*, 15 January 1972.
29. Ralph Abernathy, *And The Walls Came Tumbling Down* (New York: Harper, 1990) p. 354.
30. Greely, *The Irish Americans*, pp. 168–170.

31. Greely, *The Irish Americans*, p. 169. Greely points out that the 89 per cent of Irish Catholics who said they would vote for a black President was double the number of Protestants who said in 1958 they were prepared to vote for a Catholic President.
32. Laura Flanders, 'Principles at Stake in Duke's Bush War', *Fortnight*, July/August 1988, p. 11.
33. Formisano, *Boston Against Busing*, pp. 29, 143–144.
34. Formisano, *Boston Against Busing*, p. 139.
35. *Belfast News Letter*, 11 April 1968, p. 2.
36. Some of the most celebrated names of the 1916 Easter Rising had spent some time in America cementing contacts across the Atlantic. Tomas Ashe, Tom Clarke, Joseph Plunkett and James Connolly had all undertaken political work for Ireland in America.
37. Albert J. Menendez, *The Bitter Harvest: Church and State in Northern Ireland* (Washington DC: Robert B. Luce, 1973) p. 132.
38. Paul O'Dwyer, *Counsel for the Defense* (New York: Simon and Schuster, 1979) p. 169. Congressman John Fogarty of Rhode Island repeatedly filed the plebiscite resolution.
39. Menendez, *The Bitter Harvest*, p. 132. The US Census for 1970 listed 13,282,000 Americans of Irish ancestry.
40. Patricia McCluskey, quoted in W.H. VanVoris, *Violence in Ulster: An Oral Documentary* (Amherst University of Massachusetts Press, 1975) pp. 53–54.
41. Patricia McCluskey, interview with author, August 1996.
42. Eamonn McCann, interview with author, July 1996.
43. Michael Farrell, interview with author, July 1996. Farrell's attitude to America has mellowed. Having once been 'violently anti-American, and regarded it as something similar to the Great Satan,' he first visited the US in 1984, and no longer feels the antagonism towards America he once did.
44. *Chicago Sun-Times*, 30 November 1968.
45. See Wilson, *Irish America and the Ulster Conflict*, pp.15–16. John Dumbrell 'The United States and the Northern Irish Conflict 1969–94; from Indifference to Intervention', *Irish Studies in International Affairs*, Vol. 6 (1995) pp. 107–125.
46. Conn McCluskey, interview with author, August 1996.
47. Margie Bernard, *Daughter of Derry: The Story of Brigid Sheils Makowski* (London: Pluto, 1989) p. 52.
48. Bernard, *Daughter of Derry*, p. 65.
49. Bernard, *Daughter of Derry*, p. 5.
50. Sean Cronin, *Washington's Irish Policy 1916–1986* (Dublin: Anvil, 1987) p. 291.
51. Andrew J. Wilson, *Irish America and the Ulster Conflict 1968–1995* (Belfast: Blackstaff, 1995) p. 29.
52. Bernard, *Daughter of Derry*, p. 71.
53. Menendez, *The Bitter Harvest*, p. 142. See also *Congressional Record*, 20 October 1971.
54. Menendez, *The Bitter Harvest*, p. 145.

55. Kennedy, quoted in Wilson, *Irish American and the Ulster Crisis*, p. 64. My Lai was a village in Vietnam whose inhabitants had been massacred by American soldiers.

56. Wilson, *Irish America and the Ulster Conflict*, pp. 17–49, offers an excellent overview of the various Irish-American organisations and their responses to the developing crisis in Northern Ireland.

57. Fionnbarra Ó Dochartaigh, interview with author, September 1996.

58. Bernadette Devlin McAliskey, interview with author, August 1996.

59. G.W. Target, *Bernadette* (London: Hodder and Stoughton, 1975) p. 198.

60. Margaret Ward, 'From Civil Rights to Women's Rights', in Michael Farrell (ed.), *Twenty Years On* (Dingle: Brandon, 1988) p. 129.

61. Ward, 'From Civil Rights to Women's Rights', p. 129.

62. Inez McCormack, 'Faceless Men: Civil Rights and After', in Farrell (ed.), *Twenty Years On*, p. 27.

63. Septima Clark, quoted in Vicki Crawford et al. (eds), *Women in the Civil Rights Movement* (Indiana: Indiana University Press, 1993) p. 93 from Grace Jordan McFadden, *Oral Recollections of Septima Poinsette Clark* (Columbia: Instructional Services Center, 1980).

64. Sara Davidson, 'Bernadette Devlin: An Irish Revolutionary in America', *Harper's*, Vol. 230, No. 1436 (January 1970) pp. 78-90.

65. 'bernadette devlin: a candid conversation with the fiery young irish revolutionary', *Playboy*, No. 19 (September 1972) p. 80 and Bernadette Devlin, *The Price of My Soul* (London: Andre Deutsch, 1971) p. 143.

66. Devlin, quoted in Target, *Bernadette*, p. 225.

67. A. Carthew, 'Rebel in Armagh jail, the hater in the pulpit', *New York Times Magazine*, 9 August 1970, pp. 12–13.

68. Devlin, quoted in Target, *Bernadette*, p. 230, and Davidson, 'Bernadette Devlin: An Irish Revolutionary in America' p. 82.

69. In February 1981, Loyalist gunmen shot Bernadette McAliskey and her husband Michael in their home near Dungannon, Co. Tyrone. In August 1996, she told me 'I just have an instinct for survival, that's why I'm here'.

70. Austin Currie, interview with author, August 1996.

71. Bernadette Devlin McAliskey, interview with author, August 1996.

72. Davidson, 'Bernadette Devlin: An Irish Revolutionary in America', p. 79.

73. Davidson, 'Bernadette Devlin,: An Irish Revolutionary in Irish America', p. 78.

74. Berndatte Devlin McAliskey, interview with author, August 1996.

75. Bernadette Devlin McAliskey, 'A Peasant in the Halls of the Great', in Farrell (ed.), *Twenty Years On*, p. 87.

76. Davidson, 'Bernadette Devlin: An Irish Revolutionary in America', p. 78.

77. Bernadette Devlin McAliskey, interview with author, August 1996.

78. Bernadette Devlin McAliskey, interview with author, August 1996.

79. 'bernadette devlin: a candid conversation ...'.

80. Davidson, 'Bernadette Devlin: An Irish Revolutionary in America', p. 84. Roger Casement was executed for his part in the 1916 Easter Rising after he was captured trying to unload arms from a German submarine off the coast of Co. Kerry. Casement had worked as a British civil servant in Africa, and had written a report condemning the treatment of Africans in the Belgian Congo.
81. Bernadette Devlin McAliskey, interview with author, August 1996.
82. Steven P. Erie, *Rainbow's End: Irish-Americans and the Dilemma of Urban Machine Politics, 1840–1985* (Berkeley: University of California Press, 1988) p. 168.
83. Abernathy, *And The Walls Come Tumbling Down*, p. 365.
84. Stephen B. Oates, *Let The Trumpet Sound: The Life of Martin Luther King Jr* (New York: Harper & Row, 1982) p. 369.
85. Lentz, *Symbols, The News Magazines, and Martin Luther King*, p. 201.
86. Abernathy, *And The Walls Come Tumbling Down*, p. 363 and p. 395.
87. Davidson, 'Bernadette Devlin: An Irish Revolutionary in America', p. 84.
88. 'bernadette devlin: a candid conversation ...', p. 86.
89. Bernadette Devlin McAliskey, interview with author, August 1996.
90. Bernadette Devlin McAliskey, interview with author, August 1996.
91. Bernadette Devlin McAliskey, interview with author, August 1996.
92. Mary Holland, 'Why Bernadette left US in a hurry', the *Observer*, 7 September 1969.
93. Holland, 'Why Bernadette left US in a hurry'.
94. 'bernadette devlin: a candid conversation ...'.
95. Bernadette Devlin McAliskey, interview with author, August 1996.
96. Bernadette Devlin McAliskey, interview with author, August 1996.
97. Devlin, quoted in *Irish Independent*, 11 February 1971.
98. Bernadette Devlin McAliskey, interview with author, August 1996.
99. Angela Davis, interview with author, April 1997.
100. Bernadette Devlin McAliskey, interview with author, August 1996.
101. 'Irish Militant Criticizes US', *Los Angeles Herald-Examiner*, 12 November 1976.
102. Bernadette Devlin McAliskey, interview with author, August 1996.
103. Paddy Devlin, *Straight Left* (Belfast: Blackstaff, 1993), p. 119.

Chapter 5 Backlash

1. RUC officer, interview with author, May 1996.
2. David Boulton, *The UVF 1966–73* (Dublin: Gill and Macmillan, 1973) p. 30.
3. Boulton, *The UVF 1966–73*, p. 30.

4. A. Carthew, 'Rebel in Armagh jail, the hater in the pulpit', *New York Times Magazine*, 9 August 1970.
5. 'Dr Bob Jones tells of Paisley degree', *Belfast Telegraph*, 7 October 1969.
6. 'Dr Bob Jones tells of Paisley degree'.
7. Ed Maloney and Andy Pollak, *Paisley* (Dublin: Poolbeg, 1986) p. 247.
8. Moloney and Pollak, *Paisley*, p. 246.
9. Boulton, *The UVF 1966–73*, p. 30.
10. *Protestant Telegraph*, 11 May 1968.
11. J.D. Douglas, 'Billy Graham in Ireland: He Put It Over With Love', *Christianity Today*, Vol. 16 (20 July 1972).
12. Moloney and Pollak, *Paisley*, p. 252.
13. See *Belfast News Letter*, 13 April 1968.
14. *Protestant Telegraph*, 13 April 1968.
15. *Protestant Telegraph*, 13 April 1968.
16. *Protestant Telegraph*, 27 April 1968.
17. *Protestant Telegraph*, 19 October 1968.
18. Steve Bruce, 'The Problems of Pro-State Terrorism: Loyalist Paramilitaries in Northern Ireland', *Terrorism and Political Violence*, Vol. 4, No. 1 (Spring 1992) pp. 67–88.
19. *Unfree Citizen*, Vol. 1, No. 46, 16 June 1972; *Civil Rights*, Vol. 1, No. 17, 29 July 1972. The UDA was the largest Protestant paramilitary organisation of modern times, and was legal until 1992. It was launched in 1971 as an umbrella group for several Protestant vigilante groups, and the illegal Ulster Freedom Fighters (UFF) were closely associated with the UDA.
20. Fionnbarra Ó Dochartaigh, *Ulster's White Negroes* (Edinburgh: AK Press, 1994) p. 51.
21. Wyn Craig Wade, *The Fiery Cross: The Ku Klux Klan In America* (New York: Simon and Schuster, 1987) p. 179.
22. Wade, *The Fiery Cross*, p. 181 and Paisley quoted in Conn McCluskey, *Up Off Their Knees* (Galway: Conn McCluskey and associates, 1989) p. 157.
23. Boulton, *The UVF 1966–73*, p. 83.
24. Boulton, *The UVF 1966–73*, p. 85.
25. The Supreme Court had ruled in 1958 that segregated bus stations were illegal, but by 1961 de facto segregation in bus stations and snack bars was still normal throughout the South.
26. Wade, *The Fiery Cross*, p. 310.
27. All charges against Rainey and Price were dropped, and they were feted as Klan heroes throughout the state for years afterwards.
28. McCluskey, *Up Off Their Knees*, p. 107.
29. Tomas MacGiolla, interview with author, July 1996.
30. McCluskey, *Up Off Their Knees*, p. 23.
31. For example, in 1966, Derry's crime rate was the lowest, proportionately, for any city in Ireland or Britain. See Frank Curran, *Derry: Countdown to Disaster* (Dublin: Gill and Macmillan, 1980).
32. RUC officer, interview with author, May 1996.

33. RUC officer, interview with author, May 1996.
34. Cameron Commission, *Disturbances in Northern Ireland* (Belfast: HMSO, 1969) p. 29.
35. Bernadette Devlin, *The Price of My Soul* (London: Andre Deutsch, 1971) p. 97.
36. RUC officer, interview with author, May 1996.
37. Kerner Commission, *Report of the National Advisory Commission on Civil Disorders*, (New York: Bantam, 1968) p. 1.
38. Kerner Commission, p. 413.
39. Kerner Commission, p. 481.
40. Cameron Commission, p. 14.
41. See Cameron Commission, pp. 14, 47 and 75; Kerner Commission pp. 306, 316, 426–427.
42. Cameron Commission, p. 55.
43. *Violence and Civil Disturbances in Northern Ireland in 1969 (The Scarman Report)* (Belfast: HMSO, 1972) p. 15.
44. The reforms were announced on 19 August 1969, and were known as the 'Downing Street Declaration'.
45. The Hunt Report recommended an unarmed RUC and the disbanding of the Ulster Special Constabulary. The report's publication led to rioting in some Protestant areas of Belfast.
46. Boulton, *The UVF 1966–73* p. 126.
47. Cameron Commission, p. 84.
48. Richard Reeves, *President Kennedy* (New York: Touchstone, 1993) p. 530. Levison had, apparently, had some connection with the US Communist Party during the early 1950s, but does not appear to have been acting under orders from the Soviet Union during his involvement with the civil rights movement.
49. Richard Lentz, *Symbols, the News Magazines and Martin Luther King* (Baton Rouge; Lousiana State Press, 1990) p. 181.
50. O Dochartaigh, *Ulster's White Negroes*, p. 92.
51. Moloney and Pollak, *Paisley*, p. 199.
52. O Dochartaigh, *Ulster's White Negroes*, p. 92.
53. Bernadette Devlin McAliskey, interview with author, August 1996.
54. Enoch Powell, quoted in Anthony Lejeune 'Not Conor Cruise O'Brien', *National Review*, 9 October 1969.
55. Tom Hayden, *Reunion* (London: Hamish Hamilton, 1988) p. 433.
56. FBI memo dated 15 December 1971, quoted in Hayden, *Reunion*, p. 434.
57. Hayden, *Reunion*, p. 434.
58. Eamonn McCann, interview with author, July 1996.
59. See G.W. Target, *Bernadette: The Story of Bernadette Devlin* (London: Hodder & Stoughton, 1975) p. 20 and p. 289.
60. *Detroit Press*, 28 August 1969, and Goldwater, quoted in Robert Cielou, *Spare My Tortured People* (Lisnaskea: Whitethorn, 1983) p. 14.
61. Jeffrey St John, 'Bernadette Devlin's Words Reflect Revolutionary Links', *Columbus Dispatch*, 26 February 1971.

62. Michael Farrell, 'Long March to Freedom' in Farrell (ed.), *Twenty Years On* (Dingle: Brandon, 1988) p. 54.
63. Tomas MacGiolla, interview with author, July 1996.
64. Cameron Commission, p. 31.
65. William Craig, quoted in W.H. Van Voris, *Violence in Ulster: An Oral Documentary* (Amherst: University of Massachussets Press, 1975), p. 71.
66. Bernadette Devlin McAliskey, interview with author, August 1996.
67. Brian Moore, 'Bloody Ulster', the *Atlantic*, September 1970.
68. See Ken Ward, 'Ulster Terrorism: The US Network News Coverage of Northern Ireland 1969–1979' in Y. Alexander and A. O'Day (eds), *Terrorism in Ireland*, (New York: St Martin's Press, 1984), pp. 201–212.
69. Ward, 'Ulster Terrorism', p. 203.
70. Ward, 'Ulster Terrorism', p. 203.
71. Ward, 'Ulster Terrorism', p. 204.
72. 'The White Negroes', *Newsweek*, 2 December 1968.
73. NBC Nightly News, 15 August 1969, quoted in Ward, 'Ulster Terrorism', p. 205.
74. Ward, 'Ulster Terrorism', p. 206.
75. Russell Stetler, 'Northern Ireland', *Monthly Review*, November 1970.
76. *ABC Nightly News*, 5 June 1974, quoted in Ward, 'Ulster Terrorism', p. 207.
77. Liz Curtis, *Ireland: The Propaganda War* (London: Pluto, 1984) p. 19.
78. Curtis, *Ireland: The Propaganda War*, p. 20.
79. Curtis, *Ireland: The Propaganda War*, p. 20.
80. McCluskey, *Up Off Their Knees*, p. 99.
81. Curtis, *Ireland: The Propaganda War*, p. 22.
82. Austin Currie, interview with author, August 1996.
83. Curtis, *Ireland: The Propaganda War*, p. 25.
84. Ed Moloney, 'The Media: Asking the Right Questions?' in Farrell (ed.), *20 Years On*, p. 139.
85. Andrew Young, *An Easy Burden* (New York: HarperCollins, 1996) pp. 207–208.
86. RUC officer, interview with author, May 1996.
87. Eamonn McCann, *War and an Irish Town* (London: Pluto, 1974) p. 99.
88. *Daily Express*, 31 January 1972 and *Daily Mail*, 31 January 1972.
89. Angela Davis, interview with author, April 1997.
90. Kerner Commission, p. 374.
91. Curtis, *Ireland: The Propaganda War*, p. 31.
92. BBC minutes, reported in *Private Eye*, 15 November 1971, quoted in Curtis, *Ireland: The Propaganda War*, p. 32.
93. There are those who believe that Martin Luther King was assassinated with the help of one or more US government agencies.

94. Ward Churchill and Jim Vander Wall, *Agents of Repression* (Boston: South End Press, 1988), pp. 63–101 offers a fuller description of COINTELPRO.
95. 342 Catholics were arrested during a swoop codenamed 'Demetrius' on 9 August 1971. The terms of internment were later modified, and the first Loyalist internees were arrested in February 1973.
96. Frank Kitson, *Low Intensity Operations* (London: Faber and Faber, 1971) p. 69.
97. Churchill and Vander Wall, *Agents of Repression*, p. 49.
98. Bernadette Devlin McAliskey, interview with author, August 1996.

Chapter 6 Heirs Apparent

1. Eamonn McCann, 'Forget the myths: here's the real story', *Fortnight*, no. 266 (6 October 1988).
2. The pamphlet advertised a programme of commemorative events in Derry, 5–9 October 1968, and although the events took place, Rosa Parks was not part of them. McCann quote from interview with author, July 1996.
3. Andrew J. Wilson, *Irish America and the Ulster Conflict 1968–1995* (Belfast: Blackstaff, 1995), p. 19.
4. Michael Kilian, 'Man of Peace: John Hume, the Voice of Ulster's Catholics', *Chicago Tribune*, 18 November 1986, section 5, p. 1.
5. John Hume, *A New Ireland* (Boulder: Roberts Rinehart, 1996), p. 30.
6. Tomas MacGiolla, interview with author, July 1996.
7. Shane O'Doherty, *The Volunteer* (London: Fount, 1993) p. 42.
8. Frank Burton, *The Politics of Legitimacy* (London: Routledge, Kegan and Paul, 1987) p. 56.
9. IRA Green Book, quoted in Martin Dillon, *Killer in Clowntown* (Hutchinson, 1993), p. 260.
10. Dillon, *Killer in Clowntown*, p. 262.
11. Jacqueline Ryan, sister of Frankie Ryan, quoted in Kevin Toolis, *Rebel Hearts: Journeys Within The IRA's Soul* (London: Picador, 1993) p. 283.
12. Padraig O'Malley, *Biting at the Grave: The Irish Hunger Strikes and the Politics of Despair* (Belfast: Blackstaff, 1990), p. 167.
13. O'Malley, *Biting at the Grave*, p. 163.
14. Hoffman had been one of the New Left activists who visited Northern Ireland during the late 1960s. Eamonn McCann remembered that when Hoffman visited 'County Down were playing in the Ulster Gaelic football championship and Down's colours are red and black, the anarchist colours, and there were rosettes with "Up Down" and Abbie Hoffman was absolutely charmed by this – these anarchist's colours and people walking around saying "up Down" ... "Wow, this is really cool", says Hoffman' (interview with Eamonn McCann, July 1996). Brendan Behan had worn an 'Up Down' badge on a visit to New York some years earlier which had provoked similar fascination.

15. Jean Carey Bond, 'Northern Ireland through Black Eyes', *Freedomways*, pp. 13–20 (First Quarter 1982).
16. St Clair Bourne, interview with author, July 1997.
17. Bond, 'Northern Ireland Through Black Eyes'.
18. Kirkpatrick, interviewed in *The Black and the Green*.
19. Matt Jones, interviewed in *The Black and the Green*.
20. Daughtrey quoted in the *New York Alliance*, 5 February 1982.
21. Jim Dunn, interviewed in *The Black and the Green*.
22. St Clair Bourne, interview with author, July 1997.
23. St Clair Bourne, correspondence with author, July 1997.
24. *Irish Worker's Republic*, Vol. 1, No. 3 (Spring 1988).
25. Bernadette Devlin McAliskey, interview with author, August 1996.
26. *An Phoblacht*, 22 June 1995.
27. Not all Irish-American politicians endorsed the MacBride Principles. Figures like Senator Edward Kennedy expressed reservations about them, and they were opposed by John Hume, who claimed that the principles could scare off potential investors who 'might see them as an extra hassle and go elsewhere'. See Wilson, *Irish America and the Ulster Conflict*, 1968–1995, p. 270.
28. *An Phoblacht*, 15 August 1995.
29. *Irish People*, Vol. 26, No. 5, 5 July 1997, p. 5.
30. *An Phoblacht*, 25 July 1996.
31. *Washington Post*, 1 October 1994, p. A3.
32. Conor O'Clery, *Daring Diplomacy* (Boulder: Roberts Rinehart, 1997) p. 172.
33. O'Clery, *Daring Diplomacy*, p. 23.
34. O'Clery, *Daring Diplomacy*, p. 23.
35. Bernadette Devlin McAliskey, 'A Peasant in the Halls of the Great', in Farrell (ed.), *20 Years On*, p. 87.
36. Bernadette Devlin McAliskey, interview with author, August 1996.
37. Angela Davis statement on Roisin McAliskey, 7 March 1997.
38. Angela Davis, interview with author, April 1997.
39. Hume, *A New Ireland*, p. 52.
40. Seamus Mallon, quoted in the *Guardian*, 8 April 1997. Large numbers of arson attacks were reported in the aftermath of the previous year's marching season, when a series of conflicts had erupted over Orange Order attempts to march through largely Catholic areas. More than 80 churches (Protestant and Catholic), schools and Orange Order meeting halls had been attacked and damaged by fire in the following year.
41. *New York Times*, 30 October 1995.
42. Andrew Roth, *Enoch Powell: Tory Tribune* (London: MacDonald, 1970) pp. 340–341.
43. Associated Press report, 2 April 1982.
44. *New York Times*, 10 June 1983.
45. Bob Jones University leaflets 'FACTS: Why Christian Young Men and Women Should attend a Christian School', and 'Let Bob Jones University Change Your Life', were both sent out to prospective students in 1997.

46. *Irish America*, March/April 1997, p. 29.
47. *Irish America*, March/April 1997, pp. 96–97.
48. *Washington Post*, 27 March 1997, p. A13. However, when Daley first ran for mayor in 1991, he was backed by Chicago's influential black newspaper the *Chicago Defender*.
49. Charles Cobb, 'Black Power', *Emerge*, June 1997, pp. 38–46.
50. Cobb, 'Black Power'.
51. Patricia McCluskey, interview with author, August 1996.
52. Suzann Buckley and Pamela Lonergan, 'Women and the troubles, 1969–1980' in Alexander and A. O'Day (eds), *Terrorism in Northern Ireland* (New York: St Martin's Press, 1984) pp. 75–87.
53. Williams and Corrigan were moved to start the movement following an incident in Belfast's Andersonstown in August 1976. Two IRA gunmen, after firing on a British army patrol, escaped in a car but were chased by an army Land Rover. The driver of the fleeing car was shot and killed, and the car ploughed into a family of bystanders. Three children were killed in the crash. Betty Williams had witnessed the deaths, and Mairead Corrigan was the children's aunt. In the days following the deaths, Williams collected signatures for a petition calling for a halt to the violence, and Corrigan appeared on local television appealing for an end to the killings.
    The two founders were heavily criticised for keeping the money they were awarded by the Nobel Committee rather than putting it into the organisation. The Peace People movement still exists, and has concentrated on cross-community projects aimed and integrating Catholics and Protestants, but has been wracked by internal disputes.
54. Conn McCluskey, interview with author, August 1996.
55. In December 1972 a government-appointed committee headed by Lord Diplock recommended that, due to the possibility of juries being intimidated, only judges should determine guilt or innocence in a wide variety of paramilitary cases. RUC figure from *The Economist*, 12–18 July 1997.
56. 'With the Old Hatreds, Ulster is Braced for New Marching Season', *New York Times*, 4 July 1997.
57. 'With the Old Hatreds, Ulster is Braced for New Marching Season', *New York Times*, 4 July 1997.
58. Hume, *A New Ireland*, p. 45.
59. Austin Currie, interview with author, August 1996.
60. McCann, quoted in UPI report, 5 October 1993.
61. Edwina Stewart, interview with author, August 1997.
62. McCann quoted in 'Forget the myths: here's the real story', *Fortnight*, 6 October 1988, no. 266.
63. Edwina Stewart, interview with author, August 1997.
64. Bernadette Devlin McAliskey, interview with author, August 1996.
65. Gerry Adams, interviewed on *Fox News Sunday*, 27 July 1997.

Bibliography

Abernathy, Ralph *And The Walls Came Tumbling Down* (New York: Harper & Row, 1989).

Adams, Gerry *The Politics of Irish Freedom* (Dingle: Brandon, 1988).

Adams, Gerry *Falls Memories* (Dingle: Brandon, 1988).

Adams, James, Morgan, Robin and Bambridge, Anthony Ambush *The War Between the SAS and the IRA* (London: Pan, 1988).

Alexander, Y. and O'Day, A. (eds). *Terrorism in Northern Ireland* (New York: St Martin's Press, 1984).

Aptheker, Herbert Documentary *History of the Negro People in the United States - Volume I* (New York: Citadel, 1951).

Arthur, Paul *The People's Democracy 1968–1973* (Belfast: Blackstaff, 1974).

Bardon, Jonathan *A History of Ulster* (Belfast: Blackstaff, 1992).

Barritt, Denis P. and Carter, Charles F. *The Northern Ireland Problem* (Oxford: Oxford University Press, 1962).

Bartlett, Irving H. *Wendell and Ann Phillips* (New York: Norton, 1979).

Barton, Brian *Northern Ireland in the Second World War* (Belfast: Ulster Historical Foundation, 1995).

Behan, Brendan *Brendan Behan's New York* (London: Hutchinson, 1964).

Bennett, Ronan *Double Jeopardy: The Retrial of the Guildford Four* (London: Penguin 1993).

Beresford, David *Ten Men Dead* (London: HarperCollins, 1987).

Bernard, Margie *Daughter of Derry: The Story of Brigid Sheils Makowski* (London: Pluto, 1989).

Bishop, Patrick and Mallie, Eamonn *The Provisional IRA* (London: Heinemann, 1987).

Blackburn, Robin *The Making of New World Slavery* (London: Verso, 1997).

Blassingame, John (ed.) *The Frederick Douglass Papers Volumes I–IV* (Princeton: Yale University Press, 1985-1991).

Boulton, David *The UVF 1966–1973* (Dublin: Torc, 1973).

Bowyer Bell, J. *The Irish Troubles: A Generation of Violence 1967–1992* (Dublin: Gill and Macmillan, 1993).

Bowyer Bell, J. *The Secret Army: The IRA* (Dublin: Poolbeg, 1970, 1990 edition).

Breitman, George *The Last Year of Malcolm X* (New York: Shocken Books, 1967).

Brown, Elaine *A Taste of Power: A Black Woman's Story* (New York: Doubleday, 1992).

Bruce, Steve *God Save Ulster! The Religion and Politics of Paisleyism* (Oxford: Oxford University Press, 1986).

Burton, Frank *The Politics of Legitimacy* (London: Routledge, Kegan and Paul, 1987).

Byrnes, Timothy A. *Catholic Bishops in American Politics* (New Jersey: Princeton, 1991).

Cameron Commission *Disturbances in Northern Ireland* (Belfast: HMSO, 1969).

Carmichael, Stokely and Hamilton, Charles V. *Black Power: The Politics of Liberation In America* (New York: Random House, 1967).

Carr, James *Bad: The Autobiography of James Carr* (London: Pelagian Press, 1974).

Carson, Clayborne (ed.) *Eyes on the Prize Reader* (New York: Penguin, 1987).

Carter, Dan T. *The Politics of Rage* (New York : Simon and Schuster, 1992).

Chalmers, David M. *Hooded Americanism: The History of the Ku Klux Klan* (New York: New Viewpoints, 1965).

Christie, Kenneth *Political Protest in Northern Ireland: Continuity and Change* (Reading: Link, 1992).

Cielou, Robert *Spare My Tortured People* (Linaskea: Whitethorn, 1983).

Conlon, Gerry *Proved Innocent* (London: Hamish Hamilton, 1990).

Connolly, Colm *Herrema: Siege at Monastrevin* (Dublin: Olympic 1977).

Coogan, Tim *Pat On the Blanket: The Inside Story of the IRA Prisoners' 'Dirty' Protest* (Boulder: Roberts Rinehart, 1997, first published in 1980).

Coote, Anna and Grant, Lawrence *The NCCL Guide: Civil Liberty* (London: Penguin, 1972).

Coyle, Dominick J. *Minorities in Revolt: Political Violence in Ireland, Italy and Cyprus* (New Jersey: Fairleigh Dickinson University Press, 1983).

Crawford, Vicki et al. (eds) *Women in the Civil Rights Movement* (Indiana: Indiana University Press, 1993).

Cronin, Sean *Washington's Irish Policy 1916–1986* (Dublin: Anvil, 1987).

Curran Frank *Derry: Countdown to Disaster* (Dublin: Gill and Macmillan, 1986).

Curtis, Liz *Ireland: The Propaganda War* (London: Pluto, 1984).

Curtis, L. Perry *Apes and Angels: The Irishman in Victorian Caricature* (Washington DC: Smithsonian Institution, 1997).

Davis, Cyprian *The History of Black Catholics in the United States* (New York: Crossroads, 1995).

d'Arcy, Margaretta *Tell Them Everything* (London: Pluto, 1981).

de Paor, Liam *Divided Ulster* (London: Penguin, 1972).

Deutsch, Richard and Magowan, Vivien *Northern Ireland: A Chronology of Events 1968-1973* (Belfast: Blackstaff, 1973).

Devlin, Bernadette *The Price of My Soul* (London: Andre Deutsch, 1971).

Devlin, Paddy *Straight Left* (Belfast: Blackstaff, 1993).

Dillon, Martin *The Shankill Butchers* (London: Hutchinson, 1989).

Dillon, Martin *Stone Cold: The True Story of Martin Stone and the Milltown Massacre* (London: Hutchinson, 1992).

Dillon, Martin *Killer in Clowntown: Joe Doherty, the IRA and the Special Relationship* (London: Hutchinson, 1992).

Douglass, Frederick *My Bondage and My Freedom* (New York: Miller, Orton and Mulligan, 1885).

Duignan, Peter and Gann, L.H. *The United States and Africa* (Cambridge: Cambridge University Press, 1984).

Dunne, Derek *Out of the Maze* (Dublin: Gill and Macmillan, 1988).

Egan, Bowes and McCormack, Vincent *Burntollet* (London: LRS Publishers, 1969).

Erie, Steven P. *Rainbow's End: Irish-Americans and the Dilemma of Urban Machine Politics, 1840–1985* (Berkeley: University of California Press, 1988).

Farrell, Michael *Northern Ireland: The Orange State* (London: Pluto, 1976).

Farrell, Michael *20 Years On* (Dingle: Brandon, 1988).

Flackes, W.D. and Elliott, Sydney *Northern Ireland: A Political Directory 1968–1993* (Belfast: Blackstaff, 1994).

Formisano, Ronald P. *Boston Against Busing* (North Carolina: University of North Carolina Press, 1991).

Gallagher, Eric and Worrall, Stanley *Christians in Ulster 1968–1980* (Oxford: Oxford University Press, 1982).

Gardiner, J. *Over Here: The GIs in Wartime Britain* (London: Collins and Brown, 1992).

Garrow, David J. *Bearing the Cross: Martin Luther King Jr and the Southern Christian Leadership Conference* (New York: Jonathan Cape, 1986).

Garrow, David J. *The Montgomery Bus Boycott and the Women Who Started It: The Memoir of Jo Ann Gibson Robinson* (University of Tennessee Knoxville 1987).

Greely, Andrew M. *The Irish Americans* (New York: Harper and Row, 1981).

Hampton, Henry and Fayer, Steve *Voices of Freedom: An Oral History of the Civil Rights Movement from the 1950s to the 1980s* (New York: Bantam, 1990).

Hansen, Chadwick *Witchcraft at Salem* (New York: George Braziller, 1969).

Hayden, Tom *Reunion: A Memoir* (London: Hamish Hamilton, 1988).

Hill, Paul *Stolen Years* (London: Doubleday, 1990).

Hill, Robert A. *The Marcus Garvey and Universal Negro Improvement Association Papers, Volumes I–V* (Los Angeles: University of California Press, 1983–1986).

Holland, Jack *The American Connection* (Dublin: Poolbeg, 1987).

Hume, John *A New Ireland: Politics, Peace and Reconciliation* (Boulder: Roberts Rinehart, 1996).

Ignatiev, Noel *How the Irish Became White* (New York: Routledge, 1995).

Kerner Commission *Report of the National Advisory Commission on Civil Disorders* (New York: Bantam, 1968).

Kinealy, Christine *A Death-Dealing Famine: The Great Hunger in Ireland* (London: Pluto, 1997).

King, Desmond *Separate and Unequal: Black Americans and the US Federal Government* (Oxford: Oxford University Press, 1995).

Kingsley, Paul *Londonderry Revisited: A Loyalist Analysis of the Civil Rights Controversy* (Belfast: Belfast Publications, 1989).

Lentz, Richard Symbols, *the News Magazines, and Martin Luther King* (Baton Rouge: Louisiana State Press, 1990).

Lincoln, Eric C. *Chronicles of Black Protest* (New York: Mentor, 1969).

Maloney, Ed and Pollak, Andy *Paisley* (Dublin: Poolbeg, 1986).

McAdams, Douglas *Political Process and the Development of Black Insurgency 1930–1970* (Chicago: Chicago University Press, 1982).

McAfee, C.I. (ed.) *Concise Ulster Dictionary* (Oxford: Oxford University Press, 1996).

McCann, Eamonn *War and an Irish Town* (London: Pluto, 1974).

McCann, Eamonn *Bloody Sunday in Derry: What Really Happened* (Dingle: Brandon, 1992).

McCartney, Donal *The World of Daniel O'Connell* (Dublin: Mercier, 1980).

McCluskey, Conn *Up Off Their Knees* (Galway: Conn McCluskey and associates, 1989).

McDonald, Michael *Children of Wrath: Political Violence in Northern Ireland* (Oxford: Polity Press, 1986).

McFeely, William S. *Frederick Douglass* (London: Norton, 1991).

McGinn, Fiona *'Ignorance is Bliss'* (Queen's University Belfast thesis, 1995).

McMahon, Eileen *Which Parish Are You From?* (Kentucky: University of Kentucky, 1995).

Miller, David *Don't Mention the War* (London: Pluto, 1994).

Morgan, Michael 'The Civil Rights Movement: A Re-interpretation' (Queen's University Belfast thesis, 1984).

Morrissey, Hazel Betty Sinclair: *A Woman's Fight for Socialism* (Belfast: John Freeman, 1983).

Morrow, Tony Derry: *The War Years* (Derry: Heritage Library, 1987).

Newfield, Jack *A Prophetic Minority: The American New Left* (London: Anthony Blond, 1966).

Newton, Huey P. *Revolutionary Suicide* (New York: Writers and Readers, 1995 edition).

Nowland, Kevin B. and O'Connell, Maurice R. *Daniel O'Connell: Portrait of a Radical* (Belfast: Appletree, 1984).

Oates, Stephen B. *Let The Trumpet Sound: The Life of Martin Luther King Jr* (New York: Harper & Row, 1982).

O'Clery, Conor *Daring Diplomacy* (Colorado: Roberts Rinehart, 1997).

O Dochartaigh, Fionnbarra *Ulster's White Negroes* (Edinburgh: AK Press, 1994).

O'Doherty, Shane *The Volunteer: A Former IRA Man's True Story* (London: Fount, 1993).

O'Faolain, Sean *King of the Beggars: A Life of Daniel O'Connell* (Dublin: Poolbeg, 1938; 1990 edition).

O'Malley, Padraig *Biting at the Grave: The Irish Hunger Strikes and the Politics of Despair* (Belfast: Blackstaff, 1990).

O'Malley, Padraig *The Uncivil Wars: Ireland Today* (Boston: Beacon, 1990).

Pearson, Hugh *The Shadow of the Panther: Huey Newton and the Price of Black Power in America* (New York: Addison Wesley, 1994).

Pinkney, Alphonso *Red, Black and Green; Black nationalism in the United States* (Cambridge: Cambridge University Press, 1976).

Purdie, Bob *Politics in the Streets, the origins of the civil rights movement in Northern Ireland* (Belfast: Blackstaff, 1990).

Quarles, Benjamin (ed.) *Narrative of the Life of Frederick Douglass (An American Slave)*, (Boston: Harvard, 1967).

Rees, Merlyn *Northern Ireland: A Personal Perspective* (London: Methuen, 1985).

Reynolds, David *Rich Relations: The American Occupation of Britain 1942–1945* (London: HarperCollins, 1995).

Rose, Richard *Governing Without Consensus* (London: Faber and Faber, 1971).

Rose, Richard 'On the Priorities of Citizenship in the Deep South and Northern Ireland', *Journal of Politics*, Vol. 38 (1974).

Rowan, Brian *Behind the Lines: The Story of the IRA and Loyalist Ceasefires* (Belfast: Blackstaff, 1995).

Sands, Bobby *One Day in My Life* (London: Pluto, 1983).

Scarman Commission *Violence and Civil Disturbances in Northern Ireland in 1969* (Belfast: HMSO, 1972).

Sharp, Gene *The Politics of Nonviolent Action* (Boston: Porter Sargent, 1973).

Smith, Graham A. *When Jim Crow met John Bull: Black American Troops in World War Two in Britain* (London: IB Tauris, 1987).

Sunday Times Insight Team *Ulster* (London: Andre Deutsch, 1972).

Sweetman, Rosita *On Our Knees* (London: Pan, 1972).

Target, G.W. *Bernadette: The Story of Bernadette Devlin* (London: Hodder & Stoughton, 1975).

Taylor, Peter *Beating the Terrorists?* (London: Penguin, 1980).

Thompson, Daniel C. *The Negro Leadership Class* (New Jersey: Prentice-Hall, 1963).

Thompson, James 'The Civil Rights Movement in Northern Ireland' (Queen's University Belfast thesis, 1973).

Toolis, Kevin *Rebel Hearts: Journeys Within the IRA's Soul* (London: Picador, 1995).

Truxes, Thomas *Irish-American Trade 1660–1873* (Cambridge: Cambridge University Press, 1988).

Vann Woodward, C. *The Strange Career of Jim Crow* (Oxford: Oxford University Press, 1955).

Van Voris, W.H. *Violence in Ulster: An Oral Documentary* (Amherst: University of Massachusetts Press, 1975).

Wade, Wyn Craig *The Fiery Cross: The Ku Klux Klan In America* (New York: Simon and Schuster, 1987).

Walsh, Pat *From Civil Rights to National War* (Belfast: Athol, 1989).

Ward, Sarah 'The Genesis of the Civil Rights Movement in Northern Ireland' (Queen's University Belfast thesis, 1993).

Wilson, Andrew J. *Irish America and the Ulster Conflict 1968–1995* (Belfast: Blackstaff, 1995).

Wilson, T. *Ulster Under Home Rule* (Oxford: Oxford University Press, 1955).

Wright, Frank *Northern Ireland: A Comparative Analysis* (Dublin: Gill and Macmillan, 1987).

Young, Andrew *An Easy Burden* (New York: HarperCollins, 1996).

Zinn, Howard *SNCC, The New Abolitionists* (Boston: Beacon, 1964).

Index

Lightning Source UK Ltd.
Milton Keynes UK
UKHW010710170522
403093UK00001B/68